1851

METAMORPHOSES I-IV

In memory of

FUDGE

OVID

Metamorphoses I-IV

Edited with Translation and Notes by

D. E. HILL

ARIS & PHILLIPS
BOLCHAZY-CARDUCCI

PUBLISHERS

ISBN (UK) 0 85668 256 X (cloth)
ISBN (UK) 0 85668 257 8 (limp)
ISBN (USA) 0 86516 092 9 (cloth)
ISBN (USA) 0 86516 067 8 (limp)

Printed and published in England by Aris & Phillips Ltd., Teddington House, Warminster, Wiltshire.
Published in the United States of America by Bolchazy-Carducci Publishers Inc., 44 Lake Street, Oak Park, Illinois 60302, USA.

CONTENTS

PREFACE

It is twenty-five years since I first tried to teach classical literature in translation and I have never lost my immediate feeling of the great unfairness suffered by the students of that sort of course, the absence of the helpful annotated editions of the classics so widely available to the student who works through the original languages. It was not long before I noticed the paucity of translations prepared with any view at all to the needs of the translation student, a paucity especially evident in the case of Latin. I was, however, to my shame, content to do no more than complain, usually in private, once only in public at a meeting of the Council of University Classical Departments held in Oxford in January 1976, where I read a paper, 'What sort of Translation of Virgil do we need?', which was subsequently published in *Greece and Rome* 25 (1978) 59-68. In spite of the kind reception this work was accorded, I still did no more than complain until I was advised to discuss the issue with Mr John Aris. I already knew, of course, of his reputation and that of his publishing house, but even so I was not prepared for his kindness and generosity and for the close personal interest he has taken in this project since its inception. The debt that our discipline owes to Mr Aris is already incalculable, and it is still growing.

My second piece of great good fortune was to secure the help and support of Professor R.J. Tarrant. He is preparing the Oxford text of the *Metamorphoses* and, as I explain in greater detail in the Introduction, he very kindly let me see the draft of his text for the first four books. What I do not mention there, however, is that he also agreed to read the draft of my translation throughout. My debt to his painstaking care is enormous and it is reflected on almost every page. It is rare to find a friend who will take such pains with one's work, but Professor Tarrant and I were strangers until I approached him.

Those familiar with the profession in Britain will not need to be reminded of how lucky I am to be serving in Cardiff. Once again, my colleagues uncomplainingly took on extra teaching so that I could be granted a free term to complete this project. Not content with this, Mr Ceri Davies, Mr Kenneth Dowden and Dr N.R.E. Fisher all made penetrating comments on an earlier draft, especially of the Introduction, which saved me from myself on more occasions than I like to remember.

Another early draft was used on an undergraduate class in Cardiff and I should like to record my gratitude for their forbearance with the physical quality of the draft and for the many helpful suggestions that they made.

The labour involved in the preparation of the Index was very greatly reduced thanks to the computing skills of my son, Colin, while the proofreading owes much to the patience and hard work of Mr Cedric Littlewood, a pupil at Abingdon College, and of my daughter, Caroline.

The physical presentation of the book owes most to Miss Judith Grey who has most uncomplainingly typed and retyped and retyped again, although she must have noticed how often she was correcting not because of her errors but because of my changes of mind. I should also pay tribute to Mr Philip Mudd of Aris and Phillips whose skill and helpfulness with all the technical difficulties of production is matched only by his amazing promptness in responding to every manner of enquiry.

Finally, I am much indebted to Professor Willcock, the general editor of this series, who undertook to do some proofreading but did, in fact, do far more than that. Many years ago, when we were both in Cambridge, I was his pupil and it has been a great pleasure once again to be the beneficiary of his precise and illuminating comments as well as his undoubted skill at detecting misprints.

My debts are indeed great; I shall feel that it was all worth while, however, if the reader derives half the pleasure from reading the work as I have from preparing it. My hope is that it will be felt that the basic *rationale* of this translation and of these notes is right for the Latinless student of Roman poetry and that others will wish to develop the approach for other authors so that, in the not too distant future, no one will wish to echo my complaints of twenty-five years ago.

INTRODUCTION

1. Ovid's life and works

Ovid was born in the small Italian town of Sulmo (now Sulmona) on the 10th March 43 B.C., five days before the first anniversary of Caesar's assassination. When Octavian (soon to be known as Augustus) made himself undisputed master of the Roman world by defeating Antony and Cleopatra at Actium, Ovid was only twelve. The difference between the social and political outlook of his generation and that of Virgil, who was born only twenty-seven years before him, must have been as profound as the difference today between those who remember Europe in the tumult of the Fascist era, and those who do not.

For a century before Ovid's birth, Rome had been racked by political upheavals frequently breaking out into violence and, eventually, full civil war. Catullus (c.84-c.54 B.C.), Virgil (70-19 B.C.), Horace (65-8 B.C.), Tibullus (55/48-19 B.C.) and Propertius (54/47-16/2 B.C.) had all been touched by these upheavals and all reflect the political issues of their day to a greater or lesser extent in their poetry. The last four lived to see the end of the civil war and the establishment of the Augustan regime. Indeed, in their more optimistic moments, Virgil and Horace can dare to hope that they are witnessing the birth of a new Golden Age, though all four clearly suffer from doubts too. With Ovid, however, politics are ignored. Just as the fall of the Greek city states and the rise of the Hellenistic world some four centuries earlier had driven poetry from the centre stage of politics into the study, the countryside and the boudoir, so again, the collapse of the Roman Republic rendered politics neither interesting nor safe for any but the most robust of poets. Even so, Ovid fell disastrously foul of Augustus' authority and spent the last years of his life, from A.D. 8 until his death about a decade later, in exile.

As a boy and young man, he received the conventional education of a reasonably prosperous and ambitious Italian family. First at home, then at Rome and finally on the Grand Tour (including Athens, Sicily and Asia Minor) he was given all the training and polish necessary for a legal or political career. At the core of this training was a grounding in rhetoric achieved largely through exercises known as *controuersiae* and *suasoriae*; in the former, the student would prepare an argument based on an unusual or even exotic situation arising out of a point of law; in the latter, he would prepare a speech to sway a figure of history or mythology confronted by some dramatic or momentous decision. No reader of Ovid will be surprised to learn that Ovid preferred the latter and, for good or ill, the influence of these exercises is to be found throughout his work.

Ovid did embark briefly on the political career his father had wanted for him but his own inclinations and genius and the influence of his friends soon drove him to abandon politics and the law in favour of poetry.

All his early work was written in elegiac couplets (the metres are discussed in the next section), a medium well suited to his witty and epigrammatic style. His subject matter ranged from the plight of various mythological women in a whole range of disastrous love affairs to a number of mock didactic works purporting to give practical advice to both sexes on every aspect of the conduct of a love affair including even a poem on cosmetics. Such poetry did, however, have a more serious side. Ovid, like Catullus as well as the Augustan poets, was amazingly well read and his work is packed with witty and learned allusions to his predecessors in both Greek and Latin. Roman poets, such as Catullus, Tibullus and Propertius, as well as the almost entirely lost Gallus, had established elegiac as a prime form for amatory poetry, and Ovid's work was firmly established in that tradition.

He was exiled in A.D. 8, though we do not know precisely why. There is, however, no need to doubt his own account that it arose from *carmen et error*, 'a poem and a mistake'. For a brief discussion, see the note on 3.142. Ovid's rather cavalier attitude to authority and sexual propriety throughout his amatory elegiacs must have earned him disapprobation at a time when Augustus was constantly legislating in an attempt to enforce high moral standards. A single famous example must suffice here to make the point. In 23 B.C., M. Marcellus fell sick and died. He had recently married Augustus' daughter, Julia (they were cousins, for Marcellus' mother was Augustus' sister). The young man had clearly been marked out as Augustus' successor though he was only nineteen (he was the same age as Ovid) and the grief that followed his death was quite unrestrained. Virgil made him the final tragic figure in his famous parade of Roman heroes at the end of the sixth book of the *Aeneid* and, it is said, the boy's mother swooned when she heard Virgil recite the lines. Austin's note on *Aen.* 6.868 gives a full account of the elaborate memorials constructed for him by his grieving family. Among them was a marble portico and library dedicated by his mother. There must, accordingly, be real mischief in Ovid when, in a list of places which are particularly good for picking up a girl, he included this very monument (*Ars Amat.* 1.69-70).

However, Ovid was a man of great literary ambition. The clever trifles discussed above were so packed with wit and charm and learning that they would alone have secured him a place among the famous poets of antiquity. Nevertheless, true greatness seemed to require a major work in weighty dactylic hexameters, the metre of Homer and of Virgil whose *Aeneid* (published in 19 B.C., shortly after its author's death and when Ovid was still a young man) had come to dominate Latin letters in a wholly unprecedented way. No direct challenge to the master of epic, Virgil, was possible, but Ovid had conceived a rival plan and by the time of his exile it was essentially complete. In his *Metamorphoses*, Ovid turned to the dactylic hexameter to produce a mythological *tour de force* of epic scale that wholly transcended anything he had produced before. This, his greatest work, was essentially complete when he was sent into exile, and he had even completed the first half of another serious work, this time in elegiac couplets again, the *Fasti*, a calendar of the Roman year, which afforded ample scope for a display of religious, historical, mythological and astronomical learning.

The *Metamorphoses* is a very long poem (15 books in all) in the form of a highly idiosyncratic 'history' of the world from Creation to the death and deification of Julius Caesar. Its special peculiarity is that each of the stories it tells involves a metamorphosis (transformation) and each is so attached to the next that the whole gives the illusion of a seamless garment. There was, of course, a long tradition of more or less large poems using a single theme to unite a collection of stories. Hesiod (or, perhaps more probably, a sixth century imitator) had produced a *Catalogue of Women*, now largely lost, which consisted simply of a string of tales about women each starting with the simple formula, 'Or like...', the origin of its alternative title, *Eoiae*. This work had had a considerable influence on the Hellenistic writers. Callimachus' *Aetia*, for instance, an elegiac poem of over 4,000 lines (though only fragments survive now) was a string of legends united by the fact that all related the 'causes' (*aitia*) of some Greek custom, religious rite etc. In the 2nd century B.C., Nicander had composed a *Heteroeumena* (an alternative Greek word for *Metamorphoses*) and Ovid's older contemporaries, Parthenius and Theodorus, were also each said to have composed a *Metamorphoses*. This is a very complex issue and those who wish to follow it up should consult Wilkinson (144-46), the authorities cited by him and my own notes on 1.1 and 1.4.

One of the most obvious features of Ovid's *Metamorphoses* is the attention paid to achieving the effect of a continuous narrative, or *perpetuum...carmen* as he himself put it at 1.4. He achieved this sometimes by clever links (at 1.568-85, the Io story is linked to the Daphne story before it through an account of rivers congregating to comfort the river Peneus on the loss of his daughter, Daphne; of the rivers, only Inachus was missing and this was because of the sad tale of his daughter, Io...), sometimes by arranging for one character to narrate a story to another (at 1.689-712, Mercury begins to tell Argus the story of Syrinx and would have told it all if it had not put Argus to sleep) and sometimes by bringing together a series of stories with a common theme (from 3.1. to 4.603, the stories are linked by the common thread of Thebes). The situation is further complicated, however, by the fact that it is possible to detect other structures, such as the simple chronological one, or more subtle groupings, such as Otis's (83) four-fold division, 'The Divine Comedy' (Books 1-2), 'The Avenging Gods' (3.1-6.400), 'The Pathos of

Love' (6.401-11.795) and 'Rome and the Deified Ruler' (12-15), each section itself subdivided, according to Otis, into smaller sections as discussed in his following pages. Some readers may well find the specific analyses of Otis and others, at least in part, unconvincing, but few if any will deny that the unity of the *Metamorphoses* is achieved by Ovid's genius in relating one story to another in a bewildering variety of ways. The decision to restrict this edition to the first four books is quite arbitrary; indeed, it necessitates breaking off before the Perseus story is complete. It will, however, become obvious that there are no satisfactory breaks in this work and the whole, in this format, would make a cumbrous volume indeed. The logic of the situation suggests that, if this volume proves useful, the attempt should be made to complete the work.

In spite of Augustus' decision to banish Ovid as an offender against public morality, many readers detect a strong moral and humane theme throughout the *Metamorphoses*. Cruelty and treachery are almost invariably punished, but all the more venial of the foibles and weaknesses of human nature are depicted with a constant, gentle humour. One of the recurrent motifs is that the metamorphosis is only the revelation of some ultimate truth about the victim (see the note on 1.234) and the mediaeval writers who treated the *Metamorphoses* as a storehouse of paradigms for moral instruction (see Rand 131-37, Wilkinson 366-98) were exaggerating rather than falsifying. There are so many verbal pyrotechnics, so much showing off of learning, so much wit and humour (some subtle, some not, but none cruel) that the fundamental humanity of Ovid can be lost sight of. Many may even agree with the elder Seneca (*Contr.* 2.10.12) who complained that Ovid did not lack the judgement to restrain his excesses but the will. For my own part, I find his charm and sensitivity too overwhelming to be much exercised by his occasional blemishes. For a particularly trenchant view of Ovid's moral purpose, see W.R. Johnson in *Ancient Writers, Greece and Rome*, ed. T.J. Ince (New York, 1982) II 783-806.

Exile was a bitter pill for Ovid, the ultimate sophisticate, to swallow. The last six months of the *Fasti* were abandoned and there flowed from his pen instead a great outpouring of elegiac verse devoted largely to complaints about his punishment, nostalgia for happier days and pleadings to a variety of friends for help to secure a return home. Eventually, some four years after the death of Augustus, he died himself, still in exile at Tomis (a small town on the Black Sea, now Constanta in modern Romania). In his ten years there, he never tired of bemoaning the climate of the place and its remoteness, but he did learn the local language and he did acknowledge the kindness that his hosts had afforded him.

A much fuller account of the issues raised in this section will be found in Wilkinson and in Kenny, *Cambridge History of Classical Literature* II (Cambridge, 1982) 420-57. See also J.C. Thibault, *The Mystery of Ovid's Exile* (Beverley and Los Angeles, 1964).

2. *Metre*

English verse is based on stress; it is, essentially, a recognizable pattern of stressed and unstressed syllables.

> Mad dogs and Englishmen go out in the mid-day sun.

It would be possible to substitute for 'Englishmen' words such as 'antelopes' or 'terriers' without disturbing the metre because all three words have the same stress pattern; substitute 'alsatians', however, and the metre is lost, not because the number of syllables is wrong, but because the stress pattern is.

Classical Greek, on the other hand, had no stress so that its verse could not be stress based. It was founded instead on a pattern of 'long' (marked -) and 'short' (marked ∪) syllables, sometimes called 'heavy' and 'light', though both sets of terms are misleading because not all 'long' syllables take longer to say than 'short' syllables and 'heavy' and 'light' suggest stress which is quite wrong. It will suffice to say that the distinction for the Greek speaker between 'long' and 'short' syllables was different from, but no less important than, the distinction between stressed and unstressed syllables for the English speaker.

The Homeric poems, and all Classical epic and didactic poetry thereafter (and much more besides), were written in the dactylic hexameter. This rhythm consists of six dactyls (-∪∪) which may (in the case of the last foot, must) become spondees (--), like this:

$$— \overset{∪∪}{—} / — \overset{∪∪}{—} / — \overset{∪∪}{—} / — \overset{∪∪}{—} / — \overset{∪∪}{—} / — —$$

(As in all metres, Greek and Latin, a short syllable may count long at the end of a line). By translating length into stress, it is possible to gain some sense of the rhythm from the schoolboy mnemonic:

> Down in a deep dark ditch sat an old cow munching a turnip.

But, as the pattern above indicates and as any reading of the text will illustrate, the dactylic hexameter enjoys great inherent variety. Add to that the fact that sentences could, and more and more frequently did, run over from line to line, coming to rest at a considerable variety of points within the line, and it will be seen that this is a metre well suited for narrative poetry.

The elegiac couplet, on the other hand, is, as its name indicates, a two line metre and is a rhythm which clearly lends itself to end stopped lines. Indeed, the second line of the couplet is often no more than a restatement of the first. It is, accordingly, a superb metre for cleverness and wit, but it lacks the epic weight of the dactylic hexameters, though it never lost its role in brief epitaphs where its very simplicity could lend real dignity.

Latin, like English, is a stressed language and its very earliest verse, like much of its mediaeval or modern (*gaudeamus igitur*, for instance, or *adeste, fideles*), was based wholly on stress patterns, just like English verse. However, during the classical period and beyond, for at least a millenium from the second century B.C., Latin verse was based on the principles of Greek quantitative verse, as it is called, though, gradually, with some extra refinements that almost certainly arose because Latin was a stressed language.

The reader who wishes to know more should consult L.P. Wilkinson, *Golden Latin Artistry* (Cambridge, 1970) 89-134. Further exploration of the purely technical aspects of this section could usefully begin with W. Sidney Allen, *Accent and Rhythm* (Cambridge, 1973) and D.E. Hill, 'Quaestio Prosodiae', *Glotta* 52 (1974) 218-31.

3. *The text*

The *Metamorphoses* was one of the most popular of classical works during the Middle Ages and, as a consequence, we possess a bewildering number of mediaeval manuscripts, though none earlier than the ninth century and no complete manuscript earlier than the twelfth. In addition, we possess a translation into Greek by the 13th century monk, Maximus Planudes. All the ordinary difficulties of such a tradition are further complicated by the apparent existence from time to time of ancient alternatives which may or may not have arisen from two editions from Ovid's own hand. For the details, see R.J. Tarrant in *Texts and Transmission*, edited L.D. Reynolds, (Oxford, 1983) 276-82.

Professor Tarrant is preparing a text for the O.C.T. series and he very kindly sent me copies of his draft typescript of the text for the first four books. In choosing between well known variants or emendations I have, far more often than not, been guided by him but I have not thought it right to anticipate publication of his original ideas (except at 3.715). His text will obviously become the standard one; in view of its imminence, I have contented myself with producing a readable text without apparatus or serious pretensions to originality. The punctuation style is my own.

4. *The translation*

Before any attempt to outline the principles on which this translation is based, it may help to consider other possible approaches and discuss why they have been discarded.

It might be argued that verse for a lengthy work is as alien to a modern audience as Latin itself and any attempt, therefore, to use verse cloaks the translation with a quaintness that is quite wrong. There are, of course, translations available for anyone of that persuasion and the theoretical position is advanced in perhaps its most trenchant form in E.V. Rieu's introduction to his Penguin translation of the *Odyssey*. This translation of the *Metamorphoses*, however, is based on the proposition that the 'otherness' of Ovid is part of his importance and appeal and that to make him seem like a contemporary is not the task of his translator.

It might be argued that Ovid's verse was composed according to the strictest rules and that the appropriate English equivalent would involve strict metre at least and, probably, rhyme as well. Arthur Golding, whose translation was known to Shakespeare, and A.E. Watts (University of California Press, 1954), whose translation was lavishly praised by Otis, are among the best known to have adopted this approach. On rhyme I cannot do better than cite Milton's preamble to *Paradise Lost:*

> *The measure is* English *Heroic Verse without Rime,*
> *as that of* Homer *in* Greek, *and of* Virgil *in* Latin;
> *Rime being no necessary Adjunct or true Ornament*
> *of Poem or good Verse, in longer Works especially,*
> *but the Invention of a barbarous Age, to set off*
> *wretched matter and lame Metre; grac't indeed*
> *since by the use of some famous modern Poets,*
> *carried away by Custom, but much to thir own*
> *vexation, hindrance, and constraint to express many*
> *things otherwise, and for the most part worse than*
> *else they would have exprest them. This neglect then*
> *of Rime so little is to be taken for a defect, though*
> *it may seem so perhaps to vulgar Readers, that*
> *it rather is to be esteem'd an example set, the*
> *first in* English, *of ancient liberty recover'd to*
> *Heroic Poem from the troublesome and modern*
> *bondage of Riming.*

Furthermore, rhyme must restrict vocabulary and, therefore, fidelity and, even more important, it produces either end stopped lines or constant comic effect. For all these reasons, rhyme is possibly appropriate for Ovid's elegiacs but certainly not for his hexameter poem. Most of these arguments apply also, to a greater or lesser extent, to strict verse but, in any case, the argument for strict verse is based on something of a fallacy. While it is perfectly true that Ovidian hexameters are written to very precise rules they are, nevertheless, rules which permit an astonishing range of tempos which would be wholly lost in the strait-jacket of English strict verse. For all these reasons, I have settled on a six-beat blank verse effect though I have not scrupled, from time to time, to stretch my metre even to the point where the reader may think that it has become prose, if fidelity to Ovid's meaning was not, apparently, otherwise attainable. In broad terms, I took the view that once a rhythm had been established, it would be easier for the reader to imagine that it had been sustained than to identify and correct an infidelity. The principal advantage of the line for line translation is that it minimises the distortions inevitable in any translation. It must be wrong to use six words where Ovid uses only one, or seriously to distort the order of his ideas. I have tried to preserve either the order of Ovid's words or his sentence structure, whichever seemed more significant in each case. Where Ovid uses a common Latin word, I have sought a common English word, but where his vocabulary is highly poetic, deliberately archaic or, as so often, where he has deliberately coined a new word, I have attempted the same effect in the English. In the notes, I have tried to draw attention to particular instances where the translation has failed or might mislead. I hope that I have done this often enough so that the reader never wholly forgets that this is a translation, and not so frequently that the reader loses all trust. Ideally, the reader will so enjoy the translation and the insights that it, together with the notes, provides, that he will be driven to a desire to master the Latin. For a full account of the history of Renaissance English translations of Ovid, see Wilkinson 406-38. For more on the principles behind this particular translation, see D.E. Hill, 'What sort of Translation of Virgil do we need?', *G & R* 25 (1978) 59-68.

5. *The notes*

As has already been indicated, Ovid's *Metamorphoses* is an amazingly rich poem full of learning, allusion and wit. Apart from the very important observations on the limits of the translation, as discussed above, the main purposes of the notes are to elucidate passages likely to be unclear, to indicate something of Ovid's possible sources and to discuss how he treated them, to give some indication of how Ovid's work has influenced his successors and to add anything else which seems valuable or interesting. The notes make no pretence whatsoever of completeness and, inevitably, reflect one man's tastes and prejudices. The hope is, however, that the notes will alert readers to the sort of questions that can be asked, challenge readers to notice, from their own reading, important points that have been omitted and bring to readers' attention classical authors and modern scholarly works they might otherwise have ignored. Students of classics in translation, and some readers will surely fall into that category, are often far too diffident to approach the notes of the standard editions of classical authors. In an attempt to overcome this, I have quoted from such works extensively and directed to them very freely in the hope that any reader with access to a standard university library will feel drawn to use its resources and thus, in a relatively painless way, acquire a wider and deeper knowledge of classical literature with Ovid as the spur. However, the genius of Ovid is such that, although a full appreciation does indeed depend on a close familiarity with classical literature, much profit and pleasure can still be gained from a relatively superficial reading. Accordingly, a reader coming to the work for the first time should consult the notes only when puzzled by the translation or text. Second or subsequent readings can then be enriched by following up the leads given in the notes.

The notes include almost no linguistic discussion; it would be burdensome for those without Latin and, with a facing translation present, largely superfluous for those with Latin, especially since they can turn to Lee, Moore-Blunt and Henderson for more linguistically based notes on books 1-3.

Two points about Ovid's 'sources' should be made plain. Much classical and Hellenistic literature known to Ovid is lost to us. Accordingly, it should not be assumed that a note's reference to an earlier treatment of a myth or idea necessarily involves a suggestion that it is Ovid's source. Each case must be judged on its merits; an understanding of Ovid cannot, however, be complete without as much knowledge as possible about the ancient tradition behind him and a full appreciation of his sense of detail.

Some readers may be disappointed that the notes are not much fuller on Ovid's influence on later times. The best general treatments of this subject are to be found in Rand, Wilkinson and the essays by Robathan and Jameson in *Ovid*, edited J.W. Binns (London, 1973) 191-242. It is, however, a vast subject and no one has yet been able to do more than scratch the surface. The notes should, however, help those already well versed in the literature, music and art of the Middle Ages and beyond to develop this field. For much of the Mediaeval period, the first four books of the *Metamorphoses* were a standard part of the school syllabus, so that a large part of Ovid's influence arises from these very books. One last resource for a study of Ovid's influence was published too late to enable me to take more than superficial advantage of it in the preparation of the notes: Hanne Carlsen, *A Bibliography to the Classical Tradition in English Literature* (Copenhagen, 1985), a book that should prove invaluable to everyone interested in the *nachleben* of the Classics.

METAMORPHOSES I-IV

LIBER I

In noua fert animus mutatas dicere formas
corpora; di, coeptis (nam uos mutastis et illas)
aspirate meis primaque ab origine mundi
ad mea perpetuum deducite tempora carmen.
5   ante mare et terras et quod tegit omnia caelum
unus erat toto naturae uultus in orbe,
quem dixere Chaos, rudis indigestaque moles
nec quidquam nisi pondus iners congestaque eodem
non bene iunctarum discordia semina rerum.
10   nullus adhuc mundo praebebat lumina Titan,
nec noua crescendo reparabat cornua Phoebe,
nec circumfuso pendebat in aere Tellus
ponderibus librata suis, nec bracchia longo
margine terrarum porrexerat Amphitrite.
15   utque erat et tellus illic et pontus et aer,
sic erat instabilis tellus, innabilis unda,
lucis egens aer; nulli sua forma manebat
obstabatque aliis aliud, quia corpore in uno
frigida pugnabant calidis, umentia siccis,
20   mollia cum duris, sine pondere habentia pondus.
hanc Deus et melior litem Natura diremit;
nam caelo terras et terris abscidit undas
et liquidum spisso secreuit ab aere caelum.
quae postquam euoluit caecoque exemit aceruo,
25   dissociata locis concordi pace ligauit.
ignea conuexi uis et sine pondere caeli
emicuit summaque locum sibi fecit in arce;
proximus est aer illi leuitate locoque;
densior his tellus elementaque grandia traxit
30   et pressa est grauitate sua; circumfluus umor
ultima possedit solidumque coercuit orbem.
sic ubi dispositam quisquis fuit ille deorum
congeriem secuit sectamque in membra redegit,
principio terram, ne non aequalis ab omni
35   parte foret, magni speciem glomerauit in orbis.
tum freta diffudit rapidisque tumescere uentis
iussit et ambitae circumdare litora terrae.
addidit et fontes et stagna immensa lacusque,
fluminaque obliquis cinxit decliuia ripis;
40   quae diuersa locis partim sorbentur ab ipsa,

BOOK I

My spirit moves me to tell of shapes changed into strange
bodies; oh gods (for it was you that changed them),
inspire what I have begun and from the first beginning of the world
lead my continuous song down to my own times.
    Before the sea and the lands and the sky that covers all,   5
there was one face of nature in her whole orb
(they call it Chaos), a rough unordered mass,
nothing except inactive weight and heaped together
the discordant seeds of unassembled things.
No Titan yet provided light for the world,   10
nor did new Phoebe grow and so restore her horns,
nor was the Earth hanging in the surrounding air,
balanced by its own weight, nor had Amphitrite
stretched out her arms around the long edge of the lands.
And though there was both earth and sea and air,   15
unstable was the earth, unswimmable was the sea,
without light was the air. No part maintained its form,
and one impeded the others, because in one body
the cold were fighting with the hot, the wet with the dry,
the soft with the hard, and with the weightless those with weight.   20
    God, or more kindly Nature, settled this dispute;
for from the sky he split the lands and from the lands the waves,
and divided the clear sky from the misty air.
And after unfolding these and drawing them from their dark heap,
he bound them in their separate places with harmonious peace.   25
The fiery and weightless power of the convex sky
flashed out and made its place at the highest point of the vault;
next to that in lightness and in place is air;
earth, heavier than these, brought on its large atoms
and was pressed down by its own weight; the circling water   30
occupied the final place and confined the solid disk.
    When whichever of the gods he was had so ordered
the mass, divided it and, once it was divided, forced it into parts,
first, so that the earth might not be in any way
unequal, he rolled it into the shape of a great orb.   35
Then he scattered the seas and ordered them to swell
under the raging winds and surround the shores of the encircled earth.
He added springs, vast ponds and lakes,
he set the descending rivers into their sloping banks.   39
They, in their various places, are sometimes absorbed by the earth itself,

in mare perueniunt partim campoque recepta
liberioris aquae pro ripis litora pulsant.
iussit et extendi campos, subsidere ualles,
fronde tegi siluas, lapidosos surgere montes.
45   utque duae dextra caelum totidemque sinistra
parte secant zonae (quinta est ardentior illis),
sic onus inclusum numero distinxit eodem
cura Dei, totidemque plagae tellure premuntur.
quarum quae media est non est habitabilis aestu;
50   nix tegit alta duas; totidem inter utrumque locauit
temperiemque dedit mixta cum frigore flamma.
imminet his aer, qui quanto est pondere terrae
pondus aquae leuius tanto est onerosior igne.
illic et nebulas, illic consistere nubes
55   iussit et humanas motura tonitrua mentes
et cum fulminibus facientes fulgura uentos.
his quoque non passim mundi Fabricator habendum
aera permisit; uix nunc obsistitur illis,
cum sua quisque regant diuerso flamina tractu,
60   quin lanient mundum; tanta est discordia fratrum.
Eurus ad auroram Nabataeaque regna recessit
Persidaque et radiis iuga subdita matutinis;
uesper et occiduo quae litora sole tepescunt
proxima sunt Zephyro; Scythiam septemque Triones
65   horrifer inuasit Boreas; contraria tellus
nubibus assiduis pluuiaque madescit ab Austro.
haec super imposuit liquidum et grauitate carentem
aethera nec quidquam terrenae faecis habentem.
uix ita limitibus dissaepserat omnia certis,
70   cum quae pressa diu massa latuere sub illa
sidera coeperunt toto efferuescere caelo.
neu regio foret ulla suis animalibus orba,
astra tenent caeleste solum formaeque deorum,
cesserunt nitidis habitandae piscibus undae,
75   terra feras cepit, uolucres agitabilis aer.
        sanctius his animal mentisque capacius altae
deerat adhuc et quod dominari in cetera posset;
natus homo est; siue hunc diuino semine fecit
ille Opifex rerum, mundi melioris origo,
80   siue recens tellus seductaque nuper ab alto
aethere cognati retinebat semina caeli,
quam satus Iapeto mixtam pluuialibus undis
finxit in effigiem moderantum cuncta deorum.
pronaque cum spectent animalia cetera terram,
85   os homini sublime dedit caelumque uidere
iussit et erectos ad sidera tollere uultus.

and sometimes come down to the sea and, received by that expanse
of freer water, pound beaches instead of banks.
He ordered too the plains to be extended, the valleys to sink,
the woods to be covered by leaves and the stony mountains to rise.
And as there are two zones on the right and two   45
on the left to divide the sky (and there is a fifth hotter than them),
so has God's care marked out the burden they enclose
with the same number, and just as many regions are marked upon the earth.
Of these, the middle one cannot be lived in for the heat;
deep snow covers two; between each kind he placed two more   50
and gave them a moderate climate, flame mixed with cold.
Poised over these is the air, as much heavier than fire
as the weight of water is lighter than the weight of earth.
It was there that he told the mists to gather,
there the clouds and the thunder that was to trouble human minds,   55
and the winds that make both lightning and the thunderbolts.
The Maker of the world did not allow the air to be held
by these at whim; as it is, when each now rules his blasts
in regions far apart, there is scarcely any stopping them
from ripping the world apart; so great is the brothers' discord.   60
Eurus retreated to the dawn, to the Nabataean realms,
to Persia and the mountain range beneath the morning rays;
the evening and the shores warmed by the setting sun
are nearest to Zephyrus; Scythia and the Seven Oxen
were seized by chilling Boreas; the land directly opposite   65
is drenched with constant clouds and rain by Auster.
Over these he placed the ether clear
and weightless and having nothing of the dregs of earth.
He had scarcely thus marked all things off within their sure limits,
when, after lying long hidden beneath that mass,   70
the stars began to boil up all through the sky.
And, in case any region should be without its living things,
the stars and the forms of the gods took heaven's floor,
the waves were granted to the shimmering fish to live in,
the earth took the wild beasts, and the mobile air the birds.   75
    A holier living thing than these, with more capacity for a high mind,
one that could rule over the rest, was still required;
man was born; perhaps he was made from divine seed
by the universal Craftsman, the source of a better world;
perhaps the new earth freshly separated from the high   80
ether retained the seeds of the kindred sky,
which the son of Iapetus mixed with rain water
and shaped into the likeness of the all-controlling gods.
And while all other animals are prone and look upon the earth,
he gave to man an upright face, told him to look upon   85
the sky and raise his face aloft towards the stars.

sic modo quae fuerat rudis et sine imagine tellus
induit ignotas hominum conuersa figuras.
    aurea prima sata est aetas, quae uindice nullo,
90   sponte sua, sine lege fidem rectumque colebat.
poena metusque aberant, nec uerba minantia fixo
aere ligabantur, nec supplex turba timebat
iudicis ora sui, sed erant sine uindice tuti.
nondum caesa suis, peregrinum ut uiseret orbem,
95   montibus in liquidas pinus descenderat undas,
nullaque mortales praeter sua litora norant.
nondum praecipites cingebant oppida fossae;
non tuba derecti, non aeris cornua flexi,
non galeae, non ensis erat; sine militis usu
100   mollia securae peragebant otia gentes.
ipse quoque immunis rastroque intacta nec ullis
saucia uomeribus per se dabat omnia tellus;
contentique cibis nullo cogente creatis
arbuteos fetus montanaque fraga legebant
105   cornaque et in duris haerentia mora rubetis
et quae deciderant patula Iouis arbore glandes.
uer erat aeternum, placidique tepentibus auris
mulcebant zephyri natos sine semine flores.
mox etiam fruges tellus inarata ferebat,
110   nec renouatus ager grauidis canebat aristis;
flumina iam lactis, iam flumina nectaris ibant,
flauaque de uiridi stillabant ilice mella.
    postquam Saturno tenebrosa in Tartara misso
sub Ioue mundus erat, subiit argentea proles,
115   auro deterior, fuluo pretiosior aere.
Iuppiter antiqui contraxit tempora ueris
perque hiemes aestusque et inaequales autumnos
et breue uer spatiis exegit quattuor annum.
tum primum siccis aer feruoribus ustus
120   canduit, et uentis glacies astricta pependit;
tum primum subiere domos (domus antra fuerunt
et densi frutices et uinctae cortice uirgae);
semina tum primum longis Cerealia sulcis
obruta sunt, pressique iugo gemuere iuuenci.
125   tertia post illam successit aenea proles,
saeuior ingeniis et ad horrida promptior arma,
non scelerata tamen. de duro est ultima ferro;
protinus inrupit uenae peioris in aeuum
omne nefas; fugere pudor uerumque fidesque,
130   in quorum subiere locum fraudesque dolique
insidiaeque et uis et amor sceleratus habendi.
uela dabat uentis (nec adhuc bene nouerat illos)

So earth, which had just been rough and formless,
was changed and wore the unknown shapes of men.
        Golden was the first age born; with no avenger,
of its own free will and without law it cultivated faith and right.   90
There was no punishment or fear, no threatening words were etched
upon the fixed bronze, no crowd of suppliants
feared the judge's face, but, without an avenger, all were safe.
Not yet had the felled pine tree come down from its own mountain
to the flowing waves to visit a foreign world,   95
and mortals knew no shores besides their own.
Not yet were towns enclosed by steep ditches,
there was no bugle with straight bronze, there were no twisted horns,
no helmets and no sword; without the need for soldiers
the races lived out their peaceful leisure, free of care.   100
The earth too, unworked and untouched by the hoe,
and uninjured by any ploughs, gave everything of its own accord,
and, content with foods produced by no one's labour,
men gathered arbutus fruits and mountain strawberries,
cornels and blackberries that cling to the tough brambles,   105
and acorns which had fallen from the spreading tree of Jove.
Spring was eternal, and gentle Zephyrs with warming
breezes soothed the flowers that had sprung up unsown.
Soon even the unploughed earth was bearing corn
and the untilled field grew white with swelling ears of grain;   110
now there ran rivers of milk, now rivers of nectar
and yellow honey dripped from the green holm-oak.
        After Saturn had been sent to shadowy Tartarus
and the world was under Jupiter, there succeeded the silver race,
inferior to gold, but more precious than yellow bronze.   115
Jupiter curtailed the days of the ancient spring
and through winters, summers, inconstant autumns
and brief spring measured the year in four periods.
Then first did the air, burnt with dry heat,
glow white, and the ice hung down frozen by the winds;   120
then first did man enter houses (their houses had been caves,
thick shrubs and branches bound with bark);
then first were the seeds of Ceres buried
in long furrows, while the oxen groaned beneath the pressing yoke.
        Third after that followed the bronze race,   125
fiercer of character and readier to turn to dreadful arms,
yet not sunk in sin. From hard iron was the last race made;
at once there burst upon this age of baser vein
all evil; and shame and truth and trust fled away,
and in their place succeeded fraud and treachery   130
and plots and violence and sinful love of possession.
The sailor gave his sails to the winds (up till then he had not known

navita, quaeque diu steterant in montibus altis
fluctibus ignotis exsultauere carinae.
135 communemque prius ceu lumina solis et auras
cautus humum longo signauit limite mensor.
nec tantum segetes alimentaque debita diues
poscebatur humus, sed itum est in uiscera terrae
quasque recondiderat Stygiisque admouerat umbris
140 effodiuntur opes, inritamenta malorum.
iamque nocens ferrum ferroque nocentius aurum
prodierat; prodit bellum, quod pugnat utroque
sanguineaque manu crepitantia concutit arma.
uiuitur ex rapto; non hospes ab hospite tutus,
145 non socer a genero; fratrum quoque gratia rara est.
imminet exitio uir coniugis, illa mariti;
lurida terribiles miscent aconita nouercae;
filius ante diem patrios inquirit in annos;
uicta iacet Pietas, et Virgo caede madentes
150 ultima caelestum terras Astraea reliquit.
        neue foret terris securior arduus aether,
adfectasse ferunt regnum caeleste Gigantas
altaque congestos struxisse ad sidera montes.
tum pater omnipotens misso perfregit Olympum
155 fulmine et excussit subiectae Pelion Ossae.
obruta mole sua cum corpora dira iacerent,
perfusam multo natorum sanguine Terram
immaduisse ferunt calidumque animasse cruorem
et, ne nulla suae stirpis monimenta manerent,
160 in faciem uertisse hominum. sed et illa propago
contemptrix superum saeuaeque auidissima caedis
et uiolenta fuit; scires e sanguine natos.
        quae pater ut summa uidit Saturnius arce,
ingemit et, facto nondum uulgata recenti
165 foeda Lycaoniae referens conuiuia mensae,
ingentes animo et dignas Ioue concipit iras
conciliumque uocat; tenuit mora nulla uocatos.
est uia sublimis, caelo manifesta sereno;
Lactea nomen habet, candore notabilis ipso.
170 hac iter est superis ad magni tecta Tonantis
regalemque domum. dextra laeuaque deorum
atria nobilium ualuis celebrantur apertis
(plebs habitat diuersa locis); hac parte potentes
caelicolae clarique suos posuere penates.
175 hic locus est quem, si uerbis audacia detur,
haud timeam magni dixisse Palatia caeli.
ergo ubi marmoreo superi sedere recessu,
celsior ipse loco sceptroque innixus eburno

them well) and ships, which had before stood on
high mountains, pranced on the unfamiliar billows.
The soil, held in common before, like the light of the sun   135
or the air, was marked with a long boundary by a cautious surveyor.
And not only grain and due foods were demanded
of the rich soil, but a way was made into the bowels of the earth,
and riches, which it had concealed and moved to Stygian
shadows, were dug up to be an incitement to evils.   140
And now harmful iron, and gold more harmful than iron,
had emerged; there emerged war which fights with both
and shakes its clashing arms with bloody hand.
Men lived on pillage; no guest was safe from his host,   144
no father-in-law from his son-in-law; good will between brothers was rare.
The man is bent on the death of his wife and she on her husband's,
horrible stepmothers mix ghastly wolfsbane;
the son is too eager to cast his father's horoscope;
Piety lies conquered, and the Astraean Virgin, last
of the heavenly ones, has left the lands dripping from slaughter.   150
    And in case the lofty ether should be safer than the lands,
the Giants, they say, made an attempt upon the heavenly kingdom
and built a pile of mountains up to the high stars.
Then the almighty father dispatched his thunderbolt, shattered
Olympus and dashed Pelion from Ossa that lay underneath.   155
When the horrible bodies lay overwhelmed by their mass,
they say that Earth, drenched with much blood from her sons,
grew wet and breathed life into the warm blood,
and, in case no memorials of her offspring should remain,
turned it into the likeness of men; but that race too   160
despised the gods, was most eager for cruel slaughter
and given to violence; you could tell that they were born from blood.
    When from his citadel the Saturnian father saw these things,
he groaned and, remembering the disgusting banquet at Lycaon's table,
something not yet widely known, for it was freshly done,   165
nurtured a huge anger, worthy of Jupiter, in his heart
and called a council; no delay held up those called to it.
There is a way on high, obvious in a clear sky;
Milky is its name, for it is noted for its whiteness.
This is the gods' route to the great Thunderer's dwelling,   170
the royal home; to the right and to the left, the halls
of the noble gods have open doorways and are thronged
(the common gods live in separate areas); in this part, the powerful
and famous heavenly ones have established their penates.
This is the place which, if I may speak boldly,   175
I would not fear to speak of as great heaven's Palatine.
And so, when the gods were seated in the marble inner room,
he himself in his place on high and leaning on his ivory sceptre

terrificam capitis concussit terque quaterque
180   caesariem, cum qua terram, mare, sidera mouit.
talibus inde modis ora indignantia soluit:
'non ego pro mundi regno magis anxius illa
tempestate fui qua centum quisque parabat
inicere anguipedum captiuo bracchia caelo.
185   nam quamquam ferus hostis erat, tamen illud ab uno
corpore et ex una pendebat origine bellum.
nunc mihi qua totum Nereus circumsonat orbem
perdendum est mortale genus; per flumina iuro
infera sub terras Stygio labentia luco.
190   cuncta prius temptanda, sed immedicabile corpus
ense recidendum est ne pars sincera trahatur.
sunt mihi semidei, sunt rustica numina, Nymphae
Faunique Satyrique et monticolae Siluani;
quos, quoniam caeli nondum dignamur honore,
195   quas dedimus certe terras habitare sinamus.
an satis, o superi, tutos fore creditis illos,
cum mihi, qui fulmen, qui uos habeoque regoque,
struxerit insidias notus feritate Lycaon?'
      confremuere omnes studiisque ardentibus ausum
200   talia deposcunt. sic, cum manus impia saeuit
sanguine Caesareo Romanum exstinguere nomen,
attonitum tanto subitae terrore ruinae
humanum genus est, totusque perhorruit orbis;
nec tibi grata minus pietas, Auguste, tuorum est
205   quam fuit illa Ioui; qui postquam uoce manuque
murmura compressit, tenuere silentia cuncti.
substitit ut clamor pressus grauitate regentis,
Iuppiter hoc iterum sermone silentia rupit:
'ille quidem poenas (curam hanc dimittite) soluit;
210   quod tamen admissum, quae sit uindicta docebo.
contigerat nostras infamia temporis aures;
quam cupiens falsam summo delabor Olympo
et deus humana lustro sub imagine terras.
longa mora est quantum noxae sit ubique repertum
215   enumerare; minor fuit ipsa infamia uero.
Maenala transieram latebris horrenda ferarum
et cum Cyllene gelidi pineta Lycaei.
Arcados hinc sedes et inhospita tecta tyranni
ingredior, traherent cum sera crepuscula noctem.
220   signa dedi uenisse deum, uulgusque precari
coeperat. inridet primo pia uota Lycaon,
mox ait, "experiar deus hic discrimine aperto
an sit mortalis, nec erit dubitabile uerum."

three times or four shook the fearsome locks of hair
upon his head and with them moved earth, sea and stars.   180
Thus then he gave free rein to his indignant mouth:
'I was no more concerned for the kingdom of the world
on that occasion when each of the snake-footed ones was preparing
to lay his hundred arms on captive heaven.
For although the enemy was fierce, yet that war   185
depended on one group and on one origin.
Now I must destroy the race of mortals wherever Nereus
sounds around the whole world; I swear it by the rivers
below gliding underground in the Stygian grove.
Everything should be tried first, but the incurable body   190
must be pruned with the sword to prevent infection in the healthy part.
I have demi-gods, I have rustic spirits, the Nymphs
and the Fauns and the Satyrs and the mountain dwelling Silvans;
and since we do not yet deem them worth heavenly honour,
let us at least allow them to live in the lands we have given them!   195
Or, oh gods, do you believe that they will be safe enough
when I, who have the thunderbolt, I who rule you,
have had plots hatched against me by Lycaon, known for savagery.'
     They all muttered together and with burning passion demanded
punishment for a man of such audacity. Even so, when an impious band 200
raged to extinguish the name of Rome with Caesar's blood,
the human race was stunned by so great a fear
of sudden ruin and the whole world shuddered;
and the piety of your people, Augustus, was no less welcome to you   204
than that of Jupiter's people was to him; and after he had used his voice
                                                          and hand
to subdue their murmurs, they all kept silence together.
When the uproar had subsided, checked by the ruler's authority,
Jupiter again broke silence with this speech:
'He indeed has paid the penalty (forget that care);
but I shall tell you of his offence and of his punishment.   210
An ill report about the times had come to our ears:
I wanted it to be untrue and glided down from Olympus' height
and scoured through the lands, a god in human form.
It would take much time to specify how much mischief I discovered
everywhere: even the notoriety was less than the truth.   215
I had crossed dread Maenalos with its lairs of wild beasts
and the pine forests of cold Lycaeus together with mount Cyllene.
Next I approached the dwelling, the inhospitable roof of the Arcadian
king, while the last of the twilight was bringing in the night.
I gave a sign that a god had come and the people began   220
to pray. At first Lycaon mocked their pious prayers,
and then he said, "I shall make trial with a simple test whether he
is god or mortal; and the truth will not be doubtable."

nocte grauem somno necopina perdere morte
225   me parat; haec illi placet experientia ueri.
nec contentus eo est; missi de gente Molossa
obsidis unius iugulum mucrone resoluit,
atque ita seminecis partim feruentibus artus
mollit aquis, partim subiecto torruit igne.
230   quod simul imposuit mensis, ego uindice flamma
in domino dignos euerti tecta penates.
territus ipse fugit, nactusque silentia ruris
exululat frustraque loqui conatur; ab ipso
colligit os rabiem, solitaeque cupidine caedis
235   uertitur in pecudes et nunc quoque sanguine gaudet.
in uillos abeunt uestes, in crura lacerti;
fit lupus et ueteris seruat uestigia formae:
canities eadem est, eadem uiolentia uultus,
idem oculi lucent, eadem feritatis imago est.
240   occidit una domus, sed non domus una perire
digna fuit; qua terra patet, fera regnat Erinys.
in facinus iurasse putes; dent ocius omnes
quas meruere pati (sic stat sententia) poenas.'
      dicta Iouis pars uoce probant stimulosque frementi
245   adiciunt, alii partes adsensibus implent.
est tamen humani generis iactura dolori
omnibus, et quae sit terrae mortalibus orbae
forma futura rogant, quis sit laturus in aras
tura, ferisne paret populandas tradere terras.
250   talia quarentes (sibi enim fore cetera curae)
rex superum trepidare uetat, subolemque priori
dissimilem populo promittit origine mira.
      iamque erat in totas sparsurus fulmina terras,
sed timuit ne forte sacer tot ab ignibus aether
255   conciperet flammas longusque ardesceret axis.
esse quoque in fatis reminiscitur adfore tempus
quo mare, quo tellus correptaque regia caeli
ardeat et mundi moles operosa laboret.
tela reponuntur manibus fabricata Cyclopum;
260   poena placet diuersa, genus mortale sub undis
perdere et ex omni nimbos demittere caelo.
protinus Aeoliis Aquilonem claudit in antris
et quaecumque fugant inductas flamina nubes,
emittitque Notum. madidis Notus euolat alis,
265   terribilem picea tectus caligine uultum;

At night, when I was sound asleep, he planned to bring an unexpected
death upon me; that was the test of the truth he wanted.   225
And he was not content with that; with his sword-point he cut open
the throat of a hostage sent from the Molossian tribe,
and boiled part of the half-dead limbs
in bubbling water and roasted part over the fire.
As soon as he had placed it on the table, I with avenging flame   230
overturned his house onto penates who deserved their master.
He himself fled terrified, and when he had gained the silence of the
                                                           countryside,
he howled out and tried in vain to speak; his mouth
gathered savagery from the man himself and, with lust for his accustomed
                                                            slaughter,
he turned against his flocks and rejoiced still in blood.   235
His clothes changed into fur, his arms to legs;
he became a wolf but keeps traces of his old appearance;
his grey head is the same, the same the violence of his face,
the same eyes gleam, there is the same wild look.
One house has fallen, but it was not one house that   240
deserved to perish; the wild Erinys reigns wherever the earth stretches.
You would think that they were sworn to crime; all must the sooner pay
the penalties they deserve to suffer: so stands my decision.'
     Some voiced approval for Jove's words and pressed spurs
into his rage; others played their part with their applause.   245
Yet to discard the human race was painful
to them all, and they began to ask what would the world's shape be
deprived of mortals, who would there be to bring incense
to their altars, was he preparing to hand the world to wild beasts to
                                                            despoil.
As they questioned thus, the king of the gods told them not to fear   250
(since he would care for the rest) and promised
a race unlike the former people and from a wondrous source.
     And now he was about to shower thunderbolts on all the earth:
but he was afraid the holy ether would catch light
from so many fires and that the long sky would burn.   255
He remembered too that it was in the fates that there would be a time
when the sea and when the earth and when the kingdom of the sky would
                                                            ignite
and burn and the world's hard wrought mass would be in trouble.
The weapons fashioned by the Cyclops' hands were laid aside.
He decided on the opposite punishment, to destroy the human race   260
beneath the waters and to send storm-clouds down from the whole sky.
At once he confined Aquilo in the Aeolian caves
together with all the blasts that put the assembled clouds to flight,
and he sent Notus out: Notus flew out with dripping wings,
his terrible countenance covered with pitch-black fog;   265

barba grauis nimbis, canis fluit unda capillis,
fronte sedent nebulae, rorant pennaeque sinusque.
utque manu late pendentia nubila pressit,
fit fragor; hinc densi funduntur ab aethere nimbi.
270   nuntia Iunonis uarios induta colores
concipit Iris aquas alimentaque nubibus adfert.
sternuntur segetes et deplorata coloni
uota iacent, longique perit labor inritus anni.
      nec caelo contenta suo est Iouis ira, sed illum
275   caeruleus frater iuuat auxiliaribus undis.
conuocat hic amnes; qui postquam tecta tyranni
intrauere sui, 'non est hortamine longo
nunc,' ait, 'utendum. uires effundite uestras
(sic opus est), aperite domos ac mole remota
280   fluminibus uestris totas immittite habenas.'
iusserat; hi redeunt ac fontibus ora relaxant
et defrenato uoluuntur in aequora cursu.
ipse tridente suo terram percussit; at illa
intremuit motuque uias patefecit aquarum.
285   exspatiata ruunt per apertos flumina campos,
cumque satis arbusta simul pecudesque uirosque
tectaque cumque suis rapiunt penetralia sacris.
si qua domus mansit potuitque resistere tanto
indeiecta malo, culmen tamen altior huius
290   unda tegit, pressaeque latent sub gurgite turres.
      iamque mare et tellus nullum discrimen habebant;
omnia pontus erat, deerant quoque litora ponto.
occupat hic collem, cumba sedet alter adunca
et ducit remos illic ubi nuper arabat;
295   ille supra segetes aut mersae culmina uillae
nauigat, hic summa piscem deprendit in ulmo.
figitur in uiridi, si fors tulit, ancora prato,
aut subiecta terunt curuae uineta carinae;
et, modo qua graciles gramen carpsere capellae,
300   nunc ibi deformes ponunt sua corpora phocae.
mirantur sub aqua lucos urbesque domosque
Nereides, siluasque tenent delphines et altis
incursant ramis agitataque robora pulsant.
nat lupus inter oues, fuluos uehit unda leones,
305   unda uehit tigres; nec uires fulminis apro,
crura nec ablato prosunt uelocia ceruo;
quaesitisque diu terris ubi sistere possit,
in mare lassatis uolucris uaga decidit alis.
obruerat tumulos immensa licentia ponti,
310   pulsabantque noui montana cacumina fluctus.

his beard was heavy with storm-clouds, streams flowed from his hoary locks;
mists sat on his brow, his wings and his clothes' folds were wet with dew.
And as he squeezed the widely hanging clouds in his hand,
there was a crash; then from the ether, the thick storm-clouds poured down.
The messenger of Juno, Iris clad in varied   270
colours, drew up the waters and brought nourishment to the clouds.
The crops were flattened, the farmer wept
for his hopes laid low, and his long year's work was fruitless and dead.
    The anger of Jove, not content with the work of his sky, was
helped by his aquamarine brother and his assisting waves: 275
he summoned the rivers, and after they had entered
their king's house, 'I need not now,' he said, 'employ
a lengthy exhortation. Pour forth your strength
(that's what is needed), open up your homes, raise the starting gate
and give completely free rein to your streams.'   280
He had commanded; they returned and let their sources have their head
and with unbridled course they rolled down to the sea.
He himself struck the earth with his trident; it then
trembled and the motion opened up its waterways.
The rivers left the course and rushed through open fields,   285
and seized not only crops but trees as well and livestock,
men and houses and temples with their shrines.
If any house remained and could resist so great
an evil undemolished, its roof was still covered   289
by a higher wave and its towers were crushed and hidden underneath the
                                                                           flood.
    And now the sea and land had no distinction,
the sea was everything, a sea too that was without a shore.
One man seized on a hill, another sat in his curved skiff
and plied the oars where, just now, he had been ploughing;
one man sailed above the crops on the roof of his drowned   295
farmhouse, another caught a fish at the very top of an elm tree.
Sometimes an anchor stuck in the green meadow,
or a curved keel scraped on the vineyards beneath,
and, where the slender goats had just been browsing on the grass,
there now were lying the bodies of unsightly seals.   300
Underwater, groves and cities and houses amazed
the Nereids, dolphins occupied the woods and knocked
against high branches and shook and bumped the oaks.
The wolf swam among the sheep, the wave swept up the tawny lions,   304
the wave swept up the tigers; the strength of his flailing tusks was useless
to the boar, so were the stag's swift legs as he was carried off.
And after a long search for land on which it could alight,
the wandering bird fell down with wearied wings into the sea.
Hillocks were overwhelmed by the sea's unmeasured wantonness
and strange floods were beating at the mountain summits.   310

maxima pars unda rapitur; quibus unda pepercit,
illos longa domant inopi ieiunia uictu.
    separat Aonios Oetaeis Phocis ab aruis,
terra ferax dum terra fuit, sed tempore in illo
315   pars maris et latus subitarum campus aquarum.
mons ibi uerticibus petit arduus astra duobus,
nomine Parnasos, superantque cacumina nubes.
his ubi Deucalion (nam cetera texerat aequor)
cum consorte tori parua rate uectus adhaesit,
320   Corycidas nymphas et numina montis adorant
fatidicamque Themin, quae tunc oracla tenebat.
non illo melior quisquam nec amantior aequi
uir fuit, aut illa metuentior ulla deorum.
Iuppiter, ut liquidis stagnare paludibus orbem
325   et superesse uirum de tot modo milibus unum
et superesse uidet de tot modo milibus unam,
innocuos ambo, cultores numinis ambo,
nubila disiecit, nimbisque Aquilone remotis
et caelo terras ostendit et aethera terris.
330   nec maris ira manet, positoque tricuspide telo
mulcet aquas rector pelagi, supraque profundum
exstantem atque umeros innato murice tectum
caeruleum Tritona uocat, conchaeque sonanti
inspirare iubet fluctusque et flumina signo
335   iam reuocare dato. caua bucina sumitur illi,
tortilis in latum quae turbine crescit ab imo;
bucina quae, medio concepit ubi aera ponto,
litora uoce replet sub utroque iacentia Phoebo.
tum quoque, ut ora dei madida rorantia barba
340   contigit et cecinit iussos inflata receptus,
omnibus audita est telluris et aequoris undis,
et quibus est undis audita coercuit omnes.
iam mare litus habet, plenos capit alueus amnes,
flumina subsidunt collesque exire uidentur,
345   surgit humus, crescunt sola decrescentibus undis;
postque diem longam nudata cacumina siluae
ostendunt, limumque tenent in fronde relictum.
    redditus orbis erat; quem postquam uidit inanem
et desolatas agere alta silentia terras,
350   Deucalion lacrimis ita Pyrrham adfatur obortis:
'o soror, o coniunx, o femina sola superstes,
quam commune mihi genus et patruelis origo,
deinde torus iunxit, nunc ipsa pericula iungunt,
terrarum, quascumque uident occasus et ortus,
355   nos duo turba sumus; possedit cetera pontus.
haec quoque adhuc uitae non est fiducia nostrae

The greater part was snatched up by the water; those that the water spared
were tamed by long hunger and the scarcity of food.
    Phocis separates the Aonian from the Oetaean fields,
a fertile land, while it was land, but at that time
a part of the sea and a wide expanse of sudden waters;   315
a high mountain there seeks the stars with its two peaks,
Parnassus by name, and its summit overtops the clouds.
When Deucalion had landed here (for the sea had covered
all besides) after sailing with his marriage partner in their little boat,
they venerated the Corycian nymphs, the spirits of the mountain   320
and the prophetic Themis who at that time held the oracles.
There was not any man better than him nor more in love
with what is right, or any woman more in awe of gods than her.
When Jupiter saw the world submerged by swirling floods,
and one man surviving from so many thousands just before,   325
and saw one woman survive from so many thousands just before,
both innocent, both worshippers of god,
he dispersed the mists, and with Aquilo's help removed the storm-clouds
and revealed the lands to heaven and the ether to the lands.   329
And the sea did not stay angry, for by putting down his three-pronged fork
the marine ruler soothed the waters and called out to aquamarine
Triton, who rose above the deep, his shoulders
covered with living murex, and told him to blow
into his sounding conch-shell and give the signal to recall now
the floods and rivers: he took up the hollow horn   335
which, from the bottom of its spiral, twists and grows in width,
a horn which, whenever it is blown in the middle of the sea,
fills with its voice the shores that lie beneath each Phoebus.
Then too, as it touched the god's lips, which were wet from his dripping
beard, and once inflated sang out the retreat as ordered,   340
it was heard by all the waters of the earth and of the sea,
and it held back all the waters by which it had been heard.
Now the sea had a shore, their channels held the full streams,
the rivers fell and the hills were seen to emerge;   344
the earth rose; and with the decrease of the water the ground increased;
and after a long time the woods showed their uncovered
tree-tops, but kept the silt left on their foliage.
    The world had been restored; but after he had seen that it was empty,
and that the desolated lands were in deep silence,
Deucalion, as the tears welled up, spoke thus to Pyrrha: 350
'Oh sister, oh wife, oh only surviving woman,
a common race, and the brotherhood of our fathers, and then
the marriage bed united you to me; now we are united by our perils.
Of whatever lands are seen by the setting and the rising sun,
we two are all the population; the sea has claimed the rest.   355
Even our trust in life is not yet

certa satis; terrent etiamnunc nubila mentem.
quis tibi, si sine me fatis erepta fuisses,
nunc animus, miseranda, foret? quo sola timorem
360   ferre modo posses? quo consolante doleres?
namque ego, crede mihi, si te quoque pontus haberet,
te sequerer, coniunx, et me quoque pontus haberet.
o utinam possim populos reparare paternis
artibus atque animas formatae infundere terrae!
365   nunc genus in nobis restat mortale duobus
(sic uisum superis) hominumque exempla manemus.'
     dixerat, et flebant. placuit caeleste precari
numen et auxilium per sacras quaerere sortes.
nulla mora est; adeunt pariter Cephisidas undas,
370   ut nondum liquidas, sic iam uada nota secantes.
inde ubi libatos inrorauere liquores
uestibus et capiti, flectunt uestigia sanctae
ad delubra deae, quorum fastigia turpi
pallebant musco stabantque sine ignibus arae.
375   ut templi tetigere gradus, procumbit uterque
pronus humi gelidoque pauens dedit oscula saxo;
atque ita, 'si precibus,' dixerunt, 'numina iustis
uicta remollescunt, si flectitur ira deorum,
dic, Themi, qua generis damnum reparabile nostri
380   arte sit et mersis fer opem, mitissima, rebus.'
mota dea est sortemque dedit: 'discedite templo
et uelate caput cinctasque resoluite uestes
ossaque post tergum magnae iactate parentis.'
obstipuere diu, rumpitque silentia uoce
385   Pyrrha prior iussisque deae parere recusat,
detque sibi ueniam pauido rogat ore, timetque
laedere iactatis maternas ossibus umbras.
interea repetunt caecisque obscura latebris
uerba datae sortis secum inter seque uolutant.
390   inde Promethides placidis Epimethida dictis
mulcet, et, 'aut fallax,' ait, 'est sollertia nobis
aut pia sunt nullumque nefas oracula suadent.
magna parens terra est; lapides in corpore terrae
ossa reor dici; iacere hos post terga iubemur.'
395   coniugis augurio quamquam Titania mota est,
spes tamen in dubio est; adeo caelestibus ambo
diffidunt monitis. sed quid temptare nocebit?
discedunt uelantque caput tunicasque recingunt
et iussos lapides sua post uestigia mittunt.
400   saxa (quis hoc credat nisi sit pro teste uetustas?)
ponere duritiam coepere suumque rigorem,

sure enough; even now the clouds terrify my mind.
What would your thoughts be now, my piteous one, if you had been
snatched from the fates without me? How could you
bear the fear, alone? Who would console you in your grief?   360
For I, believe me, if the sea had you too,
would follow you, my wife, and the sea would have me too.
If only I could restore the nations with my father's
skills and pour souls into moulded earth!
Now the mortal race survives in us two   365
(so have the gods decided) and we remain as patterns of mankind.'
     He had spoken, and they wept. They decided to pray to the heavenly
power and to seek help through the sacred oracles.
Without delay, together they approached the Cephisian waters   369
which, though not yet clear, did now cut through their familiar channels.
When they had drawn water from there and bedewed
their clothes and heads with it, they turned their footsteps to the holy
goddess's shrine, where the gable was yellow
from the foul moss and the altars stood without their fires.
When they had reached the temple steps, they both fell   375
flat upon the ground in fear and kissed the cold stone,
and spoke thus: 'If gods are overcome and softened
by just prayers, if divine anger is bent aside,
tell us, Themis, by what art the loss of our race
can be repaired and bring help, oh gentlest one, to a drowned world.'   380
The goddess was moved and gave the oracle: 'Depart from the temple,
veil your heads, undo your robes' girding
and throw the bones of your great mother behind your backs.'
For a time they were struck dumb; Pyrrha's voice first
broke he silence in refusal to obey the goddess's commands,   385
and begged in fearful tones indulgence for herself, and was afraid
the throwing of her bones would harm her mother's ghost.
Meanwhile, they went over the obscure words of the oracle
given in dark riddles and turned them over in their minds and to each other.
Then Prometheus' son soothed Epimetheus' daughter   390
with gentle words saying, 'Either my skill deceives me,
or oracles are holy and urge nothing sinful.
Our great mother is the earth; I think the stones on her body
are meant by earth's bones; it is these we are told to throw behind our
                                                            backs.'
     Though Titania was moved by her husband's divination,   395
her hope was still in doubt: both so mistrusted
the heavenly advice; but how will it hurt to try?
They departed, they veiled their heads, loosened their tunics' girding
and dispatched the stones, as bidden, (behind where they were standing.
The rocks (who would believe this without the testimony of antiquity?) 400
began to shed their hardness and their rigidity

mollirique mora mollitaque ducere formam.
mox, ubi creuerunt naturaque mitior illis
contigit, ut quaedam, sic non manifesta uideri
405 forma potest hominis, sed uti de marmore coepta,
non exacta satis rudibusque simillima signis.
quae tamen ex illis aliquo pars umida suco
et terrena fuit, uersa est in corporis usum;
quod solidum est flectique nequit, mutatur in ossa;
410 quae modo uena fuit sub eodem nomine mansit;
inque breui spatio superorum numine saxa
missa uiri manibus faciem traxere uirorum,
et de femineo reparata est femina iactu.
inde genus durum sumus experiensque laborum,
415 et documenta damus qua simus origine nati.
  cetera diuersis tellus animalia formis
sponte sua peperit, postquam uetus umor ab igne
percaluit solis, caenumque udaeque paludes
intumuere aestu, fecundaque semina rerum,
420 uiuaci nutrita solo ceu matris in aluo,
creuerunt faciemque aliquam cepere morando.
sic, ubi deseruit madidos septemfluus agros
Nilus et antiquo sua flumina reddidit alueo,
aetherioque recens exarsit sidere limus,
425 plurima cultores uersis animalia glaebis
inueniunt; et in his quaedam perfecta per ipsum
nascendi spatium, quaedam modo coepta suisque
trunca uident numeris, et eodem in corpore saepe
altera pars uiuit, rudis est pars altera tellus.
430 quippe ubi temperiem sumpsere umorque calorque,
concipiunt, et ab his oriuntur cuncta duobus;
cumque sit ignis aquae pugnax, uapor umidus omnes
res creat et discors concordia fetibus apta est.
ergo, ubi diluuio tellus lutulenta recenti
435 solibus aetheriis altoque recanduit aestu,
edidit innumeras species partimque figuras
rettulit antiquas, partim noua monstra creauit.
illa quidem nollet, sed te quoque, maxime Python,
tum genuit, populisque nouis, incognite serpens,
440 terror eras; tantum spatii de monte tenebas.
hunc deus arquitenens, numquam letalibus armis
ante nisi in dammis capreisque fugacibus usus,
mille grauem telis, exhausta paene pharetra,
perdidit effuso per uulnera nigra ueneno.
445 neue operis famam possit delere uetustas,
instituit sacros celebri certamine ludos,
Pythia de domiti serpentis nomine dictos.

and after a while to be softened and, once softened, to take on a shape.
Soon, when they had grown and a gentler nature
had come upon them, a certain human form could be perceived,
though not clearly, but as if begun in marble,   405
not properly finished and very like a statue in the rough.
But the earthy part of them, damp
from some moisture, was altered to be used as flesh;
what was solid and could not be bent changed into bone;
what had just been vein kept the same name   410
and in a brief time, through the power of the gods, the rocks
dispatched by the man's hands took on the likeness of men,
and woman was restored by the woman's throwing.
And so we are a hard race that endures toil
and we give proof of the source from which we have been born.   415
     The other animals, in their various forms, were produced
spontaneously by the earth, when the lingering moisture had been warmed
by the sun's fire, and the mud and the damp marshes
had swelled up in the heat, and the fertile seeds of things
nourished in the life-supporting earth, as if in a mother's womb,   420
waited and grew and took on a particular likeness.
Just so, when the seven-mouthed Nile has left the drenched
fields and returned its streams to their original course,
and the fresh mud is heated by the ethereal star,
the farmers, as they turn the clods, find many   425
animals; and they see among them some complete and at the very
point of birth, some only just begun, stunted
and without their limbs, and often in the same body
one part is alive and the other part is raw earth.
For when a balance is formed of moisture and of heat,   430
they conceive, and from the two of them arises everything.
And though fire fights water, a moist warmth creates
all things, and a discordant concord is adept at procreation.
So, when the earth, muddied by the recent flood,
was warmed again by the ethereal sunshine, by the heat on high,   435
it gave forth countless species, partly restoring
ancient forms, partly creating wonders new.
It was then that she, unwillingly indeed, bore you too,
most great Python, and you were a terror, oh unheard of serpent,
to the new races; for you took up so great a space upon the mountain. 440
The archer-god, who had never before used his deadly
weapons except on fleeing red or yellow deer,
almost emptied his quiver to load him with a thousand arrows
and so destroyed him, as his venom flowed through his black wounds.   444
And so that the fame of his deed would not be wiped out by time's passage,
he instituted sacred games with festive competition,
called Pythian from the name of the serpent he had mastered.

hic iuuenum quicumque manu pedibusue rotaue
uicerat, aesculeae capiebat frondis honorem.
450   nondum laurus erat, longoque decentia crine
tempora cingebat de qualibet arbore Phoebus.
           primus amor Phoebi Daphne Peneia, quem non
fors ignara dedit, sed saeua Cupidinis ira.
Delius hunc, nuper uicto serpente superbus,
455   uiderat adducto flectentem cornua neruo,
'quid' que 'tibi, lasciue puer, cum fortibus armis?'
dixerat, 'ista decent umeros gestamina nostros,
qui dare certa ferae, dare uulnera possumus hosti,
qui modo pestifero tot iugera uentre prementem
460   strauimus innumeris tumidum Pythona sagittis.
tu face nescioquos esto contentus amores
inritare tua, nec laudes adsere nostras.'
filius huic Veneris, 'figat tuus omnia, Phoebe,
te meus arcus,' ait, 'quantoque animalia cedunt
465   cuncta deo, tanto minor est tua gloria nostra.'
dixit, et eliso percussis aere pennis
impiger umbrosa Parnasi constitit arce,
eque sagittifera prompsit duo tela pharetra
diuersorum operum; fugat hoc, facit illud amorem.
470   quod facit auratum est et cuspide fulget acuta;
quod fugat obtusum est et habet sub harundine plumbum.
hoc deus in nympha Peneide fixit, at illo
laesit Apollineas traiecta per ossa medullas.
protinus alter amat, fugit altera nomen amantis,
475   siluarum latebris captiuarumque ferarum
exuuiis gaudens innuptaeque aemula Phoebes.
uitta coercebat positos sine lege capillos.
multi illam petiere, illa auersata petentes
impatiens expersque uiri nemora auia lustrat,
480   nec quid Hymen, quid amor, quid sint conubia curat.
saepe pater dixit, 'generum mihi, filia, debes',
saepe pater dixit, 'debes mihi, nata, nepotes'.
illa uelut crimen taedas exosa iugales,
pulchra uerecundo suffuderat ora rubore,
485   inque patris blandis haerens ceruice lacertis,
'da mihi perpetua, genitor carissime,' dixit,
'uirginitate frui; dedit hoc pater ante Dianae.'
ille quidem obsequitur, sed te decor iste quod optas
esse uetat, uotoque tuo tua forma repugnat.
490   Phoebus amat uisaeque cupit conubia Daphnes,
quodque cupit sperat, suaque illum oracula fallunt,
utque leues stipulae demptis adolentur aristis,
ut facibus saepes ardent, quas forte uiator

There, whichever of the men had won with hand or foot
or wheel received as his reward a sprig of oak.
There was as yet no laurel and Phoebus would use any tree at all   450
to bind his graceful temples and his long hair.
    The first of Phoebus' loves was Peneian Daphne; which was given him
not by blind chance but by Cupid's fierce anger.
Recently the Delian, made haughty by his conquest of the serpent,
had seen him bending his bow with string drawn tight   455
and, 'What are these mighty arms to you, you wanton boy?',
had said, 'That equipment of yours befits my shoulders,
I can give sure wounds to beast, sure wounds to foe;
just now, as it weighed acres down under its noxious belly,
it was I with countless arrows laid low the swollen Python.   460
Be you content to stir up with your torch some
love or other and not to claim the honours that are mine.'
The son of Venus said to him, 'Let your bow, Phoebus, pierce all,
mine shall pierce you; and, by how much all creatures
yield to god, by so much is your glory less than mine.'   465
He spoke and after forcing through the air with beating wings
eagerly settled on Parnassus' shadowy peak
and from his arrow-bearing quiver plucked two shafts
of opposite effects; one routs love, the other brings it on.
Golden is the one that brings love and gleams at its sharp tip;   470
blunt is the one that routs love and has, under its reed stem, lead.
This one the god fixed in the Peneid nymph, but with the other
he drove through Apollo's bones, wounding him to the marrow.
Instantly he is in love, but she shuns the thought of a lover;
the retreats of the woods, the trophies of the beasts   475
she has caught are her delight as she vies with unwed Phoebe.
A headband held her hair set in disorder.
Many men pursued her, but she repulsed her suitors
and, stubbornly without a mate, roamed pathless copses,
and did not care what Hymen, what love or what a marriage was.   480
Often her father said, 'Daughter, you owe me a son-in-law',
often her father said, 'Child, it is grandsons you owe me'.
She hated marriage torches like a crime,
and a shy blush had spread across her beautiful face.
Clinging to her father's neck with coaxing arms,   485
'Allow me,' she said, 'parent most dear, to enjoy
being virgin for ever; Diana's father granted her that.'
Though he gave in, your loveliness forbade
what you desired, your beauty fought against your prayer.
Phoebus was in love and, seeing Daphne, wanted to marry her,   490
and what he wanted, he hoped for; his oracles deceived him.
And as light stubble is fired after the ears are cut,
as hedges catch alight from torches a traveller chances

uel nimis admouit uel iam sub luce reliquit,
495 sic deus in flammas abiit, sic pectore toto
uritur et sterilem sperando nutrit amorem.
spectat inornatos collo pendere capillos
et, 'quid si comantur?' ait; uidet igne micantes
sideribus similes oculos; uidet oscula, quae non
500 est uidisse satis; laudat digitosque manusque
bracchiaque et nudos media plus parte lacertos;
si qua latent, meliora putat. fugit ocior aura
illa leui neque ad haec reuocantis uerba resistit:
'nympha, precor, Penei, mane! non insequor hostis;
505 nympha, mane! sic agna lupum, sic cerua leonem,
sic aquilam penna fugiunt trepidante columbae,
hostes quaeque suos; amor est mihi causa sequendi.
me miserum, ne prona cadas indignaue laedi
crura notent sentes, et sim tibi causa doloris.
510 aspera qua properas loca sunt; moderatius, oro,
curre fugamque inhibe; moderatius insequar ipse.
cui placeas inquire tamen. non incola montis,
non ego sum pastor, non hic armenta gregesque
horridus obseruo. nescis, temeraria, nescis
515 quem fugias, ideoque fugis. mihi Delphica tellus
et Claros et Tenedos Patareaque regia seruit;
Iuppiter est genitor; per me quod eritque fuitque
estque patet; per me concordant carmina neruis.
certa quidem nostra est, nostra tamen una sagitta
520 certior, in uacuo quae uulnera pectora fecit.
inuentum medicina meum est, opiferque per orbem
dicor, et herbarum subiecta potentia nobis.
ei mihi, quod nullis amor est sanabilis herbis,
nec prosunt domino quae prosunt omnibus artes!'
525 plura locuturum timido Peneia cursu
fugit, cumque ipso uerba imperfecta reliquit.
tum quoque uisa decens; nudabant corpora uenti,
obuiaque aduersas uibrabant flamina uestes,
et leuis impulsos retro dabat aura capillos,
530 auctaque forma fuga est. sed enim non sustinet ultra
perdere blanditias iuuenis deus, utque monebat
ipse Amor, admisso sequitur uestigia passu.
ut canis in uacuo leporem cum Gallicus aruo
uidit, et hic praedam pedibus petit, ille salutem;
535 alter inhaesuro similis iam iamque tenere
sperat et extento stringit uestigia rostro,
alter in ambiguo est an sit comprensus et ipsis
morsibus eripitur tangentiaque ora relinquit;
sic deus et uirgo est; hic spe celer, illa timore.

to bring too close or leaves behind at daybreak,
so did the god burst into flames, so he burnt in all   495
his breast and fed his fruitless love with hope.
He looked at her hair hanging loose down her neck
and, 'What if it were put up?' he said; he saw her star-like eyes
gleaming with fire; he saw her lips, which to have seen
was not enough; he admired her fingers and her hands   500
and her arms, bare almost to her shoulders;
the parts that were covered he supposed were better still. She flew swifter
than the light breeze and did not stop when he called out to her:
'Nymph, I beg, Peneis, wait! I am no enemy in pursuit;
Thus does a lamb flee from a wolf, thus a deer from a lion,   505
doves with trembling wing flee thus from an eagle,
each from his own enemy; but love is why I pursue you.
Oh dear me, don't fall down flat or let brambles mark legs
that should never be harmed, or let me be the reason you're hurt.
Those are rough places where you are rushing; more moderately I beg you
run, restrain your flight; I shall myself pursue more moderately.   511
Do ask at least who admires you. No mountain dweller I,
no shepherd; this is no uncouth fellow watching
the herds and flocks. You do not know, rash girl, you do not know
from whom you flee, and that is why you flee. I am served   515
by the Delphic land and Claros and Tenedos and the Patarean palace;
Jupiter is my parent; through me is revealed the future,
the past and the present; through me songs harmonize on strings.
My arrow is sure indeed, but there is one arrow
surer still which has made wounds in my empty heart.   520
Medicine is my invention and I am called throughout the world
Bringer-of-help, and the power of herbs is subject to me.
Ah me, that there are no herbs that can cure love,
that the arts which help all men do not help their master!'
He was going to say more but the Peneian in timid flight   525
ran away leaving him and his unfinished words.
Then too she seemed lovely; the winds revealed her form,
and the breezes in her face met her robe, and shook it out,
a light breath of air blew her hair out behind,
and her flight enhanced her beauty. But indeed the youthful god   530
could no longer bear to waste his blandishments and, as he was urged
by Love itself, he followed her tracks with free strides.
As when a Gallic hound has seen in an empty field
a hare; one uses his feet for finding prey, the other for finding safety;
one as if just about to get a grip expects to hold on   535
right now and grazes his quarry's heels with muzzle at full stretch;
the other is in doubt as to whether he has been caught; from the very
jaws he is snatched and escapes the touch of the mouth;
thus were the god and the virgin; he swift from hope, and she from fear.

540   qui tamen insequitur, pennis adiutus Amoris
        ocior est requiemque negat tergoque fugacis
        imminet et crinem sparsum ceruicibus adflat.
        uiribus absumptis expalluit illa citaeque
        uicta labore fugae spectans Peneidas undas,
545   'fer, pater,' inquit, 'opem, si flumina numen habetis;
        qua nimium placui, mutando perde figuram.'
546a   [uicta labore fugae, Tellus,' ait, 'hisce, uel istam
547   quae facit ut laedar, mutando perde figuram.']
        uix prece finita torpor grauis occupat artus;
        mollia cinguntur tenui praecordia libro;
550   in frondem crines, in ramos bracchia crescunt;
        pes modo tam uelox pigris radicibus haeret;
        ora cacumen habet; remanet nitor unus in illa.
        hanc quoque Phoebus amat, positaque in stipite dextra
        sentit adhuc trepidare nouo sub cortice pectus
555   complexusque suis ramos ut membra lacertis
        oscula dat ligno; refugit tamen oscula lignum.
        cui deus, 'at quoniam coniunx mea non potes esse,
        arbor eris certe,' dixit, 'mea. semper habebunt
        te coma, te citharae, te nostrae, laure, pharetrae.
560   tu ducibus Latiis aderis, cum laeta Triumphum
        uox canet et uisent longas Capitolia pompas.
        postibus Augustis eadem fidissima custos
        ante fores stabis, mediamque tuebere quercum.
        utque meum intonsis caput est iuuenale capillis,
565   tu quoque perpetuos semper gere frondis honores.'
        finierat Paean; factis modo laurea ramis
        adnuit, utque caput uisa est agitasse cacumen.
           est nemus Haemoniae, praerupta quod undique claudit
        silua; uocant Tempe. per quae Peneos ab imo
570   effusus Pindo spumosis uoluitur undis,
        deiectuque graui tenues agitantia fumos
        nubila conducit, summisque aspergine siluis
        impluit, et sonitu plus quam uicina fatigat.
        haec domus, haec sedes, haec sunt penetralia magni
575   amnis; in his residens facto de cautibus antro
        undis iura dabat nymphisque colentibus undas.
        conueniunt illuc popularia flumina primum
        (nescia gratentur consolenturne parentem),
        populifer Sperchios et inrequietus Enipeus
580   Apidanosque senex lenisque Amphrysos et Aeas;
        moxque amnes alii qui, qua tulit impetus illos,
        in mare deducunt fessas erroribus undas.
        Inachus unus abest, imoque reconditus antro
        fletibus auget aquas natamque miserrimus Io

But the hunter, helped by the wings of Love,   540
was quicker and gave her no rest and leant over the fugitive's
back and breathed on her hair as it flowed from her neck.
Her strength was exhausted, she grew pale overcome
by the effort of her swift flight and, gazing at the Peneid waters,
'Bring help, father,' she said, 'if your waters have divine power;   545
since it is what made me admired too much, change and destroy my
beauty.'
Her prayer was scarcely finished, when a heavy numbness seized on her
limbs.
Her soft breast was enveloped in a thin bark,
her hair grew into foliage and her arms into branches;   550
her foot that was just now so quick was stuck in sluggish roots,
a tree top covered her face; only her radiance remained in her.
Phoebus loved her in this form too and, with his right hand upon her trunk,
felt her breast still trembling under the new grown bark,
and, putting his arms around her branches as if they were her limbs,   555
he gave his kisses to the wood; but the wood shrank from the kisses.
The god responded, 'But, since you cannot be my wife,
you will at least be my tree. There will always be
you on my hair, you on my lyres, you, laurel, on my quivers.
You will be present for the Latin leaders, when the joyful cry   560
proclaims the Triumph and the Capitol beholds the long procession.
At Augustus' porch too, a most faithful guardian
before the doors will you stand and behold the oak between,
and, as my head is youthful, my hair unshorn,
you too be always dressed in a perpetual glory of leaves.'   565
Paean had finished; the laurel assented with her branches
that had just been made, and seemed to nod her top like a head.
      There is a copse in Haemonia, shut in by a steep wood
on every side; they call it Tempe. And through it Peneus rolls
with his foaming waves, pouring out from the foot of Pindus.   570
The heavy fall produces clouds which stir up
fine mists and with its spray rains on the woods'
tops, and wearies more than the neighbourhood with its sound.
This was his house, this was his seat, this was the river's
shrine; sitting here in his cave made in the cliffs,   575
he gave laws to the waves and to the nymphs who tend the waves.
First there assembled there the local rivers
(not knowing whether to congratulate the father or console him),
the poplar-bearing Sperchios and the unresting Enipeus,
old man Apidanus, the gentle Amphrysus and the Aeas   580
and soon the other rivers, which bring their wander-weary waters,
as their current takes them, down into the sea.
Only Inachus was absent and, hidden in the bottom of his cave,
increased his waters with his weeping and most piteously mourned

585   luget ut amissam. nescit uitane fruatur
      an sit apud Manes, sed quam non inuenit usquam
      esse putat nusquam atque animo peiora ueretur.
         uiderat a patrio redeuntem Iuppiter illam
      flumine et, 'o uirgo Ioue digna tuoque beatum
590   nescioquem factura toro, pete,' dixerat, 'umbras
      altorum nemorum' (et nemorum monstrauerat umbras)
      'dum calet et medio sol est altissimus orbe.
      quod si sola times latebras intrare ferarum,
      praeside tuta deo nemorum secreta subibis,
595   nec de plebe deo, sed qui caelestia magna
      sceptra manu teneo, sed qui uaga fulmina mitto.
      ne fuge me!' (fugiebat enim.) iam pascua Lernae
      consitaque arboribus Lyrcea reliquerat arua,
      cum deus inducta latas caligine terras
600   occuluit tenuitque fugam rapuitque pudorem.
         interea medios Iuno despexit in Argos,
      et noctis faciem nebulas fecisse uolucres
      sub nitido mirata die, non fluminis illas
      esse nec umenti sensit tellure remitti;
605   atque suus coniunx ubi sit circumspicit, ut quae
      deprensi totiens iam nosset furta mariti.
      quem postquam caelo non repperit, 'aut ego fallor
      aut ego laedor,' ait, delapsaque ab aethere summo
      constitit in terris nebulasque recedere iussit.
610   coniugis aduentum praesenserat inque nitentem
      Inachidos uultus mutauerat ille iuuencam,
      (bos quoque formosa est); speciem Saturnia uaccae,
      quamquam inuita, probat, nec non et cuius et unde
      quoue sit armento, ueri quasi nescia, quaerit.
615   Iuppiter e terra genitam mentitur, ut auctor
      desinat inquiri; petit hanc Saturnia munus.
      quid faciat? crudele suos addicere amores,
      non dare suspectum est. pudor est qui suadeat illinc,
      hinc dissuadet amor. uictus pudor esset amore,
620   sed leue si munus sociae generisque torique
      uacca negaretur, poterat non uacca uideri.
      paelice donata non protinus exuit omnem
      diua metum, timuitque Iouem et fuit anxia furti
      donec Arestoridae seruandam tradidit Argo.
625   centum luminibus cinctum caput Argus habebat;
      inde suis uicibus capiebant bina quietem,
      cetera seruabant atque in statione manebant.
      constiterat quocumque modo, spectabat ad Io;
      ante oculos Io, quamuis auersus, habebat.

his daughter, Io, as lost: he did not know whether she was enjoying life,
or was among the Shades; but, as he could not find her anywhere,   586
thought that she was nowhere; and feared the worse in his heart.
    Jupiter had seen her returning from her father's
river and, 'Oh maiden worthy of Jove,' had said, 'and about to make
someone happy in the marriage bed, seek out the deep,   590
shady copses' (and he pointed out some shady copses)
'while it is hot and the sun is at its height in the middle of its course.
But in case you are afraid to enter wild beasts' lairs alone,
you will be safe going into secret copses with a god to guard you,   594
and not some common god, but with me, the one who holds the heavenly
sceptre in his mighty hand, the one who dispatches wandering thunderbolts.
Don't flee from me!' (For she was fleeing.) She had already left
Lerna's pastures and the thick tree plantations of the Lyrcean fields,
when the god spread darkness and hid the wide
lands away and stopped her flight and ravished her modesty.   600
    Meanwhile Juno looked down on the middle of Argos
and was surprised that sudden mists made it seem
like night in the shimmering day, but sensed that they were
not from a river nor had they arisen from the damp earth,
and she looked around to see where her husband was, for by now   605
she had caught him out so often in his deceitfulness.
And when she did not find him in the sky, 'Either I am mistaken,'
she said, 'or I am being wronged,' and she glided down from the highest
                                                           ether
and stood upon the earth and told the mists to disperse.
He had already sensed his wife's arrival and had transformed   610
Inachus' daughter into a gleaming heifer,
(she was a bovine beauty too); Saturnia, though unwilling,
admired the look of the cow and enquired, as if she did not know
the truth, whose she was, from where she came, and from what herd.
To bring these questions on her origin to an end, Jupiter lied   615
and said that she was born from earth; Saturnia asked for her as a favour.
What was he to do? Cruel to surrender his beloved,
not to give her, suspicious. Shame would urge him on one way,
love urged him back; shame would have been overcome by love,
but, if she who was bound to him by parentage and marriage bed   620
were refused as trivial a favour as a cow, it might not seem to be a cow.
He gave her the wench, but the goddess did not instantly cast off
all fear; she was afraid of Jove and worried by his deceitfulness
until she handed her over to be watched by Argus, Arestor's son.
    Argus' head was set all round with a hundred eyes   625
which took their rest in turns, two at a time,
while the others watched and remained on guard.
However he stood he was looking at Io.
When he turned away, he had Io before his eyes.

630 luce sinit pasci; cum sol tellure sub alta est,
     claudit et indigno circumdat uincula collo.
     frondibus arboreis et amara pascitur herba,
     proque toro terrae non semper gramen habenti
     incubat infelix limosaque flumina potat.
635 illa etiam supplex Argo cum bracchia uellet
     tendere, non habuit quae bracchia tenderet Argo;
     et conata queri mugitus edidit ore,
     pertimuitque sonos propriaque exterrita uoce est.
     uenit et ad ripas ubi ludere saepe solebat,
640 Inachidas ripas, nouaque ut conspexit in unda
     cornua, pertimuit seque exsternata refugit.
     Naides ignorant, ignorat et Inachus ipse
     quae sit. at illa patrem sequitur, sequiturque sorores
     et patitur tangi seque admirantibus offert.
645 decerptas senior porrexerat Inachus herbas;
     illa manus lambit patriisque dat oscula palmis,
     nec retinet lacrimas et, si modo uerba sequantur,
     oret opem nomenque suum casusque loquatur.
     littera pro uerbis, quam pes in puluere duxit,
650 corporis indicium mutati triste peregit.
     'me miserum!' exclamat pater Inachus, inque gementis
     cornibus et niuea pendens ceruice iuuencae,
     'me miserum!' ingeminat, 'tune es quaesita per omnes
     nata mihi terras? tu non inuenta reperta
655 luctus eras leuior. retices nec mutua nostris
     dicta refers; alto tantum suspiria ducis
     pectore, quodque unum potes, ad mea uerba remugis.
     at tibi ego ignarus thalamos taedasque parabam,
     spesque fuit generi mihi prima, secunda nepotum;
660 de grege nunc tibi uir et de grege natus habendus.
     nec finire licet tantos mihi morte dolores,
     sed nocet esse deum, praeclusaque ianua leti
     aeternum nostros luctus extendit in aeuum.'
     talia maerentem stellatus summouet Argus,
665 ereptamque patri diuersa in pascua natam
     abstrahit; ipse procul montis sublime cacumen
     occupat, unde sedens partes speculatur in omnes.
         nec superum rector mala tanta Phoronidos ultra
     ferre potest, natumque uocat quem lucida partu
670 Pleias enixa est, letoque det imperet Argum.
     parua mora est alas pedibus uirgamque potenti
     somniferam sumpsisse manu tegumenque capillis.

In the daylight he let her graze; but when the sun was under the deep
                                                                    earth,
he shut her up and put a rope around her blameless neck.   631
She grazed on the leaves of the trees and on the bitter grass,
and instead of a bed, unhappy one, she lay on not always
grassy earth and drank from muddy rivers.
When she wanted to stretch her arms out to Argus   635
in supplication, she had no arms to stretch out to Argus.
And when she tried to complain, her mouth let forth a mooing,
and she was afraid of the sound and terrified by her very own voice.
She came to the banks, where she often used to play,
to Inachus' banks, and when she saw her new horns   640
in the water, she was afraid and fled from herself in consternation.
The Naiads did not know, Inachus himself did not know
who she was. But she followed her father and she followed her sisters
and let herself be petted and offered herself to be admired.
Old Inachus plucked grass and held it out to her;   645
she licked his hands and kissed her father's palms
and did not hold back her tears: and, if only speech had come,
she would have begged for help and told her name and her misfortune.
Instead of speech, it was lettering her foot traced in the dust
that brought about the sad disclosure of her transformation.   650
'Unhappy me!' father Inachus cried out, and as he hung
on the horns and neck of the groaning snow-white heifer,
'Unhappy me!' he repeated, 'Are you the daughter I have searched for
through every land? When you had not been found you were a lighter grief
than now that you are discovered. You are silent and do not return
                                                                    answering
words to mine, you just give sighs from deep   656
in your heart, and do the only thing you can, moo back at my words.
But, in my ignorance, I was preparing the bedroom and the torches for
                                                              your wedding,
my first hope was for a son-in-law, my second for grandchildren.
Now you must have a husband from the herd, and a son from the herd. 660
And I may not end such great sorrows with death,
but it hurts to be a god, death's gate is barred to me
and stretches my griefs into an everlasting age.'
So he lamented, but the starred Argus moved him away
and snatched his daughter and dragged her away to distant   665
pastures; he himself settled down apart upon a lofty mountain
summit where he sat down and watched in all directions.
        But the ruler of the gods could no longer bear Phoronis'
great misfortunes, and called the son bright Pleias
had given birth to and ordered him to put Argus to death.   670
There was a brief delay while he put wings onto his feet, his sleep-inducing
wand into his powerful hand and a covering on his head.

haec ubi disposuit, patria Ioue natus ab arce
desilit in terras. illic tegumenque remouit
675 et posuit pennas; tantummodo uirga retenta est.
hac agit, ut pastor, per deuia rura capellas
dum uenit abductas, et structis cantat auenis.
uoce noua captus custos Iunonius, 'at tu,
quisquis es, hoc poteras mecum considere saxo,'
680 Argus ait, 'neque enim pecori fecundior ullo
herba loco est, aptamque uides pastoribus umbram.'
sedit Atlantiades et euntem multa loquendo
detinuit sermone diem, iunctisque canendo
uincere harundinibus seruantia lumina temptat.
685 ille tamen pugnat molles euincere somnos
et, quamuis sopor est oculorum parte receptus,
parte tamen uigilat. quaerit quoque (namque reperta
fistula nuper erat) qua sit ratione reperta.
  tum deus, 'Arcadiae gelidis in montibus,' inquit,
690 'inter Hamadryadas celeberrima Nonacrinas
Naias una fuit; Nymphae Syringa uocabant.
non semel et Satyros eluserat illa sequentes
et quoscumque deos umbrosaque silua feraxque
rus habet. Ortygiam studiis ipsaque colebat
695 uirginitate deam; ritu quoque cincta Dianae
falleret et posset credi Latonia, si non
corneus huic arcus, si non foret aureus illi.
sic quoque fallebat. redeuntem colle Lycaeo
Pan uidet hanc, pinuque caput praecinctus acuta
700 talia uerba refert...' restabat uerba referre,
et precibus spretis fugisse per auia nympham
donec harenosi placidum Ladonis ad amnem
uenerit; hic illam, cursum impedientibus undis,
ut se mutarent liquidas orasse sorores;
705 Panaque, cum pressam sibi iam Syringa putaret,
corpore pro nymphae calamos tenuisse palustres;
dumque ibi suspirat, motos in harundine uentos
effecisse sonum tenuem similemque querenti;
arte noua uocisque deum dulcedine captum,
710 'hoc mihi conloquium tecum,' dixisse, 'manebit,'
atque ita disparibus calamis compagine cerae
inter se iunctis nomen tenuisse puellae.
  talia dicturus uidit Cyllenius omnes
succubuisse oculos adopertaque lumina somno.
715 supprimit extemplo uocem firmatque soporem,
languida permulcens medicata lumina uirga.
nec mora, falcato nutantem uulnerat ense

When these had been arranged, Jove's son leapt from his father's
citadel down upon the earth. There he removed the covering,
laid down the wings and only kept the wand.   675
He used it, like a herdsman, to drive goats that he had stolen on the way
through the remote country, and he was playing on a set of pipes.
Juno's guard was quite taken by the strange sound. 'You there,
whoever you are,' said Argus, 'you could sit with me
upon this rock; nowhere else will your flock have   680
lusher grass and you can see the shade is right for herdsmen.'
Atlas' grandson sat down and occupied the passing day
with much conversation, and tried to overcome the wakeful
eyes by playing on his set of pipes.
He, however, fought to conquer gentle sleep   685
and, though some of his eyes accepted sleep,
others still kept awake; he asked too (for the pipe had been
only just invented) how it had been invented.
        Then the god said, 'In the cool Arcadian mountains,
there was among the Nonacrian Hamadryads   690
one very famous Naiad; the nymphs called her Syrinx.
She had escaped pursuing Satyrs more than once
as well as all the gods the shady forest and the fertile
country holds. She worshipped the Ortygian goddess with her devotion
and with her virginity too. And, when she was girt up in Diana's style, 695
she would deceive and could be thought to be Latonia, if her bow
had not been bone, if Diana's had not been golden.
Even as it was, she did deceive. On her way back from the Lycaean hill,
she was seen by Pan, his head decked out with sharp pine,
and he spoke to her words like this...'; he had still to speak the words, 700
and tell how the nymph had spurned his prayers and fled through trackless
                                                                          places
till she came to the peaceful stream of sandy
Ladon; and how there she had begged her liquid sisters,
when their waters had stopped her flight, to transform her,
and, when Pan thought Syrinx was pressed against him,   705
instead of the nymph's body he was holding marsh canes;
and how, as he sighed, the winds he had stirred in the reeds
made a low sound, like a complaint;
and how the god, taken by this new art and by the sweetness of the sound,
had said, 'This conversation with you will remain with me,'   710
and so, for unequal reeds fixed together
by a joint of wax, he had preserved the name of the girl.
        Such were to be Cyllenius' words, when he saw that all
the eyes had yielded, that the eyes were veiled in sleep.
Immediately, he checked his voice and reinforced the sleep   715
by soothing the drooping eyes with his charmed wand.
Without delay, he used his curved sword to wound him, as he nodded off,

qua collo est confine caput, saxoque cruentum ·
deicit et maculat praeruptam sanguine rupem.
720 Arge, iaces, quodque in tot lumina lumen habebas
exstinctum est, centumque oculos nox occupat una.
excipit hos uolucrisque suae Saturnia pennis
conlocat et gemmis caudam stellantibus implet.
protinus exarsit nec tempora distulit irae,
725 horriferamque oculis animoque obiecit Erinyn
paelicis Argolicae stimulosque in pectore caecos
condidit et profugam per totum exercuit orbem.
ultimus immenso restabas, Nile, labori;
quem simul ac tetigit, positisque in margine ripae
730 procubuit genibus resupinoque ardua collo,
quos potuit solos, tollens ad sidera uultus
et gemitu et lacrimis et luctisono mugitu
cum Ioue uisa queri finemque orare malorum.
coniugis ille suae complexus colla lacertis
735 finiat ut poenas tandem rogat, 'in,' que, 'futurum
pone metus,' inquit, 'numquam tibi causa doloris
haec erit;' et Stygias iubet hoc audire paludes.
ut lenita dea est, uultus capit illa priores
fitque quod ante fuit. fugiunt e corpore saetae,
740 cornua decrescunt, fit luminis artior orbis,
contrahitur rictus, redeunt umerique manusque,
ungulaque in quinos dilapsa absumitur ungues.
de boue nil superest formae nisi candor in illa.
officioque pedum nymphe contenta duorum
745 erigitur metuitque loqui, ne more iuuencae
mugiat, et timide uerba intermissa retemptat.
        nunc dea linigera colitur celeberrima turba.
huic Epaphus magni genitus de semine tandem
creditur esse Iouis perque urbes iuncta parenti
750 templa tenet. fuit huic animis aequalis et annis
Sole satus Phaethon. quem quondam magna loquentem
nec sibi cedentem Phoeboque parente superbum
non tulit Inachides, 'matri' que ait, 'omnia demens
credis et es tumidus genitoris imagine falsi.'
755 erubuit Phaethon iramque pudore repressit,
et tulit ad Clymenen Epaphi conuicia matrem;
'quo' que 'magis doleas, genetrix,' ait, 'ille ego liber,
ille ferox tacui. pudet haec opprobria nobis
et dici potuisse et non potuisse refelli.
760 at tu, si modo sum caelesti stirpe creatus,
ede notam tanti generis meque adsere caelo.'
        dixit et implicuit materno bracchia collo

where the head joins the neck, and threw him bleeding
down from the rock and staining the sheer crag with his blood.
Argus, you lie there, and whatever light you had for all your eyes   720
has been extinguished, and a single night overwhelms a hundred eyes.
Saturnia picked them up and placed them on the feathers
of her bird and filled his tail with starry gems.
She had flared up instantly and did not put off the moment of her anger,
but placed the horrific Erinys before the eyes and mind   725
of the Argive wench and planted hidden goads
in her heart, and made her flee, terrified, through the whole world.
You, oh Nile, were left to the end of her unmeasured suffering.
As soon as she reached you, she lay down with her knees set
on the edge of your bank, and with her neck bent back   730
she raised her face, which was all she could raise, to the lofty stars
and with a groan and tears and a grief-sounding moo
seemed to complain to Jove and to beg for an end to her ills.
He put his arms around his wife's neck
and begged her to bring the punishment to an end at last, and 'Have no fear
for the future,' he said, 'she will never cause   736
you pain;' and he ordered the Stygian swamps to mark these words of his.
The goddess was soothed and Io took on her former looks
and became what she had been before; the coarse hairs left her body,
the horns grew down, the circle of her eyes became more narrow,   740
the gape of her mouth was closed, her shoulders and her hands returned,
her hoof disappeared dissolving into five nails.
Nothing bovine remained in her except the brightness of her beauty.
The nymph was happy with the use of two feet and
stood upright but, afraid to speak in case she mooed   745
like a heifer, nervously tried again her interrupted use of speech.
     A most famous goddess now, she is worshipped by the linen-wearing
                                                        throng.
Epaphus, so it was believed, was born to her at last
from the seed of great Jove and, throughout the cities, he held temples
joined to his mother's. He had an equal in years and mind,   750
Sun's child, Phaethon. And once, when he was boasting
and not giving way at all as he gloried in his father, Phoebus,
Inachides, past endurance, said, 'You are insane to trust your mother
wholly, you have a false and inflated notion of your parentage.'
Phaethon blushed, his shame suppressed his anger,   755
and he brought Epaphus' insults to his mother, Clymene,
saying, 'To upset you, mother, more, I, the frank one,
I, the defiant one, was silent. This taunt shames us
both because it could be said and because it could not be refuted.
But if I am really sprung from heavenly stock,   760
give me a token of my great origin and confirm my claim to heaven.'
     He spoke and wrapped his arms around his mother's neck

perque suum Meropisque caput taedasque sororum
traderet orauit ueri sibi signa parentis.
765 ambiguum Clymene precibus Phaethontis an ira
mota magis dicti sibi criminis utraque caelo
bracchia porrexit, spectansque ad lumina solis,
'per iubar hoc,' inquit, 'radiis insigne coruscis,
nate, tibi iuro, quod nos auditque uidetque,
770 hoc te, quem spectas, hoc te, qui temperat orbem,
Sole satum. si ficta loquor, neget ipse uidendum
se mihi, sitque oculis lux ista nouissima nostris.
nec longus labor est patrios tibi nosse penates;
unde oritur domus est terrae contermina nostrae.
775 si modo fert animus, gradere, et scitabere ab ipso.'
emicat extemplo laetus post talia matris
dicta suae Phaethon et concipit aethera mente,
Aethiopasque suos positosque sub ignibus Indos
sidereis transit, patriosque adit impiger ortus.

and begged her, by Merops' head and by his own, and by his sisters'
marriages, to give him signs of his true father.
It is uncertain whether Clymene was moved more by the prayers   765
of Phaethon or by her anger at the spoken accusation; she stretched
both arms towards heaven and, gazing at the sun's light,
said, 'I swear to you, my son, by this bright radiance,
with its flashing beams, which hears and sees us,
that you were fathered by the Sun that you behold, by him   770
who regulates the world. If I speak falsely, let him refuse to let
me see him, let this be my eyes' last light.
It would not be a great task for you to know the penates of your father:
the house from where he rises borders on our land.
If your spirit moves you, go and you can question him face to face.'   775
Upon such words from his mother, Phaethon at once
sprang up in joy and set his thoughts on the ether.
He passed through his Ethiopians, and the Indians who live
under the starry fires and impatiently approached his father's rising-place.

LIBER II

    Regia Solis erat sublimibus alta columnis,
clara micante auro flammasque imitante pyropo,
cuius ebur nitidum fastigia summa tegebat,
argenti bifores radiabant lumine ualuae.
5   materiam superabat opus; nam Mulciber illic
aequora caelarat medias cingentia terras
terrarumque orbem caelumque quod imminet orbi.
caeruleos habet unda deos, Tritona canorum
Proteaque ambiguum ballenarumque prementem
10 Aegaeona suis immania terga lacertis
Doridaque et natas, quarum pars nare uidetur,
pars in mole sedens uirides siccare capillos,
pisce uehi quaedam; facies non omnibus una,
non diuersa tamen, qualem decet esse sororum.
15 terra uiros urbesque gerit siluasque ferasque
fluminaque et nymphas et cetera numina ruris.
haec super imposita est caeli fulgentis imago
signaque sex foribus dextris totidemque sinistris.
    quo simul accliui Clymeneia limite proles
20 uenit et intrauit dubitati tecta parentis,
protinus ad patrios sua fert uestigia uultus
consistitque procul; neque enim propiora ferebat
lumina. purpurea uelatus ueste sedebat
in solio Phoebus claris lucente smaragdis.
25 a dextra laeuaque Dies et Mensis et Annus
Saeculaque et positae spatiis aequalibus Horae,
Verque nouum stabat cinctum florente corona;
stabat nuda Aestas et spicea serta gerebat,
stabat et Autumnus, calcatis sordidus uuis,
30 et glacialis Hiemps, canos hirsuta capillos.
ipse loco medius rerum nouitate pauentem
Sol oculis iuuenem quibus aspicit omnia uidit,
'quae' que 'uiae tibi causa? quid hac,' ait, 'arce petisti,
progenies, Phaethon, haud infitianda parenti?'
35 ille refert, 'o lux immensi publica mundi,
Phoebe, pater, si das usum mihi nominis huius
nec falsa Clymene culpam sub imagine celat,
pignora da generis per quae tua uera propago
credar, et hunc animis errorem detrahe nostris.'

BOOK II

The palace of the Sun was tall with lofty columns,
and bright with flashing gold and pyrope that mimics flames;
its gable top was covered with gleaming ivory,
the double doors radiated the brightness of their silver,
but the artistry outdid the medium; for on them Mulciber   5
had carved the seas that surround the earth within them,
the earth's disk and the sky which hangs above the disk.
The water held the aquamarine gods, melodious Triton,
unstable Proteus, Aegaeon with his arms
pressed round the vast backs of whales,   10
Doris and her daughters, some of whom seemed to be swimming,
some to be sitting on a rock to dry their green hair,
and one to be riding on a fish. They were not all alike in looks,
and yet not very different, as is right for sisters.
The land had men and cities, woods and beasts,   15
rivers and nymphs and all the spirits of the countryside.
Above these were portrayed the resplendent heavens,
six signs on the right hand doors and as many on the left.
As soon as Clymene's offspring had arrived by the steep
path and entered the house of his disputed parent,
immediately he took his steps towards his father's face,   20
but stopped far off; for he could not bear the light
too close. Wrapped in a purple cloak sat
Phoebus on a throne that shone with emeralds bright.
To right and left stood Day and Month and Year
and Centuries and Hours placed at equal intervals,   25
and new Spring wreathed in a floral crown;
naked Summer stood there carrying her garland of corn-stalks,
Autumn stood there too, filthy from treading grapes,
and icy Winter with his hoary, bristling locks.   30
The Sun himself, with the eyes with which he looks on everything, saw
from his central position the young man frightened by the strangeness of
                                                                 it all
and said, 'What is the reason for your journey? What do you seek from
                                                        this citadel,
oh Phaethon, a child your parent could not disown?'
And he replied, 'Oh universal light of the immeasurable world,   35
Phoebus, father, if you let me use that word
and Clymene is not giving a false picture to conceal her guilt,
give me proofs of my birth by which I may be believed truly to be your
offspring, and take away this confusion from my mind.'

40   dixerat, at genitor circum caput omne micantes
deposuit radios propiusque accedere iussit
amplexuque dato, 'nec tu meus esse negari
dignus es, et Clymene ueros,' ait, 'edidit ortus.
quoque minus dubites, quoduis pete munus, ut illud
45   me tribuente feras. promissi testis adesto
dis iuranda palus, oculis incognita nostris.'
uix bene desierat, curros rogat ille paternos
inque diem alipedum ius et moderamen equorum.
       paenituit iurasse patrem; qui terque quaterque
50   concutiens illustre caput, 'temeraria,' dixit,
'uox mea facta tua est. utinam promissa liceret
non dare! confiteor, solum hoc tibi, nate, negarem.
dissuadere licet: non est tua tuta uoluntas.
magna petis, Phaethon, et quae nec uiribus istis
55   munera conueniant nec tam puerilibus annis.
sors tua mortalis; non est mortale quod optas.
plus etiam quam quod superis contingere fas sit
nescius adfectas; placeat sibi quisque licebit,
non tamen ignifero quisquam consistere in axe
60   me ualet excepto. uasti quoque rector Olympi,
qui fera terribili iaculatur fulmina dextra,
non aget hos currus: et quid Ioue maius habemus?
       ardua prima uia est et qua uix mane recentes
enituntur equi; medio est altissima caelo,
65   unde mare et terras ipsi mihi saepe uidere
fit timor et pauida trepidat formidine pectus.
ultima prona uia est et eget moderamine certo;
tunc etiam, quae me subiectis excipit undis,
ne ferar in praeceps Tethys solet ipsa uereri.
70   adde quod adsidua rapitur uertigine caelum
sideraque alta trahit celerique uolumine torquet.
nitor in aduersum, nec me, qui cetera, uincit
impetus, et rapido contrarius euehor orbi.
finge datos currus; quid ages? poterisne rotatis
75   obuius ire polis, ne te citus auferat axis?
forsitan et lucos illic urbesque deorum
concipias animo delubraque ditia donis
esse; per insidias iter est formasque ferarum,
utque uiam teneas nulloque errore traharis,
80   per tamen aduersi gradieris cornua Tauri

He had spoken. But his father took off the rays that flashed   40
all round his head and told him to approach closer,
and, giving him an embrace, said, 'You do not deserve that I deny
that you are mine, and Clymene has told the truth about your origin.
And, to reduce your doubts, ask any favour you would like
me to grant and you to take. May there be present as witness to my   45
                                                            promises
the swamp that gods must swear by, unknown as it is to my eyes.'
He had scarcely finished when Phaethon asked for his father's chariot
and the right to drive the wing-footed horses for a day.
        Then the father regretted he had sworn; three times or four
he shook his shining head saying, 'How reckless   50
have your words made mine. If only I could break
my promises! I admit, my son, that that's the only thing I would deny you.
But I may dissuade you: what you want to do is not safe.
It's a great favour you are asking, Phaethon, and one not suited
to your strength or to your boyish years.   55
You are a mortal, what you want is not for mortals!
In your ignorance, you are attempting more than it would be right to grant
even to the gods; though each of them is free to please himself,
none has the strength to stand upon the fiery
wagon, except for me! Even the ruler of vast Olympus,   60
who hurls fierce thunderbolts from his terrible right hand,
will not drive this chariot: and what have we greater than Jupiter?
        The first part of the way is steep; though it's morning and they're
                                                            fresh,
the horses scarcely struggle up; the highest part is in the middle of the sky
and to look upon the sea and lands from there often makes   65
even me afraid, and my breast tremble in fearful dread.
The last part of the way is sheer and needs a sure control;
then even Tethys herself, who receives me in her waters
underneath, tends to fear I'll be brought down head first.
And what is more, the sky is seized by a continuous whirl   ·   70
and drags along the stars on high and twists them round in rapid
                                                            revolutions.
I struggle against it, and its impetus defeats all things
except me and I drive through in opposition to the rapid motion of the
                                                            sphere.
Suppose you are given the chariot; what will you do? Will you be able to go
against the revolving poles and see that their swift axis does not carry
                                                            you away?
Perhaps in your mind you imagine groves up there   76
and cities of the gods and temples rich
with gifts; the route takes you in sight of ambushes and wild beasts.
And, if you hold your course and are not diverted from it in confusion,
even so you will proceed through the horns of advancing Taurus,   80

Haemoniosque arcus uiolentique ora Leonis
saeuaque circuitu curuantem bracchia longo
Scorpion atque aliter curuantem bracchia Cancrum.
nec tibi quadripedes animosos ignibus illis,
85   quos in pectore habent, quos ore et naribus efflant,
in promptu regere est; uix me patiuntur, ubi acres
incaluere animi ceruixque repugnat habenis.
at tu, funesti ne sim tibi muneris auctor,
nate, caue, dum resque sinit, tua corrige uota.
90   scilicet ut nostro genitum te sanguine credas
pignora certa petis: do pignora certa timendo,
et patrio pater esse metu probor. aspice uultus
ecce meos; utinamque oculos in pectora posses
inserere et patrias intus deprendere curas.
95   denique quidquid habet diues circumspice mundus
eque tot ac tantis caeli terraeque marisque
posce bonis aliquid; nullam patiere repulsam.
deprecor hoc unum, quod uero nomine poena,
non honor est; poenam, Phaethon, pro munere poscis.
100   quid mea colla tenes blandis, ignare, lacertis?
ne dubita, dabitur (Stygias iurauimus undas)
quodcumque optaris; sed tu sapientius opta.'
      finierat monitus; dictis tamen ille repugnat
propositumque premit flagratque cupidine currus.
105   ergo qua licuit genitor cunctatus ad altos
deducit iuuenem, Vulcania munera, currus.
aureus axis erat, temo aureus, aurea summae
curuatura rotae, radiorum argenteus ordo;
per iuga chrysolithi positaeque ex ordine gemmae
110   clara repercusso reddebant lumina Phoebo.
dumque ea magnanimus Phaethon miratur opusque
perspicit, ecce uigil nitido patefecit ab ortu
purpureas Aurora fores et plena rosarum
atria; diffugiunt stellae, quarum agmina cogit
115   Lucifer et caeli statione nouissimus exit.
quem petere ut terras mundumque rubescere uidit
cornuaque extremae uelut euanescere lunae,
iungere equos Titan uelocibus imperat Horis.
iussa deae celeres peragunt ignemque uomentes
120   ambrosiae suco saturos praesepibus altis
quadripedes ducunt adduntque sonantia frena.
tum pater ora sui sacro medicamine nati
contigit et rapidae fecit patientia flammae
imposuitque comae radios praesagaque luctus

the Haemonian bows, the mouth of savage Leo,
Scorpio bending his cruel arms in a long
arc and Cancer bending his arms from the other side.
And you will not readily control steeds that draw
their spirit from the fires in their breast   85
breathed out from their mouths and nostrils; they scarcely tolerate me
when their keen spirits are inflamed and their necks fight back against the
                                                                      reins.
But you, my son, so that I may not be to blame for granting you a deadly
favour, take care, and change your prayer, while you still can.
Of course you want sure proofs to believe   90
that you were born from my blood: I give sure proofs by my fear,
my fatherly alarm proves my fatherhood. Look, gaze into
my face; if only you could put your eyes
into my breast and discover there my fatherly concern.
So look around at everything the rich world holds   95
and ask for something from all the great good things
of heaven and earth and sea. You will not be rebuffed.
It's only this I plead against which by its true name is a punishment,
not an honour; it's punishment you ask for, Phaethon, not a favour.
Why do you put your coaxing arms around my neck, oh foolish one?   100
Have no doubt, you will be given (I have sworn by the Stygian waters)
whatever you will choose, but, please choose more wisely.'
        He had finished his warning; but Phaethon fought back against his
                                                                      words,
pressed his idea and was aflame with desire for the chariot.
And so, after delaying him as much as he was able, his father led   105
the young man down to the high chariot, the handiwork of Vulcan.
It had a golden axle, a golden pole, a golden rim
on the edge of the wheels and ranks of silver spokes.
Along the yoke, chrysolites and gems arranged in ranks
returned a shining light as they reflected Phoebus.   110
And while high-spirited Phaethon admired these things and wondered
at their workmanship, look, Dawn, who watches from the gleaming East,
opened up her crimson doors and her halls that are filled
with roses: the stars fled away, with Lucifer to bring up
the rear, the very last to leave his posting in the sky.   115
And when Titan saw him nearing the earth, while the world
grew red and the horns of the waning moon were vanishing,
he commanded the rapid Hours to yoke the horses.
The swift goddesses carried out their orders and led the fire-
spewing steeds who had drunk their fill of ambrosia juice   120
from their high stalls and added the noisy bridles.
Then the father touched his son's face with holy
medicine and made it tolerant of the raging flame
and placed the rays upon his head and, as he drew from his troubled

125 pectore sollicito repetens suspiria dixit,
'si potes his saltem monitis parere parentis,
parce, puer, stimulis et fortius utere loris;
sponte sua properant; labor est inhibere uolentes.
nec tibi derectos placeat uia quinque per arcus;
130 sectus in obliquum est lato curuamine limes
zonarumque trium contentus fine polumque
effugit australem iunctamque aquilonibus Arcton.
hac sit iter, manifesta rotae uestigia cernes.
utque ferant aequos et caelum et terra calores,
135 nec preme nec summum molire per aethera cursum.
altius egressus caelestia tecta cremabis,
inferius terras; medio tutissimus ibis.
neu te dexterior tortum declinet ad Anguem,
neue sinisterior pressam rota ducat ad Aram:
140 inter utrumque tene. Fortunae cetera mando,
quae iuuet et melius quam tu tibi consulat opto.
dum loquor, Hesperio positas in litore metas
umida nox tetigit. non est mora libera nobis.
poscimur, et fulget tenebris Aurora fugatis.
145 corripe lora manu, uel, si mutabile pectus
est tibi, consiliis, non curribus utere nostris.
dum potes et solidis etiamnunc sedibus astas,
dumque male optatos nondum premis inscius axes,
quae tutus spectes, sine me dare lumina terris.'
150   occupat ille leuem iuuenali corpore currum
statque super manibusque datas contingere habenas
gaudet et inuito grates agit inde parenti.
interea uolucres Pyrois et Eous et Aethon,
Solis equi, quartusque Phlegon hinnitibus auras
155 flammiferis implent pedibusque repagula pulsant.
quae postquam Tethys, fatorum ignara nepotis,
reppulit et facta est immensi copia caeli,
corripuere uiam pedibusque per aera motis
obstantes scindunt nebulas pennisque leuati
160 praetereunt ortos isdem de partibus Euros.
sed leue pondus erat nec quod cognoscere possent
Solis equi, solitaque iugum grauitate carebat;
utque labant curuae iusto sine pondere naues
perque mare instabiles nimia leuitate feruntur,
165 sic onere adsueto uacuus dat in aere saltus
succutiturque alte similisque est currus inani.

breast sighs that foretold his grief, he said,   125
'If you can heed at least these warnings from your father,
be sparing with the goad, my boy, and use the reins quite strongly;
they hurry of their own accord; as they fly along the task is to hold them
                                                                              back.
And do not choose the direct route through the five bands;
your path cuts aslant in a broad curve   130
and is confined within the boundaries of three zones and avoids
the South Pole and the North together with its winds.
Let that be your route, you will clearly see my wheel tracks.
So that heaven and earth endure the heat fairly,
don't push your course down and do not drive it through the highest ether.
You will burn heaven's houses if you go up too high;   136
too low, and it will be the earth; you will go safest in the middle.
Don't let your right wheel veer towards the coiled Snake,
nor your left pull you towards the Altar down below:
keep between the two. I trust the rest to Fortune,   140
who, I pray, may help you and think for you better than you do for
                                                                           yourself.
While I speak, moist Night has reached the boundary stones
set on the Western shore. We are free to delay no more.
We are summoned and Dawn's gleam has made the shadows flee.
Grasp the reins with your hand or, if you have a mind   145
that can be changed, take my advice and not my chariot.
Even now, while you are able to and have a solid place to stand on,
while you are not yet pressing down foolishly upon the axles you unwisely
                                                                              want,
watch in safety and let me give the lands their light.'
        He settled his youthful body onto the light chariot   150
and, standing up in it, delighted at the touch of the reins as they were put
into his hands, for which he then gave thanks to his unwilling father.
Meanwhile, the flying horses of the Sun, Pyrois, Eous
and Aethon, with Phlegon to make a fourth, filled the air
with their flame-producing neighs and beat against the barriers with their
                                                                              feet.
But after Tethys, who did not know about her grandson's fate,   156
had thrust these back and given access to the immeasurable sky,
the horses rushed upon their way and, as their feet moved through the air,
they ripped apart the obstructing clouds and, lifted on their wings,
went past the East winds that spring up in the same regions.   160
But their load was light and one the horses of the Sun could not
recognize, for the yoke was missing its usual heaviness.
And, as curved ships totter without their proper load,
and are borne unsteadily over the sea because they are too light,
so, free of its accustomed load, the chariot gave a leap   165
into the air and jerked up high as if it were unoccupied.

quod simul ac sensere, ruunt tritumque relinquunt
quadriiugi spatium nec quo prius ordine currunt.
ipse pauet nec qua commissas flectat habenas
170 nec scit qua sit iter nec, si sciat, imperet illis.
tum primum radiis gelidi caluere Triones
et uetito frustra temptarunt aequore tingi,
quaeque polo posita est glaciali proxima Serpens,
frigore pigra prius nec formidabilis ulli,
175 incaluit sumpsitque nouas feruoribus iras.
te quoque turbatum memorant fugisse, Boote,
quamuis tardus eras et te tua plaustra tenebant.
   ut uero summo despexit ab aethere terras
infelix Phaethon penitus penitusque patentes,
180 palluit et subito genua intremuere timore
suntque oculis tenebrae per tantum lumen obortae.
et iam mallet equos numquam tetigisse paternos,
iam cognosse genus piget et ualuisse rogando;
iam Meropis dici cupiens ita fertur, ut acta
185 praecipiti pinus Borea, cui uicta remisit
frena suus rector, quam dis uotisque reliquit.
quid faciat? multum caeli post terga relictum,
ante oculos plus est; animo metitur utrumque
et modo, quos illi fatum contingere non est,
190 prospicit occasus, interdum respicit ortus;
quidque agat ignarus, stupet et nec frena remittit
nec retinere ualet nec nomina nouit equorum.
sparsa quoque in uario passim miracula caelo
uastarumque uidet trepidus simulacra ferarum.
195 est locus in geminos ubi bracchia concauat arcus
Scorpius et cauda flexisque utrimque lacertis
porrigit in spatium signorum membra duorum;
hunc puer ut nigri madidum sudore ueneni
uulnera curuata minitantem cuspide uidit,
200 mentis inops gelida formidine lora remisit.
   quae postquam summum tetigere iacentia tergum,
exspatiantur equi nulloque inhibente per auras
ignotae regionis eunt quaque impetus egit,
hac sine lege ruunt altoque sub aethere fixis
205 incursant stellis rapiuntque per auia currum,
et modo summa petunt, modo per decliue uiasque
praecipites spatio terrae propiore feruntur,
inferiusque suis fraternos currere Luna

As soon as they felt that, the steeds rushed to leave
their worn track and did not run in the way they had before.
Their driver panicked; he did not know how to ply the reins entrusted   169
to him, or where his route was, nor, if he had known, would he have
                                            controlled the horses.
That was the first time that the cold Oxen grew hot from the sun's rays
and tried in vain to plunge into the forbidden sea,
and that the Serpent, which lies next to the icy pole
and was sluggish from the cold before and feared by nobody,
grew hot and caught a strange new anger from the fires.   175
They say that you too, Boötes, were disturbed and fled,
slow as you were and though your wagon held you back.
    But when, from the highest ether, unhappy Phaethon
picked out the lands stretched out below, so far below,
he blanched, his knees trembled in sudden fear   180
and darkness rose across his eyes because of all that light.
And now he would prefer never to have touched his father's horses,
now he was sorry he had learnt his origin and had succeeded with his
                                            request.
Now, wanting to be known as Merops' son, he was borne along just like a
                                            boat
driven by headlong Boreas while its captain, who has lost   185
control and given up, has left it to the gods and to his prayers.
What was he to do? Much of the sky was left behind his back;
but there was more before his eyes: in his mind he measured both,
and now he looked forward towards the west, which it was not
his fate to reach, and sometimes he looked back towards the east.   190
Unaware of what to do, he froze and neither let the reins go,
nor was strong enough to keep them, nor did he know the horses' names.
And in his fear, too, he saw marvels scattered everywhere
throughout the sky and images of huge wild beasts.
There is a place where Scorpio bows out his Claws into twin   195
arcs and with his tail and his arms bent on both sides
stretches his body into the space of two signs;
when the boy saw him dripping with the sweat of black poison
and threatening injury with his curved sting,
out of his wits with cold fear he dropped the reins.   200
    And once they felt them lying on the surface of their backs,
the horses left their course and, with no one to restrain them, went
through the air of an unfamiliar region and rushed, where the urge
took them, out of control and ran amongst the stars set
in the high ether and dragged the chariot through trackless places,   205
and sometimes sought the highest points and were sometimes brought
                                            through slopes
and sheer paths to a place too near the earth,
and the Moon was astonished that her brother's horses were running

admiratur equos ambustaque nubila fumant.
210 corripitur flammis, ut quaeque altissima, tellus
fissaque agit rimas et sucis aret ademptis;
pabula canescunt, cum frondibus uritur arbor,
materiamque suo praebet seges arida damno.
    parua queror: magnae pereunt cum moenibus urbes,
215 cumque suis totas populis incendia gentes
in cinerem uertunt; siluae cum montibus ardent,
ardet Athos Taurusque Cilix et Tmolus et Oete
et tum sicca, prius creberrima fontibus, Ide
uirgineusque Helicon et (nondum Oeagrius) Haemus.
220 ardet in immensum geminatis ignibus Aetne
Parnasosque biceps et Eryx et Cynthus et Othrys,
et tandem niuibus Rhodope caritura, Mimasque
Dindymaque et Mycale natusque ad sacra Cithaeron.
nec prosunt Scythiae sua frigora: Caucasus ardet
225 Ossaque cum Pindo maiorque ambobus Olympus
aeriaeque Alpes et nubifer Appenninus.
    tum uero Phaethon cunctis e partibus orbem
aspicit accensum nec tantos sustinet aestus
feruentesque auras uelut e fornace profunda
230 ore trahit currusque suos candescere sentit;
et neque iam cineres eiectatamque fauillam
ferre potest calidoque inuoluitur undique fumo,
quoque eat aut ubi sit, picea caligine tectus,
nescit et arbitrio uolucrum raptatur equorum.
235 sanguine tum credunt in corpora summa uocato
Aethiopum populos nigrum traxisse colorem;
tum facta est Libye raptis umoribus aestu
arida, tum nymphae passis fontesque lacusque
defleuere comis: quaerit Boeotia Dircen,
240 Argos Amymonen, Ephyre Pirenidas undas.
nec sortita loco distantes flumina ripas
tuta manent: mediis Tanais fumauit in undis,
Peneosque senex Teuthranteusque Caicus
et celer Ismenos cum Phegiaco Erymantho
245 arsurusque iterum Xanthus flauusque Lycormas
quique recuruatis ludit Maeandros in undis
Mygdoniusque Melas et Taenarius Eurotas.
arsit et Euphrates Babylonius, arsit Orontes
Thermodonque citus Gangesque et Phasis et Hister.
250 aestuat Alpheos, ripae Spercheides ardent.
quodque suo Tagus amne uehit fluit ignibus aurum,
et quae Maeonias celebrabant carmine ripas

lower than her own and the clouds caught fire and smoked.
And the earth, in all its highest parts, was set aflame,   210
and split and developed cracks and dried as its moisture was dispelled.
The pastures turned white, trees and their foliage were burnt,
and the dry crops supplied the fuel for their own destruction.
  These are small complaints: great cities perished with their walls,
and the fires turned whole nations with their peoples   215
into ash; the woods blazed with their mountains,
Athos blazed and Cilician Taurus and Tmolus and Oete
and Ida, dry then, but previously abounding in springs,
and Helicon of the Virgins and Haemus (not yet Oeagrian).
Etna's fires were doubled and blazed immeasurably,   220
twin-peaked Parnassus too, and Eryx and Cynthus and Othrys,
and Rhodope, at last about to lose its snows, and Mimas,
Dindyma and Mycale, and Cithaeron born for sacred rites.
Nor was Scythia helped by her cold: the Caucasus blazed
and Ossa together with Pindus, and Olympus bigger than both of them, 225
and the airy Alps, and the beclouded Appenines.
  Then indeed Phaethon saw that the world was ignited
on every side and he could not take such heat,
and through his mouth he drew in searing air
as if from a deep furnace, and he felt his chariot glowing white.   230
And he could no longer bear the ashes
and the embers belching out, and he was wrapped on every side in hot
                   smoke,
and, covered in pitchy darkness, he did not know where he was going to
or where he was, but was dragged off at the whim of his flying horses.
It was then, they think, that, as the blood was drawn to the surface of
                   their bodies,
the Ethiopian peoples took on their black colour;
it was then that Libya, its moisture snatched up by the heat, became
a desert; it was then that the nymphs loosed their hair and bewailed
their springs and lakes: Boeotia looked for Dirce,
Argos for Amymone and Ephyre for the waters of Pirene.   240
Nor did the rivers, though they were allotted banks set far apart,
stay safe: the Tanais smoked in the midst of its waters,
and so did old man Peneus, Teuthrantean Caicus,
swift Ismenus, Phegiacan Erymanthus,
Xanthus, that was to burn again, yellow Lycormas,   245
Meander that plays among its twisting waters,
Mygdonian Melas and Taenarian Eurotas;
Babylonian Euphrates burnt, Orontes burnt,
and fast Thermodon, Ganges, Phasis and the Danube.
Alpheus boiled and the banks of Spercheus burnt.   250
And the gold which Tagus bears in its stream melted in the fires,
and the river birds that used to sing the praises

flumineae uolucres medio caluere Caystro.
Nilus in extremum fugit perterritus orbem
255   occuluitque caput, quod adhuc latet; ostia septem
puluerulenta uacant, septem sine flumine ualles.
fors eadem Ismarios Hebrum cum Strymone siccat
Hesperiosque amnes, Rhenum Rhodanumque Padumque
cuique fuit rerum promissa potentia, Thybrim.
260   dissilit omne solum, penetratque in Tartara rimis
lumen et infernum terret cum coniuge regem.
et mare contrahitur siccaeque est campus harenae,
quod modo pontus erat, quosque altum texerat aequor,
exsistunt montes et sparsas Cycladas augent.
265   ima petunt pisces nec se super aequora curui
tollere consuetas audent delphines in auras.
corpora phocarum summo resupina profundo
exanimata natant. ipsum quoque Nerea fama est
Doridaque et natas tepidis latuisse sub antris.
270   ter Neptunus aquis cum toruo bracchia uultu
exserere ausus erat; ter non tulit aeris ignes.
        alma tamen Tellus, ut erat circumdata ponto,
inter aquas pelagi contractosque undique fontes,
qui se condiderant in opacae uiscera matris,
275   sustulit oppressos collo tenus arida uultus
opposuitque manum fronti magnoque tremore
omnia concutiens paulum subsedit et infra,
quam solet esse, fuit sacraque ita uoce locuta est:
'si placet hoc meruique, quid o tua fulmina cessant,
280   summe deum? liceat periturae uiribus ignis
igne perire tuo clademque auctore leuare.
uix equidem fauces haec ipsa in uerba resoluo;'
(presserat ora uapor) 'tostos en aspice crines
inque oculis tantum, tantum super ora fauillae.
285   hosne mihi fructus, hunc fertilitatis honorem
officiique refers, quod adunci uulnera aratri
rastrorumque fero totoque exerceor anno,
quod pecori frondes alimentaque mitia, fruges
humano generi, uobis quoque tura ministro?
290   sed tamen exitium fac me meruisse: quid undae,
quid meruit frater? cur illi tradita sorte
aequora decrescunt et ab aethere longius absunt?
quod si nec fratris nec te mea gratia tangit,
at caeli miserere tui! circumspice utrumque:

of the Maeonian banks, sweltered in the middle of the Cayster.
The Nile fled to the ends of the earth in terror
and concealed his head (it is hidden still); his seven mouths   255
lay dusty and empty, seven riverless valleys.
The same fate dried the Ismarian streams, Hebrus
and Strymon, and in the West, the Rhine, the Rhone and the Po,
and, though it had been promised power over the world, the Tiber.
        The ground was all split open, and through the cracks light
                                                                penetrated
into Tartarus and terrified the king below together with his wife.   261
The sea contracted, there was an expanse of dry sand
where it had just been; mountains, that the water's depth
had covered, emerged and increased the scattered Cyclades.
The fishes sought the depths and the dolphins did not dare to raise   265
and bend their bodies above the waters into the air, as they usually did.
Seals' bodies floated lifeless and on their backs
upon the surface of the deep. And Nereus himself, the story goes,
and Doris and their daughters lay hidden in caves grown warm.
Three times Neptune dared to thrust his arms and stern   270
face above the waters; three times he could not bear the fires in the air.
        But bounteous Earth, surrounded as she was by the sea,
between the waters of the ocean and the springs that had packed in
                                                together from every side
and hidden in the bowels of their dark mother,
raised her drooping head from the neck and, parched,   275
put her hand before her face and, with a great tremor,
shook everything and settled down a little and lay
lower than she usually was and, in her holy voice, spoke thus:
'If this is your will, if I have deserved it, why are your thunderbolts
                                                                inactive,
oh highest of the gods? May I who am to perish in fire's might   280
perish in your fire and lighten the disaster with the thought of who had
                                                                caused it.
I can scarcely open my throat for these very words;'
(the smoke had pressed against her face) 'look at my burnt hair,
and all this ash in my eyes and all this ash upon my face.
Are these the returns you pay me, is this my reward   285
for fertility and service, for enduring wounds inflicted by the curved
ploughshare and by hoes, for being worked all through the year,
for supplying fodder to the flocks and gentle nourishment,
grain for human kind, and incense for you gods too?
But, suppose I have deserved destruction: what have the waves   290
deserved, and what has your brother? Why have the seas, his portion
of the allotment, shrunk down to be more distant from the ether?
But if neither your brother's good will nor mine mean anything to you,
at least pity your own heaven! Look all around you:

295　fumat uterque polus, quos si uitiauerit ignis,
　　atria uestra ruent. Atlans en ipse laborat
　　uixque suis umeris candentem sustinet axem.
　　si freta, si terrae pereunt, si regia caeli,
　　in chaos antiquum confundimur. eripe flammis
300　si quid adhuc superest et rerum consule summae.'
　　　　dixerat haec Tellus (neque enim tolerare uaporem
　　ulterius potuit nec dicere plura) suumque
　　rettulit os in se propioraque manibus antra.
　　　　at pater omnipotens superos testatus et ipsum
305　qui dederat currus, nisi opem ferat, omnia fato
　　interitura graui, summam petit arduus arcem,
　　unde solet nubes latis inducere terris,
　　unde mouet tonitrus uibrataque fulmina iactat.
　　sed neque quas posset terris inducere nubes
310　tunc habuit nec quos caelo demitteret imbres.
　　intonat et dextra libratum fulmen ab aure
　　misit in aurigam pariterque animaque rotisque
　　expulit et saeuis compescuit ignibus ignes.
　　consternantur equi et saltu in contraria facto
315　colla iugo eripiunt abruptaque lora relinquunt.
　　illic frena iacent, illic temone reuulsus
　　axis, in hac radii fractarum parte rotarum,
　　sparsaque sunt late laceri uestigia currus.
　　　　at Phaethon, rutilos flamma populante capillos,
320　uoluitur in praeceps longoque per aera tractu
　　fertur, ut interdum de caelo stella sereno,
　　etsi non cecidit, potuit cecidisse uideri.
　　quem procul a patria diuerso maximus orbe
　　excipit Eridanus fumantiaque abluit ora.
325　Naides Hesperiae trifida fumantia flamma
　　corpora dant tumulo signantque hoc carmine saxum:
　　HIC . SITVS . EST . PHAETHON . CVRRVS . AVRIGA .
　　　　　　　　　　　　　　　　　　　　　PATERNI
　　QVEM . SI . NON . TENVIT . MAGNIS . TAMEN .
　　　　　　　　　　　　　　　　　EXCIDIT . AVSIS.
　　　　nam pater obductos luctu miserabilis aegro
330　condiderat uultus et, si modo credimus, unum
　　isse diem sine sole ferunt; incendia lumen
　　praebebant aliquisque malo fuit usus in illo.
　　　　at Clymene, postquam dixit quaecumque fuerunt
　　in tantis dicenda malis, lugubris et amens
335　et laniata sinus totum percensuit orbem
　　exanimesque artus primo, mox ossa requirens
　　repperit ossa tamen peregrina condita ripa,
　　incubuitque loco nomenque in marmore lectum

both poles are smoking and, if the fire ruins them,   295
your halls will collapse. Look, even Atlas is struggling
and can hardly hold the white-hot world upon his shoulders.
If the seas and the lands and the palace of heaven perish,
we are sunk into primaeval Chaos. If there is anything still left,
snatch it from the flames and take some thought for the universe.'   300
      Earth had had her say (for she could endure
the heat no longer and could say no more) and she returned
her face into herself and to her caves nearer to the Shades.
      But the almighty father called the gods to witness, and him especially
who had given the chariot, that unless he brought help, everything would
                                                                die
in a grievous fate; and then he sought the top of his citadel on high,   306
from where he draws the clouds over the wide lands,
from where he sends the thunder and shakes and hurls the lightning bolt.
But then he had no clouds that he could draw
across the lands, no showers that he might send down from the sky.   310
He thundered and balanced the lightning bolt by his right ear
and sent it against the charioteer and drove him all at once from life
and from his wheels and quenched the fires with his savage fires.
The startled horses leapt in opposite directions,
wrenching their necks from the yoke and leaving the torn off reins behind.
There lay their harnesses, there the axles ripped from   316
the pole, over here the spokes of the broken wheels,
and remnants of the wrecked chariot were scattered far and wide.
      But Phaethon, while the fire still ravaged his russet hair,
was rolled over headlong and borne with a long trail   320
through the air, as from time to time a star could seem
to have fallen from a clear sky, even if it did not fall.
He was caught, far from his native land in a different part of the world,
by the great Eridanus which bathed his smoking face.
His body, smoking from the three-pronged flame, was given   325
burial by the western Naiads who carved these lines upon the stone:
HERE LIES PHAETHON, DRIVER OF HIS FATHER'S CHARIOT.
IF HE COULD NOT CONTROL IT, EVEN SO HE PERISHED DARING
                                  GREATLY.

      His father, pitiable in the pain of his grief, veiled
and hid his face; and they say, if we can believe them,   330
that one day went by without the sun; light was provided
by the fires, so, in that ill, there was some use.
      As for Clymene, after she had said whatever
had to be said in such great ills, insane with sorrow,
she tore her breasts and searched through all the earth,   335
and, seeking first his lifeless limbs, and soon his bones,
she found his bones, at least, buried on a far off bank.
She lay down on the spot and, as she read his name upon the marble,

perfudit lacrimis et aperto pectore fouit.
340 nec minus Heliades lugent et inania morti
munera dant lacrimas et caesae pectora palmis
non auditurum miseras Phaethonta querelas
nocte dieque uocant asternunturque sepulcro.
luna quater iunctis implerat cornibus orbem;
345 illae more suo, nam morem fecerat usus,
plangorem dederant. e quis Phaethusa, sororum
maxima, cum uellet terra procumbere, questa est
deriguisse pedes; ad quam conata uenire
candida Lampetie subita radice retenta est;
350 tertia, cum crinem manibus laniare pararet,
auellit frondes; haec stipite crura teneri,
illa dolet fieri longos sua bracchia ramos.
dumque ea mirantur, complectitur inguina cortex
perque gradus uterum pectusque umerosque manusque
355 ambit et exstabant tantum ora uocantia matrem.
quid faciat mater, nisi, quo trahit impetus illam,
huc eat atque illuc et, dum licet, oscula iungat?
non satis est, truncis auellere corpora temptat
et teneros manibus ramos abrumpit; at inde
360 sanguineae manant, tamquam de uulnere, guttae.
'parce, precor, mater,' quaecumque est saucia clamat,
'parce, precor; nostrum laceratur in arbore corpus.
iamque uale--' cortex in uerba nouissima uenit.
inde fluunt lacrimae, stillataque sole rigescunt
365 de ramis electra nouis, quae lucidus amnis
excipit et nuribus mittit spectanda Latinis.
adfuit huic monstro proles Stheneleia Cycnus,
qui tibi materno quamuis a sanguine iunctus,
mente tamen, Phaethon, propior fuit. ille relicto
370 (nam Ligurum populos et magnas rexerat urbes)
imperio, ripas uirides amnemque querelis
Eridanum implerat siluamque sororibus auctam,
cum uox est tenuata uiro canaeque capillos
dissimulant plumae collumque a pectore longe
375 porrigitur digitosque ligat iunctura rubentes,
penna latus uelat, tenet os sine acumine rostrum.
fit noua Cycnus auis nec se caeloque Iouique
credit, ut iniuste missi memor ignis ab illo;
stagna petit patulosque lacus ignemque perosus
380 quae colat elegit contraria flumina flammis.
squalidus interea genitor Phaethontis et expers
ipse sui decoris, qualis, cum deficit orbem,
esse solet, lucemque odit seque ipse diemque

bathed it with her tears and caressed it with her breasts bared.
    And the Heliades grieved no less and gave to his corpse   340
the vain offering of their tears, striking their hands upon their breasts,
they called on Phaethon night and day, though he was not to hear
their sad complaints, and they lay prostrate upon his tomb.
The moon had filled her orb and joined her horns four times,
and they, as was their habit, for practice had created a habit,   345
had given way to lamentation. One of them, Phaethusa, the eldest
of the sisters, when she wanted to lie down upon the ground, complained
that her feet had stiffened; and, when fair Lampetie tried
to come to her, she was held back by a sudden root.
A third, setting out to tear her hair with her hands,   350
pulled leaves away; one over here grieved that her legs were held
by a tree-trunk, one over there that her arms were being made into long
                                                                 branches.
And while they stood amazed at this, bark covered up their thighs
and encircled, step by step, their womb, their breast, their shoulders
and their hands, and only their mouths were left calling for their mother.
What was their mother to do, except to go this way and that,   356
wherever impulse drove her, and exchange kisses while she might?
It was not enough, she tried to pull their bodies from the trunks,
and broke off their tender branches with her hands; but drops
of blood, as if from a wound, flowed out.   360
'Spare me, I beg you, mother,' whichever one was being hurt cried out,
'Spare me, I beg you. It is my body being torn inside the tree.
And now, farewell --' the bark came over her last words.
Their tears flowed on, and dripped from the new branches
as amber which hardened in the sun and was taken off by the clear   365
stream and sent to be admired by Latin brides.
    There was present at this miracle Sthenelus' offspring, Cycnus,
who, though related to you, Phaethon, on his mother's
side, was closer still in spirit; he left his position
of power (for he had ruled the peoples of Liguria and their great   370
cities) and had filled with his complaints the river Eridanus
and its green banks and the wood to which his sisters had been added,
and then his voice grew thin, his hair took on the guise
of white feathers, his neck was stretched out far
from his breast, a linkage joined his reddening fingers,   375
a wing covered up his flank, a beak without a point possessed his mouth.
Cycnus became a new bird; but he did not entrust himself to the sky
or to Jove, remembering as he did the fire unjustly sent by him;
he sought the ponds and spreading lakes and, detesting fire,
he chose to dwell upon the rivers, the very opposite of flames.   380
    Meanwhile, the father of Phaethon, dishevelled and without
his normal radiance, but as he tends to be when his orb
is in eclipse, hated the light and himself and the day,

datque animum in luctus et luctibus adicit iram
385   officiumque negat mundo. 'satis,' inquit, 'ab aeui
sors mea principiis fuit inrequieta; pigetque
actorum sine fine mihi, sine honore laborum.
quilibet alter agat portantes lumina currus.
si nemo est omnesque dei non posse fatentur.
390   ipse agat, ut saltem, dum nostras temptat habenas,
orbatura patres aliquando fulmina ponat.
tum sciet, igniferum uires expertus equorum,
non meruisse necem qui non bene rexerit illos.'
talia dicentem circumstant omnia Solem
395   numina, neue uelit tenebras inducere rebus,
supplice uoce rogant; missos quoque Iuppiter ignes
excusat precibusque minas regaliter addit.
colligit amentes et adhuc terrore pauentes
Phoebus equos stimuloque dolens et uerbere saeuit
400   (saeuit enim) natumque obiectat et imputat illis.
at pater omnipotens ingentia moenia caeli
circuit et, ne quid labefactum uiribis ignis
corruat, explorat. quae postquam firma suique
roboris esse uidet, terras hominumque labores
405   perspicit. Arcadiae tamen est impensior illi
cura suae, fontesque et nondum audentia labi
flumina restituit, dat terrae gramina, frondes
arboribus, laesasque iubet reuirescere siluas.
dum redit itque frequens, in uirgine Nonacrina
410   haesit, et accepti caluere sub ossibus ignes.
non erat huius opus lanam mollire trahendo
nec positu uariare comas; ubi fibula uestem,
uitta coercuerat neglectos alba capillos,
et modo leue manu iaculum, modo sumpserat arcum,
415   miles erat Phoebes, nec Maenalon attigit ulla
gratior hac Triuiae; sed nulla potentia longa est.
ulterius medio spatium sol altus habebat,
cum subit illa nemus, quod nulla ceciderat aetas.
exuit hic umero pharetram lentosque retendit
420   arcus inque solo, quod texerat herba, iacebat
et pictam posita pharetram ceruice premebat.
Iuppiter ut uidit fessam et custode uacantem,
'hoc certe furtum coniunx mea nesciet,' inquit,
'aut si rescierit, sunt, o sunt iurgia tanti!'
425   protinus induitur faciem cultumque Dianae

and gave his spirit up to grief, with anger added to his grief,   384
and refused to perform his duty to the world. 'It's been my lot,' he said,
'to go without a rest from the beginning of time; and it's enough. I'm tired
of working endlessly with my efforts unrewarded.
Anyone else you like may drive the chariot that brings the light.
If there is no one, and all the gods admit they cannot do it,
let Jove himself do it, so that at least for some time, while he is trying
out
my reins, he will put down his father-bereaving lightning bolts.   391
Then he will know, when he has felt the strength of my fire-bearing
horses,
that he did not deserve death for not controlling them well.'
        All the gods stood around the Sun as he spoke
thus, and, in entreating tones, asked him not to want   395
to bring darkness on the world; Jove too defended his sending
of the fires and in regal manner added threats to his entreaties.
        The horses, frantic and still trembling with fear,
were rounded up by Phoebus and, in his grief, he savaged them with goad
and whip
(for he felt savage) and held them responsible for his son's death and
blamed them for it.
        But the almighty father went round heaven's huge   401
walls and inspected them in case in the might of his fire any of them
had weakened and collapsed. When he saw that they were firm,
with their normal sturdiness, he examined the lands and works
of men. But Arcadia was his more particular   405
concern, and he restored the springs and the rivers that did not yet
dare flow, he gave grass to the earth, foliage
to the trees and told the ravaged woods to grow green again.
As he was going constantly to and fro, he was transfixed by a Nonacrian
maiden, and the fires, caught in his bones, grew hot.   410
It was not her style to soften wool by drawing it out,
nor to keep changing the arrangement of her hair; once a pin had fastened
her dress and a white headband her disregarded hair,
and she had taken in her hand a smooth javelin perhaps, or perhaps a bow,
she was Phoebe's soldier; and there was no girl that reached Maenalos 415
more cherished by Trivia than she was; but no favour lasts for long.
        The sun on high was holding a place just past the midpoint
as she entered a copse which no generation had cut down.
Here, she slipped her quiver off her shoulder, unstrung her supple
bow and lay down upon the grass-covered ground   420
and rested her neck against her painted quiver.
When Jupiter saw her tired and unprotected,
'Well this deceit, at least, my wife will not know of,' he said,
'or, if she does find out -- her abuse is worth it, oh it is well worth it.'
He at once put on Diana's face and her dress   425

atque ait, 'o comitum, uirgo, pars una mearum,
in quibus es uenata iugis?' de caespite uirgo
se leuat et, 'salue numen, me iudice,' dixit,
'audiat ipse licet, maius Ioue.' ridet et audit
430   et sibi praeferri se gaudet et oscula iungit
nec moderata satis nec sic a uirgine danda.
      qua uenata foret silua narrare parantem
impedit amplexu, nec se sine crimine prodit.
illa quidem contra, quantum modo femina posset
435   (aspiceres utinam, Saturnia; mitior esses),
illa quidem pugnat; sed quem superare puella,
quisue Iouem poterat? superum petit aethera uictor
Iuppiter; huic odio nemus est et conscia silua.
unde pedem referens paene est oblita pharetram
440   tollere cum telis et quem suspenderat arcum.
      ecce suo comitata choro Dictynna per altum
Maenalon ingrediens et caede superba ferarum
aspicit hanc uisamque uocat. clamata refugit
et timuit primo, ne Iuppiter esset in illa.
445   sed postquam pariter nymphas incedere uidit,
sensit abesse dolos numerumque accessit ad harum.
heu quam difficile est crimen non prodere uultu!
uix oculos attollit humo nec, ut ante solebat,
iuncta deae lateri nec toto est agmine prima;
450   sed silet et laesi dat signa rubore pudoris;
et, nisi quod uirgo est, poterat sentire Diana
mille notis culpam. nymphae sensisse feruntur.
      orbe resurgebant lunaria cornua nono,
cum dea, uenatu fraternis languida flammis,
455   nacta nemus gelidum, de quo cum murmure labens
ibat et attritas uersabat riuus harenas.
ut loca laudauit, summas pede contigit undas.
his quoque laudatis, 'procul est,' ait, 'arbiter omnis:
nuda superfusis tingamus corpora lymphis.'
460   Parrhasis erubuit; cunctae uelamina ponunt,
una moras quaerit; dubitanti uestis adempta est,
qua posita nudo patuit cum corpore crimen.
attonitae manibusque uterum celare uolenti,
'i procul hinc,' dixit, 'nec sacros pollue fontes,'
465   Cynthia deque suo iussit secedere coetu.
      senserat hoc olim magni matrona Tonantis
distuleratque graues in idonea tempora poenas.
causa morae nulla est, et iam puer Arcas (id ipsum

and said, 'Oh maiden, one from my band of companions,
which slopes have you been hunting on?' The maiden raised herself
from the turf and said, 'Welcome, oh divinity, greater, if I am
the judge, than Jupiter, though he himself hears me.' He laughed as he
                                                    heard her
and rejoiced that he was preferred to himself, and exchanged kisses,   430
not particularly restrained ones, and not the sort to be given by a maiden.
    She was preparing to tell what wood she had been hunting in,
when he stopped her with his embrace and, not without a guilty act, gave
                                                    himself away.
She, indeed, as much, at least, as a woman could
(if only you had seen, Saturnia; you would have been more lenient),   435
she indeed fought back; but who could a girl overcome,
or who could overcome Jove? Victorious Jupiter sought the ether
up on high: she hated the copse and the wood that knew her guilt.
She withdrew from there and almost forgot to pick up
her quiver with its arrows and the bow she had hung up. .   440
    Look, Dictynna accompanied by her chorus was approaching
through high Maenalos and, proud from the killing of wild beasts,
noticed her and, as she saw her, called. Hearing the shout, she fled
and was afraid at first that Jupiter was in her.
But when she saw the nymphs advancing along beside her,   445
she realized there was no trickery and added herself to their number.
Alas, how difficult it is not to give guilt away by one's expression.
She could hardly raise her eyes up from the ground, and she was not, as
                                                    she used to be before,
close to the goddess and first in the whole procession;
but she was silent and, with a blush, gave the signs of injured shame;   450
and, but for her virginity, Diana could have sensed
her guilt from a thousand indications. They say the nymphs did sense it.
    The lunar horns had grown again in their ninth orb,
when the goddess, weary from hunting under her brother's rays,
reached a cool copse from which a brook came murmuring   455
and gliding by and stirring up the smooth worn sand.
She praised the spot and touched the surface of the waters with her foot.
These too she praised and, 'Every onlooker,' she said, 'is far away:
let's bathe and dip our naked bodies in the water.'
Parrhasis blushed; the others took off their clothes;   460
she alone sought delay; while she hesitated, they took off her clothes
and, as they put them down, exposed not just her naked body but her guilt.
She was stunned and, as she tried to hide her womb with her hands,
Cynthia said to her, 'Go far from here, do not pollute
my sacred streams,' and she ordered her to leave her company.   465
    The great Thunderer's matron had sensed this long ago,
but had delayed stern punishments until the times were suitable.
Now, there was no reason to delay; a boy, Arcas, (this too

indoluit Iuno) fuerat de paelice natus.
470 quo simul obuertit saeuam cum lumine mentem,
    'scilicet hoc unum restabat, adultera,' dixit,
    'ut fecunda fores fieretque iniuria partu
    nota Iouisque mei testatum dedecus esset.
    haud impune feres; adimam tibi namque figuram,
475 qua tibi quaque places nostro, importuna, marito.'
        dixit et aduersa prensis a fronte capillis
    strauit humi pronam; tendebat bracchia supplex:
    bracchia coeperunt nigris horrescere uillis
    curuarique manus et aduncos crescere in ungues
480 officioque pedum fungi laudataque quondam
    ora Ioui lato fieri deformia rictu.
    neue preces animos et uerba precantia flectant,
    posse loqui eripitur; uox iracunda minaxque
    plenaque terroris rauco de gutture fertur.
485 mens antiqua manet (facta quoque mansit in ursa)
    adsiduoque suos gemitu testata dolores
    qualescumque manus ad caelum et sidera tollit
    ingratumque Iouem, nequeat cum dicere, sentit.
    a quotiens, sola non ausa quiescere silua,
490 ante domum quondamque suis errauit in agris!
    a quotiens per saxa canum latratibus acta est
    uenatrixque metu uenantum territa fugit!
    saepe feris latuit uisis, oblita quid esset;
    ursaque conspectos in montibus horruit ursos,
495 pertimuitque lupos, quamuis pater esset in illis.
        ecce Lycaoniae proles ignara parentis
    Arcas adest, ter quinque fere natalibus actis,
    dumque feras sequitur, dum saltus eligit aptos
    nexilibusque plagis siluas Erymanthidas ambit,
500 incidit in matrem, quae restitit Arcade uiso
    et cognoscenti similis fuit. ille refugit
    immotosque oculos in se sine fine tenentem
    nescius extimuit propiusque accedere auenti
    uulnifico fuerat fixurus pectora telo.
505 arcuit omnipotens pariterque ipsosque nefasque
    sustulit et uolucri raptos per inania uento
    imposuit caelo uicinaque sidera fecit.
        intumuit Iuno postquam inter sidera paelex
    fulsit, et ad canam descendit in aequora Tethyn
510 Oceanumque senem, quorum reuerentia mouit

pained Juno) had been born to the wench.
And as she turned a savage mind and eye upon the scene,   470
'Yes, of course, that was all that was left, adulteress,' she said,
'that you should conceive and make it known that I've been wronged
by giving birth, and testify to the misconduct of my Jove.
You will not get away unpunished: for I shall strip away your beauty   474
with which, wanton girl, you give pleasure to yourself and to my husband.'
    She spoke, and, as the girl faced round, she grasped her hair at the
                                                                         forehead
and struck her flat upon the ground; she began to stretch her arms in
                                                                      supplication:
her arms began to bristle with black hairs,
her hands to bend and grow into curved claws
and to perform the task of feet, and her mouth, once   480
praised by Jove, became misshapen, gaping wide.
In case her prayers and praying words might move his heart,
her power of speech was snatched away. An angry, threatening voice
came terrifyingly from her hoarse throat.
Her original mind remained (and has remained too in what became a bear)
and she testified to her sorrows with a persistent groan,   486
and raised whatever sort of hands she had to heaven and to the stars,
feeling, although she could not say it, that Jupiter was ungrateful.
Oh, how often she did not dare to rest in the lonely wood
but wandered in front of her former home and its fields!   490
Oh, how often was she driven through the rocks by the baying of the dogs,
and, though a huntress, fled terrified in fear of the huntsmen!
Often, on seeing wild beasts, she hid, forgetting what she was;
and, though a she-bear, she shuddered when she noticed he-bears on the
                                                                       mountains,
and she feared the wolves, although her father was among them.   495
    Look, Arcas, her offspring, was there, unaware of
his Lycaonian mother; he had passed thrice five birthdays or thereabouts,
and while he was pursuing wild beasts, while he was picking likely glades
and encircling the Erymanthian woods with his intertwining nets,
he chanced upon his mother; she stood still on seeing Arcas,   500
like someone who knew him. He fled back
and in his ignorance was terrified of her as she ceaselessly held her
                                                                        unmoving
eyes upon him, and, as she became eager to approach more closely,
he got set to pierce her breast with a wound-inducing weapon.
The almighty one took control, suspending both them   505
and the sinful act and also, using the wind to drive them through the void,
he set them in the sky and made them into neighbouring stars.
    Juno was enraged when the wench began to shine
amongst the stars, and she went down into the sea to white-haired Tethys
and to the old man Ocean, who have often been the objects   510

saepe deos, causamque uiae scitantibus infit;
'quaeritis aetheriis quare regina deorum
sedibus hic adsim? pro me tenet altera caelum.
mentior, obscurum nisi nox cum fecerit orbem,
515 nuper honoratas summo, mea uulnera, caelo
uideritis stellas illic, ubi circulus axem
ultimus extremum spatioque breuissimus ambit.
et uero quisquam Iunonem laedere nolit
offensamque tremat, quae prosum sola nocendo?
520 o ego quantum egi! quam uasta potentia nostra est!
esse hominem uetui: facta est dea. sic ego poenas
sontibus impono, sic est mea magna potestas.
uindicet antiquam faciem uultusque ferinos
detrahat, Argolica quod in ante Phoronide fecit.
525 cur non et pulsa ducit Iunone meoque
conlocat in thalamo socerumque Lycaona sumit?
at uos si laesae tangit contemptus alumnae,
gurgite caeruleo Septem prohibete Triones
sideraque in caelo stupri mercede recepta
530 pellite, ne puro tingatur in aequore paelex.'
      di maris adnuerant; habili Saturnia curru
ingreditur liquidum pauonibus aethera pictis,
tam nuper pictis caeso pauonibus Argo,
quam tu nuper eras, cum candidus ante fuisses,
535 corue loquax, subito nigrantes uersus in alas.
      nam fuit haec quondam niueis argentea pennis
ales, ut aequaret totas sine labe columbas
nec seruaturis uigili Capitolia uoce
cederet anseribus nec amanti flumina cycno.
540 lingua fuit damno: lingua faciente loquaci,
qui color albus erat, nunc est contrarius albo.
      pulchrior in tota quam Larisaea Coronis
non fuit Haemonia: placuit tibi, Delphice, certe,
dum uel casta fuit uel inobseruata; sed ales
545 sensit adulterium Phoebeius, utque latentem
detegeret culpam, non exorabilis index
ad dominum tendebat iter; quem garrula motis
consequitur pennis, scitetur ut omnia, cornix
auditaque uiae causa, 'non utile carpis,'
550 inquit, 'iter: ne sperne meae praesagia linguae.
quid fuerim quid simque uide, meritumque require.
inuenies nocuisse fidem. nam tempore quodam
Pallas Erichthonium, prolem sine matre creatam,

of the gods' respect, and when they wanted to know the reason for her
journey, she began,
'Do you ask why I, the queen of the gods, am present here
from my ethereal dwelling? Another is holding sway in heaven instead of me.
If I'm not lying, when the night has made the world dark,
you will see freshly appointed stars, wounding to me, there   515
at the top of the sky where the last circle,
shortest in extent, goes round the edge of the pole.
And, truly, would anyone be unwilling to harm Juno
or tremble when she is offended, since I alone help by harming?
Oh, what a great thing I have done! How enormous is my power!   520
I have stopped her being human: she has become a goddess. That's how I
inflict
punishments on the guilty, that is my great authority.
Let him restore her original likeness and strip away her bestial
appearance, as he did before with Argive Phoronis.
Why does he not drive Juno out and marry this one and settle her   525
in my bedroom and take Lycaon for his father-in-law?
But, if you are touched by the insult to your wronged foster-child,
bar the Seven Oxen from your aquamarine flood
and drive off stars that have been taken into heaven as a reward   529
for shamelessness, so that the wench can never bathe in your pure waters.'
The gods of the sea had nodded their assent; Saturnia proceeded
through the clear
ether in her trim chariot with its painted peacocks,
peacocks as recently painted from the killing of Argus
as you had recently and suddenly been turned into a black winged
bird, oh talkative raven, although you had been white before.   535
For once this bird was silver with snowy
wings, the equal of wholly unblemished doves,
and not inferior to the geese that were to save the Capitol
with their watchful voice, nor to the river loving swan.
His tongue was his ruin: through the action of his talkative tongue,   540
his colour that was white is now the opposite to white.
In all Haemonia, there was no girl more beautiful
than Larissaean Coronis: she certainly gave pleasure to you, oh Delphic one,
while she was true, or unwatched; but Phoebus'
bird noticed her adultery and the relentless   545
tell-tale, pressed on his way to his master
to reveal her hidden guilt; the chattering crow
pursued him with flapping wings so as to find out everything,
and, when she had heard the reason for the journey, said, 'It is no profitable
journey you are taking: do not despise my tongue's forewarning.   550
See what I was and what I am, then ask about my deserts.
You will find it was my good faith that hurt me. For, once,
Pallas had shut Erichthonius, a child born without

          clauserat Actaeo texta de uimine cista
555   uirginibusque tribus gemino de Cecrope natis
          et legem dederat, sua ne secreta uiderent.
          abdita fronde leui densa speculabar ab ulmo,
          quid facerent: commissa duae sine fraude tuentur,
          Pandrosos atque Herse; timidas uocat una sorores,
560   Aglauros, nodosque manu diducit, et intus
          infantemque uident adporrectumque draconem.
          acta deae refero; pro quo mihi gratia talis
          redditur, ut dicar tutela pulsa Mineruae
          et ponar post noctis auem. mea poena uolucres
565   admonuisse potest, ne uoce pericula quaerant.
          at, puto, non ultro nec quidquam tale rogantem
          me petiit? ipsa licet hoc a Pallade quaeras.
          quamuis irata est, non hoc irata negabit.
          nam me Phocaica clarus tellure Coroneus
570   (nota loquor) genuit fueramque ego regia uirgo
          diuitibusque procis (ne me contemne) petebar;
          forma mihi nocuit. nam cum per litora lentis
          passibus, ut soleo, summa spatiarer harena,
          uidit et incaluit pelagi deus; utque precando
575   tempora cum blandis absumpsit inania uerbis,
          uim parat et sequitur. fugio densumque relinquo
          litus et in molli nequiquam lassor harena.
          inde deos hominesque uoco, nec contigit ullum
          uox mea mortalem: mota est pro uirgine uirgo
580   auxiliumque tulit. tendebam bracchia caelo:
          bracchia coeperunt leuibus nigrescere pennis;
          reicere ex umeris uestem molibar: at illa
          pluma erat inque cutem radices egerat imas;
          plangere nuda meis conabar pectora palmis:
585   sed neque iam palmas nec pectora nuda gerebam;
          currebam, nec ut ante pedes retinebat harena,
          sed summa tollebar humo. mox alta per auras
          euehor et data sum comes inculpata Mineruae.
          quid tamen hoc prodest, si diro facta uolucris
590   crimine Nyctimene nostro successit honori?
          an quae per totam res est notissima Lesbon
          non audita tibi est, patrium temerasse cubile
          Nyctimenen? auis illa quidem, sed conscia culpae
          conspectum lucemque fugit tenebrisque pudorem
595   celat et a cunctis expellitur aethere toto.'
                  talia dicenti, 'tibi,' ait, 'reuocamina,' coruus
          'sint precor ista malo; nos uanum spernimus omen.'

a mother, in a chest of Actaean wicker-work
and had given him to the three maiden daughters of two-formed   555
Cecrops together with a rule not to look at what she had secreted.
Hidden in the light foliage of a leafy elm, I began to keep a watch
on what they did: two, Pandrosos and Herse, guarded their charge
without deceit; one, Aglauros, called her sisters
timid and undid the knots with her hand, and they saw   560
the baby inside and a snake stretched out beside him.
I told the goddess what they had done; for which, the sort of gratitude
I was returned was that I be declared expelled from the protection of
                                                              Minerva
and ranked below the bird of night. My punishment could
have warned birds not to invite punishment with their voice.   565
And, as I think, did she not seek me of her own accord when I was asking
for nothing of the sort? You may question Pallas herself on this.
Angry though she is, she will not, because she is angry, deny it.
I was born to famous Coroneus in the territory
of Phocis (as you know) and I was a royal maiden   570
and was sought (don't mock me) by wealthy suitors.
My beauty hurt me. For while I was strolling across the beach
with leisurely steps, as I used to, on the surface of the sand,
the sea-god saw me and caught fire; and, when he had spent
the time vainly in entreaty and coaxing words,   575
he prepared for violence and pursued me; I fled and left the hard
beach and vainly wearied myself in the soft sand.
Then I called on gods and men, but my voice
did not reach any mortal: but a maiden was moved by a maiden
and brought her help. I stretched my arms up to the sky: 580
my arms began to grow black with light feathers;
I struggled to pull my clothing from my shoulders: but it
was plumage and had driven roots deep into my skin;
I tried to use my hands to beat my naked breasts:
but now I had neither hands nor naked breasts;   585
I ran, but the sand did not hold my feet back as before,
but I was carried along the surface of the ground. Soon I was driven
                                                        through the air
and carried up and given to Minerva as an undefiled companion.
But what good is that, if Nyctimene, who was made into a bird
because of terrible sin, has succeeded to my office?   590
Or, haven't you heard what is very well known
throughout all Lesbos, that Nyctimene defiled her father's
bed? Now she is a bird, but she feels her guilt
and avoids being seen in the light, hiding her shame
in the darkness and driven by all from the whole ether.'   595
      To such words the raven said, 'I pray your calling back
turns out ill for you; I scorn your vain foreboding.'

nec coeptum dimittit iter dominoque iacentem
cum iuuene Haemonio uidisse Coronida narrat.
600 laurea delapsa est audito crimine amantis,
et pariter uultusque deo plectrumque colorque
excidit; utque animus tumida feruebat ab ira,
arma adsueta capit flexumque a cornibus arcum
tendit et illa suo totiens cum pectore iuncta
605 indeuitato traiecit pectora telo.
icta dedit gemitum tractoque a corpore ferro
candida puniceo perfudit membra cruore
et dixit, 'potui poenas tibi, Phoebe, dedisse,
sed peperisse prius; duo nunc moriemur in una.'
610 hactenus, et pariter uitam cum sanguine fudit.
corpus inane animae frigus letale secutum est.
paenitet, heu, sero poenae crudelis amantem,
seque, quod audierit, quod sic exarserit, odit;
odit auem, per quam crimen causamque dolendi
615 scire coactus erat; nec non arcumque manumque
odit cumque manu temeraria tela, sagittas.
conlapsamque fouet seraque ope uincere fata
nititur et medicas exercet inaniter artes.
quae postquam frustra temptata rogumque parari
620 uidit et arsuros supremis ignibus artus,
tum uero gemitus (neque enim caelestia tingi
ora licet lacrimis) alto de corde petitos
edidit, haud aliter quam cum, spectante iuuenca,
lactentis uituli dextra libratus ab aure
625 tempora discussit claro caua malleus ictu.
ut tamen ingratos in pectora fudit odores
et dedit amplexus iniustaque iusta peregit,
non tulit in cineres labi sua Phoebus eosdem
semina, sed natum flammis uteroque parentis
630 eripuit geminique tulit Chironis in antrum,
sperantemque sibi non falsae praemia ·linguae
inter aues albas uetuit consistere coruum.
semifer interea diuinae stirpis alumno
laetus erat mixtoque oneri gaudebat honore.
635   ecce uenit rutilis umeros protecta capillis
filia Centauri, quam quondam nympha Chariclo
fluminis in rapidi ripis enixa uocauit
Ocyroen; non haec artes contenta paternas
edidicisse fuit: Fatorum arcana canebat.
640 ergo ubi uaticinos concepit mente furores
incaluitque deo quem clausum pectore habebat,
aspicit infantem, 'toto' que 'salutifer orbi

And he did not put off the journey he had begun, but told his master
he had seen Coronis sleeping with a young Haemonian.
The lover's laurel slipped off when he heard of the offence,   600
and the god lost his expression, his plectrum and his colour
all at once and, as his spirit seethed with boiling anger,
he took his customary weapons and stretched his bow bent
from its horns and, with his ineludible arrow, pierced
that breast so often joined with his breast.   605
She was struck and gave a groan and, as she pulled the shaft out from her
                                                                          body,
she drenched her fair limbs with crimson blood
and said, 'Phoebus, I could have paid the penalty to you,
but given birth first. Now two of us will die in one.'
She got so far and then poured out her life together with her blood.   610
Her body was emptied of its soul and a deathly chill came over it.
Alas, too late, the lover regretted the cruel penalty
and hated himself for listening, for becoming so incensed;
he hated the bird who had forced him to know of the offence
and that he had cause to grieve; he also hated his bow   615
and his hand, and with his hand, those reckless weapons, his arrows.
He caressed the fallen girl and, with tardy help, struggled to overcome
her fate and vainly exercised his skills in medicine.
After these futile attempts, he realized that the pyre
was being readied and that her limbs would burn in those last fires;   620
then indeed (for it is not permitted for heavenly faces to be bathed
with tears), he uttered groans summoned up from the bottom
of his heart, just as when, with the heifer looking on,
a hammer, balanced by the right ear, smashes
the hollow temples of a suckling calf with a resounding blow.   625
But when he had poured thankless perfumes on her breast
and given her an embrace and performed the rites that were not right,
Phoebus could not bear that his seed disappear into the same
ashes, but snatched his son from the flames and from his mother's
womb and bore him to the cave of two-formed Chiron,   630
and forbade the raven, who was hoping to be rewarded
for his undeceitful tongue, to keep his place amongst white birds.
Meanwhile, the half-beast was happy with a foster child
of divine stock and rejoiced at so onerous an honour.
          Look, here comes the Centaur's daughter, her shoulders covered   635
by her russet hair. The nymph, Chariclo, bore her
once on the banks of a swift river and called her
Ocyroe; she was not content to have learnt
her father's skills: she used to sing the secrets of the Fates.
And so, when she had caught the prophetic frenzy in her mind   640
and was on fire with the god whom she held closed in her breast,
she saw the child and said, 'Grow, boy,

cresce, puer,' dixit; 'tibi se mortalia saepe
corpora debebunt; animas tibi reddere ademptas
645 fas erit, idque semel dis indignantibus ausus,
posse dare hoc iterum flamma prohibebere auita,
eque deo corpus fies exsangue deusque,
qui modo corpus eras, et bis tua fata nouabis.
tu quoque, care pater, nunc immortalis et aeuis
650 omnibus ut maneas nascendi lege creatus,
posse mori cupies, tum cum cruciabere dirae
sanguine serpentis per saucia membra recepto,
teque ex aeterno patientem numina mortis
efficient, triplicesque deae tua fila resoluent.'
655 restabat fatis aliquid; suspirat ab imis
pectoribus, lacrimaeque genis labuntur obortae,
atque ita, 'praeuertunt,' inquit, 'me Fata, uetorque
plura loqui, uocisque meae praecluditur usus.
non fuerant artes tanti, quae numinis iram
660 contraxere mihi; mallem nescisse futura.
iam mihi subduci facies humana uidetur,
iam cibus herba placet, iam latis currere campis
impetus est. in equam cognataque corpora uertor.
tota tamen quare? pater est mihi nempe biformis.'
665 talia dicenti pars est extrema querelae
intellecta parum, confusaque uerba fuerunt.
mox nec uerba quidem nec equae sonus ille uidetur,
sed simulantis equam, paruoque in tempore certos
edidit hinnitus et bracchia mouit in herbas.
670 tum digiti coeunt et quinos alligat ungues
perpetuo cornu leuis ungula, crescit et oris
et colli spatium, longae pars maxima pallae
cauda fit, utque uagi crines per colla iacebant,
in dextras abiere iubas, pariterque nouata est
675 et uox et facies; nomen quoque monstra dedere.
    flebat opemque tuam frustra Philyreius heros,
Delphice, poscebat. nam nec rescindere magni
iussa Iouis poteras, nec, si rescindere posses,
tunc aderas: Elin Messeniaque arua colebas.
680 illud erat tempus, quo te pastoria pellis
texit onusque fuit baculum siluestre sinistrae,
alterius dispar septenis fistula cannis.
dumque amor est curae, dum te tua fistula mulcet,

health bringer to all the world; mortal bodies will often
owe you their existence. And it will be your right to restore   644
souls that have been carried off, but you will dare it once when the gods
                                                        begrudge it,
and you will be stopped from being able to grant this again by your
                                        grandfather's flame,
and, instead of a god, you will become a bloodless body, and then a god
who was just now a body, and you will twice renew your fates.
You too, dear father, immortal now and begotten
and born on the understanding that you would endure for all the ages,   650
you will desire the ability to die then, when you are being tortured by the
                                                        dreadful
snake's blood admitted through the injuries in your limbs,
and the gods will bring you from immortality to be one that suffers
death, and the three-fold goddesses will undo your threads.'
Something of his fate was left: she sighed from the bottom   655
of her heart and tears welled up and flowed down her cheeks
and she spoke thus, 'The Fates forestall me and I am forbidden
to say more and my use of speech is blocked.
The skills by which I have provoked god's anger
were not worth so much; I would rather not have known the future.   660
Now I seem to be losing my human likeness,
now I want grass for food, now I have an urge to run
on the broad plains. I am being turned into a mare, a body I am related to.
But, why all of me? My father, as you know, is two-formed.'
So she spoke, but the last part of her complaint   665
was scarcely understood and her words became confused.
Soon it seemed like neither words nor the sound of a mare,
but like one imitating a mare, and, after a little while she clearly
gave forth whinnies and moved her arms into the grass.
Then her fingers came together and a light hoof bound   670
her five finger nails in solid horn, the length of her face
and of her neck grew and the greater part of her long cloak
became a tail, and as her straying tresses lay along her neck
they turned into a mane on the right, and both her voice and likeness
were changed together; this wonder gave her a name as well.   675
     The Philyrean hero wept and demanded your help,
oh Delphic one, in vain. For you could not have revoked
the orders of great Jupiter, nor, if you could have revoked them,
were you there at that time: you were living in Elis and the Messenian
                                                        fields.
That was the time when a shepherd's leather cloak   680
covered you and you bore a staff from the woods in your left hand,
and in the other an unequal set of pipes with seven reeds.
And while you were concerned with love, while your pipes were soothing
                                                        you,

incustoditae Pylios memorantur in agros
685   processisse boues. uidet has Atlantide Maia
natus et arte sua siluis occultat abactas.
senserat hoc furtum nemo nisi notus in illo
rure senex: Baîtum uicinia tota uocabant.
diuitis hic saltus herbosaque pascua Nelei
690   nobiliumque greges custos seruabat equarum.
hunc timuit blandaque manu seduxit et illi,
'quisquis es, hospes,' ait, 'si forte armenta requiret
haec aliquis, uidisse nega; neu gratia facto
nulla rependatur, nitidam cape praemia uaccam.'
695   et dedit. accepta uoces has reddidit hospes:
'tutus eas. lapis iste prius tua furta loquetur.'
et lapidem ostendit. simulat Ioue natus abire.
mox redit et uersa pariter cum uoce figura,
'rustice, uidisti si quas hoc limite,' dixit,
700   'ire boues, fer opem furtoque silentia deme.
iuncta suo pariter dabitur tibi femina tauro.'
at senior, postquam est merces geminata, 'sub illis
montibus,' inquit, 'erunt.' et erant sub montibus illis.
risit Atlantiades et, 'me mihi, perfide, prodis?
705   me mihi prodis?' ait. periuraque pectora uertit
in durum silicem, qui nunc quoque dicitur index,
inque nihil merito uetus est infamia saxo.
        hinc se sustulerat paribus Caducifer alis
Munychiosque uolans agros gratamque Mineruae
710   despectabat humum cultique arbusta Lycei.
illa forte die castae de more puellae
uertice supposito festas in Palladis arces
pura coronatis portabant sacra canistris.
inde reuertentes deus aspicit ales iterque
715   non agit in rectum, sed in orbem curuat eundem.
ut uolucris uisis rapidissima miluus extis,
dum timet et densi circumstant sacra ministri,
flectitur in gyrum nec longius audet abire
spemque suam motis auidus circumuolat alis;
720   sic super Actaeas agilis Cyllenius arces
inclinat cursus et easdem circinat auras.
quanto splendidior quam cetera sidera fulget
Lucifer et quanto quam Lucifer aurea Phoebe,
tanto uirginibus praestantior omnibus Herse

it is said that your unguarded cows advanced
into the fields of Pylos. The son of Maia, Atlas' daughter,   685
saw them and drove them off and artfully hid them in the woods.
No one had noticed the theft except an old man well known
in the country there: the whole neighbourhood called him Battus.
He was a herdsman and looked after the glades of wealthy Neleus
and his grassy pastures and his famous herds of mares.   690
Mercury was afraid of him and, drawing him aside with a coaxing hand,
                                                                                                            said
to him, 'Stranger, whoever you are, if someone happens to be looking for
these cattle, say that you have not seen them, and, to recompense your act
with some gratitude, take a sleek cow for your reward.'
And he gave him one. The stranger accepted it and replied in these words:
'You may go safely. That stone will tell of your theft before I do.'   696
And he pointed out a stone. Jove's son pretended to depart.
Soon he returned, with his voice as well as his appearance changed,
and said, 'Peasant, if you have seen any cattle going
along this path, help me by refusing to be silent on the theft.   700
You will be given a bull together with its mate.'
But the old man, now that the reward was doubled, said,
'They will be at the foot of those mountains.' And they were at the foot
                                                                                            of those mountains.
Atlas' grandson laughed and said, 'Are you betraying me to myself, you
                                                                                                            cheat?
Are you betraying me to myself?' And he turned his perjured breast   705
into the hard stone which is even now called touch-stone,
and on the stone that deserved it not at all there is that old stigma.
        The Staffbearer took himself up away from here on his balanced
                                                                                                            wings
and, as he flew, looked down upon the Munychian fields and Minerva's
favourite earth and the woods of the cultured Lyceum.   710
It happened on that day that chaste girls, in accordance with the custom,
were carrying on the top of their heads pure and sacred objects
in garlanded baskets to the citadel of Pallas on her festival.
The winged god noticed them as they were coming back from there and
                                                                                                            did not take
a straight path but veered round into the same arc.   715
Just as the kite, swiftest of birds when it has seen entrails,
wheels round in a circle while it is afraid and the priests
stand crowding around the sacrifice, and it dares not go too far away
but, with flapping wings, flies eagerly around what it is hoping for;
even so the eager Cyllenian diverts his course above   720
the Actaean citadels and circles through the same air.
Just as Lucifer shines more brightly than the other
stars, and just as golden Phoebe outshines Lucifer,
even so was Herse outstanding over all the maidens

725   ibat eratque decus pompae comitumque suarum.
    obstipuit forma Ioue natus et aethere pendens
    non secus exarsit, quam cum Balearica plumbum
    funda iacit: uolat illud et incandescit eundo,
    et quos non habuit sub nubibus inuenit ignis.
730   uertit iter caeloque petit terrena relicto
    nec se dissimulat, tanta est fiducia formae.
    quae quamquam iusta est, cura tamen adiuuat illam
    permulcetque comas chlamydemque, ut pendeat apte,
    conlocat, ut limbus totumque appareat aurum,
735   ut teres in dextra, qua somnos ducit et arcet,
    uirga sit, ut tersis niteant talaria plantis.
    pars secreta domus ebore et testudine cultos
    tres habuit thalamos, quorum tu, Pandrose, dextrum,
    Aglauros laeuum, medium possederat Herse.
740   quae tenuit laeuum, uenientem prima notauit
    Mercurium nomenque dei scitarier ausa est
    et causam aduentus; cui sic respondit, 'Atlantis
    Pleionesque nepos ego sum, qui iussa per auras
    uerba patris porto; pater est mihi Iuppiter ipse.
745   nec fingam causas; tu tantum fida sorori
    esse uelis prolisque meae matertera dici.
    Herse causa uiae; faueas oramus amanti.'
    aspicit hunc oculis isdem, quibus abdita nuper
    uiderat Aglauros flauae secreta Mineruae,
750   proque ministerio magni sibi ponderis aurum
    postulat; interea tectis excedere cogit.
    uertit ad hanc torui dea bellica luminis orbem
    et tanto penitus traxit suspiria motu,
    ut pariter pectus positamque in pectore forti
755   aegida concuteret. subit hanc arcana profana
    detexisse manu tum cum sine matre creatam
    Lemnicolae stirpem contra data foedera uidit,
    et gratamque deo fore iam gratamque sorori
    et ditem sumpto, quod auara poposcerat, auro.
760   protinus Inuidiae nigro squalentia tabo
    tecta petit; domus est imis in uallibus huius
    abdita, sole carens, non ulli peruia uento,
    tristis et ignaui plenissima frigoris et quae
    igne uacet semper, caligine semper abundet.
765   huc ubi peruenit belli metuenda uirago,

as she went and was the glory of the procession and of her companions.
Jove's son was dumbfounded by her beauty and, as he hung in the ether,
caught fire no differently than lead thrown by a Balearic
sling: it flies and, as it goes, becomes white hot
and finds, beneath the clouds, fires it did not have before.
He altered course and, leaving heaven behind, sought earthly things,   730
and he did not disguise himself, so great was his confidence in his looks.
Though this was justified, he still took care to help them further
by smoothing down his hair and arranging his cloak so that it would hang
properly, and the fringe and all the gold would show,   734
by seeing that the wand in his right hand, the one that brings and takes
                                              away our sleep,
was polished and that his feet were scrubbed and that his sandals gleamed.
In a secluded part of the house there were three bedrooms
decked with ivory and tortoiseshell; of these, yours, Pandrosos, was on the
                                              right,
Aglauros had the left hand one and Herse the one in the middle.
It was she who held the room on the left who first realized that Mercury
was coming and dared to question him about his name   741
and the reason for his arrival there; and he replied to her like this, 'I am
Atlas' and Pleione's grandson, the one who carries my father's words,
as bidden, through the air; my father is Jupiter himself.
And I shall not lie about my reasons; may you just be willing to be   745
loyal to your sister and to be spoken of as my offspring's aunt.
Herse is the reason for my journey; I pray that you may look favourably
                                              on a lover.'
Aglauros looked at him with the same eyes with which
she had recently seen the secrets of fair-haired Minerva,
and demanded, for her services, a great weight   750
of gold; meanwhile, she compelled him to withdraw from the house.
The warrior-goddess turned to her with a grim look in her eye
and drew from deep within sighs with such emotion
that her breast and the aegis lying on her strong breast   754
were shaken up together. It came to her that this one had uncovered her
                                              secrets
with a sacrilegious hand then, when she had broken the undertaking she
                                              had given
and seen the Lemnos-dweller's offspring born without a mother,
and that she would be cherished by a god now and cherished by her sister
and rich, once she had procured the gold which she had greedily demanded.
        Immediately, she sought the house of Envy, which is smothered   760
in black slime: her home hidden in the depths
of a sunless valley where no wind can penetrate,
a sad place, filled with numbing cold and which
always lacks fire and always abounds in darkness.
When the fearsome manly-maid of war arrived here,   765

constitit ante domum (neque enim succedere tectis
fas habet) et postes extrema cuspide pulsat.
concussae patuere fores; uidet intus edentem
uipereas carnes, uitiorum alimenta suorum,
770 Inuidiam, uisaque oculos auertit; at illa
surgit humo pigra semesarumque relinquit
corpora serpentum passuque incedit inerti;
utque deam uidit formaque armisque decoram,
ingemuit uultumque ima ad suspiria duxit.
775 pallor in ore sedet, macies in corpore toto,
nusquam recta acies, liuent rubigine dentes,
pectora felle uirent, lingua est suffusa ueneno.
risus abest, nisi quem uisi mouere dolores,
nec fruitur somno, uigilacibus excita curis,
780 sed uidet ingratos intabescitque uidendo
successus hominum carpitque et carpitur una
suppliciumque suum est. quamuis tamen oderat illam,
talibus adfata est breuiter Tritonia dictis:
'infice tabe tua natarum Cecropis unam,
785 sic opus est; Aglauros ea est.' haud plura locuta
fugit et impressa tellurem reppulit hasta.
    illa deam obliquo fugientem lumine cernens
murmura parua dedit successurumque Mineruae
indoluit baculumque capit, quod spinea totum
790 uincula cingebant, adopertaque nubibus atris,
quacumque ingreditur, florentia proterit arua
exuritque herbas et summa cacumina carpit
adflatuque suo populos urbesque domosque
polluit, et tandem Tritonida conspicit arcem
795 ingeniis opibusque et festa pace uirentem,
uixque tenet lacrimas, quia nil lacrimabile cernit.
sed postquam thalamos intrauit Cecrope natae,
iussa facit pectusque manu ferrugine tincta
tangit et hamatis praecordia sentibus implet
800 inspiratque nocens uirus piceumque per ossa
dissipat et medio spargit pulmone uenenum;
neue mali causae spatium per latius errent,
germanam ante oculos fortunatumque sororis
coniugium pulchraque deum sub imagine ponit
805 cunctaque magna facit; quibus irritata dolore
Cecropis occulto mordetur et anxia nocte,
anxia luce gemit lentaque miserrima tabe
liquitur, ut glacies incerto saucia sole,
felicisque bonis non lenius uritur Herses

she stopped before the house (for she did not think it right
to step into the building) and struck the doorposts with the very tip of her
                                                            spear.
The doors, once struck, stood open: she saw within eating
the flesh of vipers, nourishment for her vileness,
Envy, and on seeing her turned her eyes away; but she   770
rose up from the barren ground, leaving the bodies
of half-eaten snakes and advanced with sluggish tread;
and, when she saw the goddess resplendent in beauty and in arms,
she groaned and screwed up her expression in a deep sigh.
Her face has a settled pallor, she is gaunt in all her body,   775
her gaze is never straight, her teeth are foul with decay,
her breasts are green with bile and her tongue is drenched in poison.
She has no smile, except one brought by the sight of others' sorrows,
and she never enjoys sleep, roused as she is by wakeful cares,
but she looks at men's unwelcome success   780
and wastes away as she looks; gnawing and gnawed together,
she is her own punishment. But, however much she hated her,
Tritonia still spoke briefly to her with words like this:
'Infect one of Cecrops' daughters with your corruption,
that is your task; Aglauros is the one.' She spoke no more   785
but left, pressing down upon her spear to push up from the earth.
     She watched askance as the goddess left
and, giving a low murmur, was pained that Minerva
would succeed, but she took her staff, the one all set about
with thorny chains, and, veiled by dark clouds   790
wherever she stepped, trampled down the flowering fields,
burnt up the grass and tore at the highest tree tops,
and polluted peoples, cities and homes
with her breath, and at last beheld Tritonis' citadel
flourishing with its talents, wealth and festive peace,   795
and she scarcely kept from crying, for she could see nothing to cry about.
But after she had entered the bedroom of Cecrops' daughter,
she did as she had been told and touched the girl's breast with a hand
                                                         steeped
in rottenness and filled her bosom with prickly brambles
and breathed a noxious, pitchy venom through her bones,   800
scattering and spreading poison deep into her lungs;
and in case the reasons for this evil should be lost in too broad a range,
she placed her sister before her eyes, her sister's
lucky marriage, and the god in his handsome appearance,
and magnified them all; these things stung Cecropis,   805
she was gnawed by hidden grief and, troubled by night
and troubled by day, she groaned and began to fade away most miserably
with a slow wasting, like ice stricken by uncertain sunshine,
and she was no less consumed by Herse's good luck

810 　　　quam cum spinosis ignis supponitur herbis,
　　　　　quae neque dant flammas lenique tepore cremantur.
　　　　　saepe mori uoluit, ne quidquam tale uideret,
　　　　　saepe, uelut crimen, rigido narrare parenti;
　　　　　denique in aduerso uenientem limine sedit
815 　　　exclusura deum; cui blandimenta precesque
　　　　　uerbaque iactanti mitissima, 'desine,' dixit,
　　　　　'hinc ego me non sum nisi te motura repulso.'
　　　　　'stemus,' ait, 'pacto,' uelox Cyllenius, 'isto,'
　　　　　caelestique fores uirga patefecit; at illi
820 　　　surgere conanti partes, quascumque sedendo
　　　　　flectitur, ignaua nequeunt grauitate moueri.
　　　　　illa quidem pugnat recto se attollere trunco,
　　　　　sed genuum iunctura riget, frigusque per ungues
　　　　　labitur, et pallent amisso sanguine uenae.
825 　　　utque malum late solet immedicabile cancer
　　　　　serpere et inlaesas uitiatis addere partes,
　　　　　sic letalis hiemps paulatim in pectora uenit
　　　　　uitalesque uias et respiramina clausit,
　　　　　nec conata loqui est nec, si conata fuisset,
830 　　　uocis habebat iter; saxum iam colla tenebat,
　　　　　oraque duruerant, signumque exsangue sedebat;
　　　　　nec lapis albus erat, sua mens infecerat illum.
　　　　　　　　has ubi uerborum poenas mentisque profanae
　　　　　cepit Atlantiades, dictas a Pallade terras
835 　　　linquit et ingreditur iactatis aethera pennis.
　　　　　seuocat hunc genitor nec causam fassus amoris.
　　　　　'fide minister,' ait, 'iussorum, nate, meorum,
　　　　　pelle moram solitoque celer delabere cursu,
　　　　　quaeque tuam matrem tellus a parte sinistra
840 　　　suspicit (indigenae Sidonida nomine dicunt),
　　　　　hanc pete, quodque procul montano gramine pasci
　　　　　armentum regale uides, ad litora uerte.'
　　　　　dixit, et expulsi iamdudum monte iuuenci
　　　　　litora iussa petunt, ubi magni filia regis
845 　　　ludere uirginibus Tyriis comitata solebat.
　　　　　non bene conueniunt nec in una sede morantur
　　　　　maiestas et amor; sceptri grauitate relicta,
　　　　　ille pater rectorque deum, cui dextra trisulcis
　　　　　ignibus armata est, qui nutu concutit orbem,
850 　　　induitur faciem tauri mixtusque iuuencis
　　　　　mugit et in teneris formosus obambulat herbis.
　　　　　quippe color niuis est, quam nec uestigia duri

than when fire is applied to prickly grasses   810
and they do not burst out in flames but burn in a slow heat.
Often she wished to die, and so see nothing of this sort,
often to tell their stern father, as if it were a crime;
at last, she sat at the doorway opposite, to bar
the god from coming; and when he plied her with coaxings,   815
prayers and the gentlest of words, 'Stop,' she said,
'I am not going to move myself from here unless you have been driven off.'
'Let us abide,' the swift Cyllenian said, 'by that agreement,'
and opened the doors with his heavenly staff; but when she
tried to rise a numbing heaviness prevented her   820
from moving any of the parts she bends in sitting down.
Of course she fought to lift herself erect,
but her knee joints were stiff and a chill flowed through her
to her finger-nails, and her veins were pallid from losing blood.
And as an evil, incurable cancer tends to creep   825
extensively, adding undamaged parts to diseased ones,
so a lethal cold came little by little to her breast
and closed off the vital passages and respiration
and she did not try to speak, nor, if she had tried,
did she have a pathway for her voice; stone was already possessing her
                                                                        throat
and her mouth had hardened and she sat there, a bloodless statue;   831
but the stone was not white, her mind had infected it.
      When Atlas' grandson had punished her thus for her words
and sacrilegious mind, he left the lands called after
Pallas and beating his wings proceeded to the ether.   835
His father called him aside, but did not admit that love was his reason.
'My son,' he said, 'faithful servant of my biddings,
do not delay, but glide down quickly at your usual pace;
you know the land that looks up towards your mother from the left-hand
side (its inhabitants give it the name Sidon),   840
make for that, and when you see the royal herd grazing
far off on the mountain pasture, turn it towards the shore.'
He had spoken, and the bullocks were already being driven from the
                                                                        mountain
and were making for the shore that he had ordered where the great king's
                                                                        daughter
usually played with the Tyrian maidens for company.   845
Majesty and love do not go well together and will not stay
in a single place; he left his solemn sceptre behind,
did the father and ruler of the gods, he whose right arm is equipped
with three-pronged fires and who shakes the world with his nod,
and he put on the appearance of a bull and, mingling with the bullocks,
he bellowed and ambled through the soft grass, a handsome sight.   851
He had the colour of snow that has not been trampled by the tracks

calcauere pedis nec soluit aquaticus Auster.
colla toris exstant, armis palearia pendent,
855 cornua parua quidem, sed quae contendere possis
facta manu, puraque magis perlucida gemma.
nullae in fronte minae, nec formidabile lumen,
pacem uultus habet. miratur Agenore nata,
quod tam formosus, quod proelia nulla minetur.
860 sed quamuis mitem metuit contingere primo.
mox adit et flores ad candida porrigit ora.
gaudet amans et, dum ueniat sperata uoluptas,
oscula dat manibus; uix iam, uix cetera differt.
et nunc adludit uiridique exsultat in herba,
865 nunc latus in fuluis niueum deponit harenis,
paulatimque metu dempto modo pectora praebet
uirginea plaudenda manu, modo cornua sertis
impedienda nouis, ausa est quoque regia uirgo,
nescia quem premeret, tergo considere tauri,
870 cum deus a terra siccoque a litore sensim
falsa pedum primis uestigia ponit in undis;
inde abit ulterius mediique per aequora ponti
fert praedam. pauet haec litusque ablata relictum
respicit et dextra cornum tenet, altera dorso
875 imposita est; tremulae sinuantur flamine uestes.

of rough feet nor melted by the watery Auster.
Muscles stood out upon his neck, a dewlap hung from the point of his
shoulder,
his horns were small, but you would insist that they   855
were made by hand, and they gleamed more than a flawless gem.
There was no menace in his forehead, his look was not ferocious,
he had a peaceful face. Agenor's daughter wondered at him
because he was so handsome, because he was not menacing or aggressive.
But, however gentle he might be, at first she was afraid to touch him. 860
Soon she approached him and proffered flowers to his white mouth.
The lover rejoiced and, until the delights he hoped for came along,
gave kisses to her hands; scarcely now, scarcely could he put off the rest
as he now frolicked by her and pranced upon the green grass,
and now lay his snowy flank upon the yellow sand   865
as, little by little, he took her fear away and offered first his chest
to be petted by her maiden's hand and then his horns to be entwined
with fresh garlands. The royal maiden even dared
to sit upon the bull's back, not knowing who she was resting on,
while the god gradually put his false footsteps away from the land   870
and from the dry shore and in the nearest waves,
and then went further out, carrying his prize into the middle
of the sea's expanse. She was afraid and, as she was carried off, looked
back to the shore
she had left behind, holding his horn in her right hand, and putting her
other hand
upon his back; her dress billowed and fluttered in the breeze.   875

LIBER III

Iamque deus, posita fallacis imagine tauri,
se confessus erat Dictaeaque rura tenebat,
cum pater ignarus Cadmo perquirere raptam
imperat et poenam, si non inuenerit, addit
5   exilium, facto pius et sceleratus eodem.
orbe pererrato (quis enim deprendere possit
furta Iouis?) profugus patriamque iramque parentis
uitat Agenorides Phoebique oracula supplex
consulit et quae sit tellus habitanda requirit.
10 'bos tibi,' Phoebus ait, 'solis occurret in aruis,
nullum passa iugum curuique immunis aratri.
hac duce carpe uias et, qua requieuerit herba,
moenia fac condas Boeotiaque illa uocato.'
uix bene Castalio Cadmus descenderat antro,
15 incustoditam lente uidet ire iuuencam
nullum seruitii signum ceruice gerentem.
subsequitur pressoque legit uestigia gressu
auctoremque uiae Phoebum taciturnus adorat.
iam uada Cephisi Panopesque euaserat arua:
20 bos stetit et tollens speciosam cornibus altis
ad caelum frontem mugitibus impulit auras
atque ita respiciens comites sua terga sequentes
procubuit teneraque latus submisit in herba.
Cadmus agit grates peregrinaeque oscula terrae
25 figit et ignotos montes agrosque salutat.
sacra Ioui facturus erat: iubet ire ministros
et petere e uiuis libandas fontibus undas.
     silua uetus stabat nulla uiolata securi
et specus in medio, uirgis ac uimine densus,
30 efficiens humilem lapidum compagibus arcum,
uberibus fecundus aquis, ubi conditus antro
Martius anguis erat, cristis praesignis et auro;
igne micant oculi, corpus tumet omne uenenis,
tres uibrant linguae, triplici stant ordine dentes.
35 quem postquam Tyria lucum de gente profecti
infausto tetigere gradu demissaque in undas
urna dedit sonitum, longo caput extulit antro
caeruleus serpens horrendaque sibila misit.
effluxere urnae manibus sanguisque reliquit

BOOK III

The god had already laid aside the deceitful guise of a bull,
and admitted who he was and arrived at the Dictaean countryside,
while her father, in his ignorance, was ordering Cadmus to seek out
his ravished daughter, adding that he would punish him with exile if he did
          not
find her, being by that same token dutiful and wicked.   5
Agenor's son wandered throughout the world, a fugitive (for who
could discover Jove's thefts?), and avoided both his native land
and his father's anger, and, as a suppliant, consulted Phoebus'
oracle to find out what land he ought to dwell in.
'You will be met,' Phoebus said, 'in the lonely fields by a cow   10
which has never endured the yoke and has been exempt from the curved
           plough.
Pick your way, with her to lead, and where she rests upon the grass
see that you establish city walls, and call them Boeotian.'
Cadmus had scarcely made good his descent from the Castalian cave,
when he saw, coming slowly, an untended heifer   15
that bore no mark of servitude upon her neck.
He followed after with a deliberate tread, keeping to her tracks
and silently worshipping Phoebus, his journey's guide.
By now he had already passed Cephisos' shallows and the fields of Panope:
the cow stopped and lifted her lovely forehead with its tall   20
horns towards the sky and, disturbing the air with her lowing
as she looked back to her companions following on behind,
she sank down, lowering her side onto the soft grass.
Cadmus gave thanks and planted kisses on this alien
land and greeted the unfamiliar fields and mountains.   25
He was about to sacrifice to Jupiter: he ordered his attendants to go
and get water for libations from a running spring.
  An ancient wood stood there, defiled by no axe,
and in its midst a grotto, thick with twigs and branches,
making a low arch with close-fitting stones,   30
a prolific source of water. Concealed there in the cave
was the snake of Mars, distinguished by its golden crest;
its eyes gleamed with fire, all its body swelled with venom,
its three tongues flickered and its teeth stood in triple ranks.
When the descendants of the Tyrian race had reached   35
the grove with their unpropitious step, and the pitcher they let down
into the water had made a sound, the blue-green serpent raised its head
from the long cave and gave out a horrible hissing.
The pitchers slipped from their hands, the blood left

40 corpus et attonitos subitus tremor occupat artus.
ille uolubilibus squamosos nexibus orbes
torquet et immensos saltu sinuatur in arcus,
ac media plus parte leues erectus in auras
despicit omne nemus tantoque est corpore, quanto,
45 si totum spectes, geminas qui separat Arctos.
nec mora, Phoenicas, siue illi tela parabant
siue fugam, siue ipse timor prohibebat utrumque,
occupat: hos morsu, longis complexibus illos,
hos necat adflatu funesti tabe ueneni.
50 fecerat exiguas iam sol altissimus umbras:
quae mora sit sociis miratur Agenore natus
uestigatque uiros. tegimen derepta leoni
pellis erat, telum splendenti lancea ferro
et iaculum, teloque animus praestantior omni.
55 ut nemus intrauit letataque corpora uidit
uictoremque supra spatiosi corporis hostem
tristia sanguinea lambentem uulnera lingua,
'aut ultor uestrae, fidissima corpora, mortis,
aut comes,' inquit, 'ero.' dixit, dextraque molarem
60 sustulit et magnum magno conamine misit.
illius impulsu cum turribus ardua celsis
moenia mota forent: serpens sine uulnere mansit,
loricaeque modo squamis defensus et atrae
duritia pellis ualidos cute reppulit ictus.
65 at non duritia iaculum quoque uicit eadem,
quod medio lentae spinae curuamine fixum
constitit et totum descendit in ilia ferrum.
ille dolore ferox caput in sua terga retorsit
uulneraque aspexit fixumque hastile momordit,
70 idque, ubi ui multa partem labefecit in omnem,
uix tergo eripuit; ferrum tamen ossibus haesit.
tum uero, postquam solitas accessit ad iras
causa recens, plenis tumuerunt guttura uenis,
spumaque pestiferos circumfluit albida rictus,
75 terraque rasa sonat squamis, quique halitus exit
ore niger Stygio uitiatas inficit auras.
ipse modo immensum spiris facientibus orbem
cingitur, interdum longa trabe rectior astat,
impete nunc uasto ceu concitus imbribus amnis
80 fertur et obstantes proturbat pectore siluas.
cedit Agenorides paulum spolioque leonis
sustinet incursus instantiaque ora retardat
cuspide praetenta; furit ille et inania duro

their bodies and a sudden shaking seized their stunned limbs.   40
The snake twisted its scaly coils in writhing
knots and, with a spring, bent itself into immeasurable loops,
then raised up more than half its length into the air
and looked down on the whole copse with a body as large as,
were you to see it all, is the one that separates the twin Bears.   45
Without delay, the Phoenicians, whether they were preparing arms
or flight, or whether fear itself was keeping them from either,
were brought up short: some were killed by its bite, others by a drawn out
crushing, others by the corrupting exhalation of its deadly venom.
    The sun, now at its highest, had made the shadows very small: 50
Agenor's son was wondering what the delay was with his companions
and he went to track them down. His shield was a skin
stripped from a lion, his weaponry a lance with a tip of shining iron,
a javelin, and a spirit too surpassing any weaponry.
As he entered the copse and saw the slain bodies   55
and, on top, their victorious enemy with its vast body
licking their bitter wounds with its bloody tongue,
'Either I shall be an avenger of your death, most faithful
bodies,' he said, 'or a companion.' As he spoke, he picked up in his right
          hand
a massive stone and sent the great thing off with great exertion.   60
The blow would have moved high city walls
with lofty towers: the serpent remained uninjured,
and was protected by its scales as if by a breastplate, for the hardness
of its hide repulsed the mighty blows from its skin.
But with that hardness it could not defeat the javelin too,   65
which lodged in the middle of its stiffly curving spine
and stayed there, while the whole iron tip sank down into its guts.
The snake, maddened with pain, twisted its head round onto its back,
inspected its injuries and bit into the spear lodged there
and, even when with much force it had loosened it on every side,   70
it could hardly wrench it from its back; even so, the iron tip stuck in its
          bones.
Then indeed, when this fresh grievance had been added to its
usual anger, its throat swelled up with full veins,
and a whitish foam flowed round its noxious jaws;
its scales scraped noisily on the earth, and black breath   75
came from its Stygian mouth to infect the corrupted air.
The snake would at one point curl up with its coils making a vast
circle, then it would stand up straighter than a length of planking,
or be carried forward in a mighty rush, like a stream swollen
by rainstorms, and with its breast push aside the woods standing in its way.
Agenor's son withdrew a little and absorbed the onrush   81
with his lion skin, and slowed the jaw's assaults
by thrusting out his spear; it raged and inflicted vain

uulnera dat ferro figitque in acumine dentes.
85 iamque uenenifero sanguis manare palato
coeperat et uirides aspergine tinxerat herbas;
sed leue uulnus erat, quia se retrahebat ab ictu
laesaque colla dabat retro plagamque sedere
cedendo arcebat nec longius ire sinebat,
90 donec Agenorides coniectum in guttura ferrum
usque sequens pressit, dum retro quercus eunti
obstitit et fixa est pariter cum robore ceruix.
pondere serpentis curuata est arbor et ima
parte flagellari gemuit sua robora caudae.
95 dum spatium uictor uicti considerat hostis,
uox subito audita est (neque erat cognoscere promptum
unde, sed audita est): 'quid, Agenore nate, peremptum
serpentem spectas? et tu spectabere serpens.'
ille diu pauidus pariter cum mente colorem
100 perdiderat, gelidoque comae terrore rigebant;
ecce uiri fautrix superas delapsa per auras
Pallas adest motaeque iubet supponere terrae
uipereos dentes, populi incrementa futuri.
paret et, ut presso sulcum patefecit aratro,
105 spargit humi iussos, mortalia semina, dentes.
inde (fide maius) glaebae coepere moueri,
primaque de sulcis acies apparuit hastae,
tegmina mox capitum picto nutantia cono,
mox umeri pectusque onerataque bracchia telis
110 exsistunt, crescitque seges clipeata uirorum.
sic, ubi tolluntur festis aulaea theatris,
surgere signa solent primumque ostendere uultus,
cetera paulatim, placidoque educta tenore
tota patent imoque pedes in margine ponunt.
115 territus hoste nouo Cadmus capere arma parabat;
'ne cape,' de populo quem terra creauerat unus
exclamat, 'nec te ciuilibus insere bellis.'
atque ita terrigenis rigido de fratribus unum
comminus ense ferit; iaculo cadit eminus ipse.
120 hunc quoque qui leto dederat non longius illo
uiuit et exspirat modo quas acceperat auras;
exemploque pari furit omnis turba, suoque
Marte cadunt subiti per mutua uulnera fratres.
iamque breuis uitae spatium sortita iuuentus
125 sanguineam tepido plangebant pectore matrem
quinque superstitibus, quorum fuit unus Echion.

injuries on the hard iron by pressing its teeth against the point.
By now the blood had begun to flow from its venom-bearing   . 85
palate and had bespattered and stained the green grass;
but its injury was slight, for it was retreating from the blow
and bringing its hurt neck back and, by withdrawing, keeping
the stroke from going home and letting it go no further,
till Agenor's son, following through, pressed in the iron tip   90
that he had hurled against its throat, until an oak blocked its
retreat and its neck and the trunk were pierced together.
The weight of the serpent bent the tree which groaned out,
for its trunk was being scourged by the last part of the tail.
While the victor was gazing at the size of his vanquished enemy,   · 95
a voice was suddenly heard (it was not easy to know
from where, but it was heard): 'Why, son of Agenor, are you looking at
the serpent you destroyed? You too will be a serpent to be looked at.'
     For a long time he was fearful and lost his colour together with
his presence of mind, and his hair began to stand up straight with chilling
                                                             fright;
but look, his patroness had glided down through the upper air,   101
Pallas was there telling him to turn the earth over and plant
the viper's teeth, from which his people was to grow.
He obeyed and, as he drove his plough and exposed a furrow,
he scattered the teeth, the seeds of mortals, as bidden, on the ground. 105
And then (it is beyond belief) the ploughed field began to be disturbed;
first to appear from the furrows was a spear tip,
soon there were head-pieces with dyed plumes nodding,
there soon emerged shoulders and a breast and arms loaded
with weapons, and a crop of shield-bearing men began to grow.   110
Even so, when the curtains are brought up in a theatre on a feast day,
figures rise, showing their faces first,
and gradually the rest of them, and they are drawn up in a smooth glide
till fully displayed with their feet set on the bottom edge.
Cadmus was terrified by this new enemy and was preparing to take up his
                                                             arms;
'Don't take them up,' cried out one of the people created   116
by the earth, 'and do not plant yourself in our civil war.'
And with that, he struck one of his earth-born brothers
with his firm sword at close range; and fell himself to a javelin from long
                                                             range.
And that one too who had sent him to his death did not live longer   120
than him, but expired on the breath he had just taken in;
and the whole throng raged in the same fashion, as the sudden
brothers fell in their own war from mutual injuries.
And now these young men, whose lot had been so brief a span of life,
were striking their blood-stained mother on her warm breast,   125
and there were five surviving, of whom one was Echion.

is sua iecit humo monitu Tritonidis arma
fraternaeque fidem pacis petiitque deditque.
hos operis comites habuit Sidonius hospes,
130　cum posuit iussus Phoebeis sortibus urbem.
　　　iam stabant Thebae; poteras iam, Cadme, uideri
exilio felix: soceri tibi Marsque Venusque
contigerant; huc adde genus de coniuge tanta,
tot natas natosque et, pignora cara, nepotes,
135　hos quoque iam iuuenes. sed scilicet ultima semper
exspectanda dies hominis, dicique beatus
ante obitum nemo supremaque funera debet.
prima nepos inter tot res tibi, Cadme, secundas
causa fuit luctus, alienaque cornua fronti
140　addita, uosque, canes, satiatae sanguine erili.
at bene si quaeras, fortunae crimen in illo,
non scelus inuenies; quod enim scelus error habebat?
　　　mons erat infectus uariarum caede ferarum,
iamque dies medius rerum contraxerat umbras
145　et sol ex aequo meta distabat utraque,
cum iuuenis placido per deuia lustra uagantes
participes operum compellat Hyantius ore:
'lina madent, comites, ferrumque cruore ferarum,
fortunamque dies habuit satis. altera lucem
150　cum croceis inuecta rotis Aurora reducet,
propositum repetemus opus; nunc Phoebus utraque
distat idem meta finditque uaporibus arua;
sistite opus praesens nodosaque tollite lina.'
iussa uiri faciunt intermittuntque laborem.
155　　　uallis erat piceis et acuta densa cupressu,
nomine Gargaphie, succinctae sacra Dianae,
cuius in extremo est antrum nemorale recessu
arte laboratum nulla; simulauerat artem
ingenio natura suo, nam pumice uiuo
160　et leuibus tofis natiuum duxerat arcum.
fons sonat a dextra tenui perlucidus unda,
margine gramineo patulos incinctus hiatus.
hic dea siluarum uenatu fessa solebat
uirgineos artus liquido perfundere rore.
165　quo postquam subiit, nympharum tradidit uni
armigerae iaculum pharetramque arcusque retentos;
altera depositae subiecit bracchia pallae;
uincla duae pedibus demunt; nam doctior illis
Ismenis Crocale sparsos per colla capillos

He, at Tritonis' behest, threw down his weapons to the ground
and both sought and gave a pledge of peace with his brothers.
The Sidonian exile took them as companions in his task
of establishing a city, as ordered by the oracle of Phoebus.   130
     Thebes was now standing; Cadmus, you could now be seen
as lucky in your exile: you had Mars and Venus
for your in-laws; to this, add a family from your noble wife,
so many sons and daughters, and grandchildren, dear tokens of affection,
these too young men by now. But of course we should always   135
wait for a man's last day, and no one should
be called happy before his death and his last rites.
Your first cause, Cadmus, for grief, among so many favourable things,
was your grandson and the strange horns added
to his forehead and you, his dogs, glutted with your master's blood.   140
But if you look into it well, you will find him guilty
of bad luck, not of a crime; for what crime was there in a mistake?
     There was a mountain stained with the slaughter of many kinds of
                 beast,
and already it was midday, so that the shadows of things had drawn in,
and the sun was equidistant from both its turning-points,   145
when the Hyantian young man called out in a friendly tone
to his companions of the chase while they were roaming through remote
                 haunts:
'The nets and swords are drenched, my comrades, with the blood of wild
                 beasts;
the day has given us enough good luck. When tomorrow's Dawn,
riding on saffron wheels, brings the light back   150
we shall take up our chosen task again; now Phoebus is the same
distance from both turning-points and is cracking the earth with his heat;
stop the chase for now and pick up the knotted lines.'
The men did as they were told and broke off their toil.
     There was a valley thick with spruce and tapering cypress trees, 155
called Gargaphie and sacred to girt-up Diana,
and there was, in its furthest recess, a woodland cave
constructed by no art but by nature, in her genius,
imitating art; for she had shaped a natural
arch out of light tufa and the native pumice stone.   160
To the right, there was the sound of a limpid spring and a narrow stream
with its spreading pool surrounded by a grassy bank.
Here, the goddess of the woods, when exhausted from the hunt, used to
bathe her virgin limbs in the clear and dew-fresh water.
And when she entered the cave, she passed to one of her nymphs,   165
to her armour-bearer, her javelin, her quiver and her unstrung bows;
another nymph slipped an arm under her cloak as she took it off,
while two of them removed the thongs from her feet; for Ismenian Crocale,
more skilled than them, tied up her hair, which was streaming

170   colligit in nodum, quamuis erat ipsa solutis.
       excipiunt laticem Nepheleque Hyaleque Rhanisque
       et Psecas et Phiale funduntque capacibus urnis.
       dumque ibi perluitur solita Titania lympha,
       ecce nepos Cadmi dilata parte laborum
175   per nemus ignotum non certis passibus errans
       peruenit in lucum: sic illum fata ferebant.
       qui simul intrauit rorantia fontibus antra,
       sicut erant nudae uiso sua pectora nymphae
       percussere uiro subitisque ululatibus omne
180   impleuere nemus circumfusaeque Dianam
       corporibus texere suis; tamen altior illis
       ipsa dea est colloque tenus supereminet omnes.
       qui color infectis aduersi solis ab ictu
       nubibus esse solet aut purpureae aurorae,
185   is fuit in uultu uisae sine ueste Dianae.
       quae, quamquam comitum turba est stipata suarum,
       in latus obliquum tamen astitit oraque retro
       flexit et, ut uellet promptas habuisse sagittas,
       quas habuit sic hausit aquas uultumque uirilem
190   perfudit spargensque comas ultricibus undis
       addidit haec cladis praenuntia uerba futurae:
       'nunc tibi me posito uisam uelamine narres,
       si poteris narrare, licet.' nec plura minata
       dat sparso capiti uiuacis cornua cerui,
195   dat spatium collo summasque cacuminat aures,
       cum pedibusque manus, cum longis bracchia mutat
       cruribus et uelat maculoso uellere corpus;
       additus et pauor est. fugit Autonoeius heros
       et se tam celerem cursu miratur in ipso.
200   ut uero uultus et cornua uidit in unda,
       'me miserum!' dicturus erat: uox nulla secuta est.
       ingemuit: uox illa fuit, lacrimaeque per ora
       non sua fluxerunt; mens tantum pristina mansit.
       quid faciat? repetatne domum et regalia tecta,
205   an lateat siluis? pudor hoc, timor impedit illud.
       dum dubitat, uidere canes primique Melampus
       Ichnobatesque sagax latratu signa dedere,
       Cnosius Ichnobates, Spartana gente Melampus.
       inde ruunt alii rapida uelocius aura,
210   Pamphagos et Dorceus et Oribasos, Arcades omnes,
       Nebrophonosque ualens et trux cum Laelape Theron
       et pedibus Pterelas et naribus utilis Agre
       Hylaeusque fero nuper percussus ab apro
       deque lupo concepta Nape pecudesque secuta

over her neck, into a knot, although her own was loose.   170
Water was collected by Nephele and Hyale and Rhanis,
by Psecas and by Phiale, and poured out from capacious urns.
And while Titania was washing there in the water, as was her custom,
look, Cadmus' grandson, who had put off his part of the toil,
wandered through an unfamiliar copse with aimless steps   175
and arrived at the grove: that is how the fates were driving him.
As soon as he had entered the spring-drenched cave,
the naked nymphs, just as they were, beat their breasts,
for they had seen a man, and filled the whole copse
with a sudden screaming and, pouring round Diana,   180
they covered her with their bodies; but the goddess
was taller than them, standing head and shoulders above them all.
There is a colour seen in clouds tinged
from the impact of the facing sun or of the rosy dawn;
that was the colour on Diana's face when she was seen without her dress,
and although she had a throng of her companions clustered round her,   186
yet she stood sideways and bent her head
back and, though she could wish she had her arrows to hand,
still she drew what was to hand, the water, and soaked the man's
face and showered his hair with avenging streams,   190
adding these words, prophetic of the disaster that was to be:
'Now you may tell that you have seen me with my clothes
removed, if you can tell.' She threatened him no more,
but gave to the head that she had showered the horns of a long-lived stag,
she gave length to his neck and sharpened the tops of his ears,   195
she changed his hands to feet and his arms to long
legs, and covered his body with a dappled hide;
she added fear too. Autonoe's hero fled
and, even as he ran, he marvelled that he was so fast.
But when he saw his face and horns in water,   200
'Unhappy me,' he would have said: but no speech came.
He gave a groan: that was his speech, and his tears flowed down
cheeks that were not his own; only his mind remained in its original state.
What should he do? Should he make for home, for the royal palace,
or should he hide in the woods? Fear stopped one course and shame the
                                                                    other.
While he was hesitating, he was seen by his dogs; Melampus and keen   206
Ichnobates were the first to give the signal with their bark,
Ichnobates was a Cnossian and Melampus of Spartan breed.
Then others rushed up, swifter than a raging wind,
Pamphagos, Dorceus and Oribasus, all Arcadians,   210
strong Nebrophonos, Laelaps and savage Theron,
swift-footed Pterelas and keen-scented Agre,
and Hylaeus, recently mauled by a wild boar,
and Nape, born from a she-wolf, and Poemenis who tended

215   Poemenis et natis comitata Harpyia duobus
      et substricta gerens Sicyonius ilia Ladon
      et Dromas et Canache Sticteque et Tigris et Alce
      et niueis Leucon et uillis Asbolos atris
      praeualidusque Lacon et cursu fortis Aello
220   et Thoos et Cyprio uelox cum fratre Lycisce
      et nigram medio frontem distinctus ab albo
      Harpalos et Melaneus hirsutaque corpore Lachne
      et patre Dictaeo sed matre Laconide nati
      Labros et Agriodus et acutae uocis Hylactor
225   quosque referre mora est; ea turba cupidine praedae
      per rupes scopulosque aдituque carentia saxa,
      quaque est difficilis quaque est uia nulla, sequuntur.
      ille fugit per quae fuerat loca saepe secutus,
      heu, famulos fugit ipse suos. clamare libebat,
230   'Actaeon ego sum, dominum cognoscite uestrum.'
      uerba animo desunt; resonat latratibus aether.
      prima Melanchaetes in tergo uulnera fecit,
      proxima Therodamas, Oresitrophos haesit in armo
      (tardius exierant, sed per compendia montis
235   anticipata uia est); dominum retinentibus illis
      cetera turba coit confertque in corpore dentes.
      iam loca uulneribus desunt, gemit ille sonumque,
      etsi non hominis, quem non tamen edere possit
      ceruus, habet maestisque replet iuga nota querelis
240   et genibus pronis supplex similisque roganti
      circumfert tacitos tamquam sua bracchia uultus.
      at comites rapidum solitis hortatibus agmen
      ignari instigant oculisque Actaeona quaerunt
      et uelut absentem certatim Actaeona clamant
245   (ad nomen caput ille refert) et abesse queruntur
      nec capere oblatae segnem spectacula praedae.
      uellet abesse quidem, sed adest, uelletque uidere,
      non etiam sentire canum fera facta suorum.
      undique circumstant mersisque in corpore rostris
250   dilacerant falsi dominum sub imagine cerui,
      nec nisi finita per plurima uulnera uita
      ira pharetratae fertur satiata Dianae.
            rumor in ambiguo est: aliis uiolentior aequo
      uisa dea est, alii laudant dignamque seuera
255   uirginitate uocant; pars inuenit utraque causas.
      sola Iouis coniunx non tam culpetne probetne
      eloquitur quam clade domus ab Agenore ductae
      gaudet et a Tyria conlectum paelice transfert

the flocks, and Harpyia, accompanied by two puppies,   215
and Sicyonian Ladon with the hollow flanks,
and Dromas, Canache, Sticte, Tigris and Alce,
and white-haired Leucon and black Asbolos,
and Lacon, who was outstandingly strong, and Aello the strong runner,
and Thoos and swift Lycisce with Cyprius, her brother,   220
and Harpalos, distinguished by a white patch in the middle of his black
forehead, and Melaneus and shaggy Lachne,
Labros and Agriodus, born to a Dictaean father
but a Laconian mother, and Hylactor with his shrill bark,
and others it would take too long to tell; that pack, in its lust for prey,
chased through crags and boulders and inaccessible rocks,   226
where it was difficult and where there was no way.
He was fleeing through the places where he had often chased,
alas, the master was fleeing from his servants. He wanted to cry out,
'I am Actaeon, recognize your lord.'   230
Words failed his spirit, the ether resounded with barking.
The first wounds on his back were made by Melanchetes,
the next by Therodamas, Oresitrophos clung to his shoulder
(they had set off later, but by a short cut through the mountain
had got in front); and while they were holding their lord down,   235
the rest of the pack collected and sank their teeth in his body.
There was now no room to wound him, he groaned and the sound,
even if it was not human was still not the sort a stag
could produce, and he filled the familiar ridges with mournful complaints,
and, supplicating down upon his knees, like a man at prayer,   240
he cast his silent face around as if it were his arms.
But his companions, in their ignorance, urged on the savage pack
with their usual encouragements, and looked around to find Actaeon,
and outdid one another in shouting for Actaeon as if he were not there 244
(he turned his head round at his name), and they complained he was not
                                                               there
and that he was too slow to catch sight of the prey they had met up with.
He would have wished, indeed, not to be there, but he was there, and
                                       would have wished to see,
and not to feel as well the cruel deeds of his dogs.
They surrounded him on every side, their muzzles buried in his body,
and they tore their master apart in his false guise as a stag,   250
and it is said that not until his life was ended by so very many
wounds was the anger of Diana of the quiver satisfied.
      Opinion was divided: to some the goddess seemed
more savage than was fair, others praised her and called her worthy
of her strict virginity; both sides could find their reasons.   255
Jove's wife alone did not so much declare whether she faulted her
or approved of her as she rejoiced at the disaster of the house descended
from Agenor, and she transferred her pent up hatred from the Tyrian

in generis socios odium. subit ecce priori
260 causa recens, grauidamque dolet de semine magni
esse Iouis Semelen; dum linguam ad iurgia soluit,
'profeci quid enim totiens per iurgia?' dixit,
'ipsa petenda mihi est; ipsam, si maxima Iuno
rite uocor, perdam, si me gemmantia dextra
265 sceptra tenere decet, si sum regina Iouisque
et soror et coniunx, certe soror. at, puto, furto est
contenta et thalami breuis est iniuria nostri.
concipit (id deerat) manifestaque crimina pleno
fert utero et mater, quod uix mihi contigit, uno
270 de Ioue uult fieri: tanta est fiducia formae.
fallat eam faxo, nec sum Saturnia, si non
ab Ioue mersa suo Stygias penetrabit in undas.'
surgit ab his solio fuluaque recondita nube
limen adit Semeles, nec nubes ante remouit
275 quam simulauit anum posuitque ad tempora canos
sulcauitque cutem rugis et curua trementi
membra tulit passu, uocem quoque fecit anilem,
ipsaque erat Beroe, Semeles Epidauria nutrix.
ergo ubi captato sermone diuque loquendo
280 ad nomen uenere Iouis, suspirat et, 'opto
Iuppiter ut sit,' ait, 'metuo tamen omnia: multi
nomine diuorum thalamos iniere pudicos.
nec tamen esse Iouem satis est; det pignus amoris,
si modo uerus is est, quantusque et qualis ab alta
285 Iunone excipitur, tantus talisque rogato
det tibi complexus suaque ante insignia sumat.'
talibus ignaram Iuno Cadmeida dictis
formarat: rogat illa Iouem sine nomine munus.
cui deus, 'elige:' ait, 'nullam patiere repulsam.
290 quoque magis credas, Stygii quoque conscia sunto
numina torrentis; timor et deus ille deorum est.'
laeta malo nimiumque potens perituraque amantis
obsequio Semele, 'qualem Saturnia,' dixit,
'te solet amplecti, Veneris cum foedus initis,
295 da mihi te talem.' uoluit deus ora loquentis
opprimere: exierat iam uox properata sub auras.

wench to those linked to her by blood. Look, a fresh grievance   259
had been added to the earlier one, it rankled with her that Semele was
                                                                  pregnant
from the seed of great Jove; then even as she loosed her tongue for insults,
it was, 'For what have I achieved from insults all those times?' that she
                                                                      said.
'It is she herself that I must seek; it is she herself, if I am rightly called
Juno most great, I shall destroy, if I am fit to hold
the bejewelled sceptre in my right hand, if I am the queen and Jove's 265
sister and wife, well sister certainly. But, I suppose, she is satisfied
with her deceit and the wrong done to my marriage bed is slight.
She has conceived (that's all that was left) and she carries her flagrant
                                                                      crime
in her full womb, and wants to be made a mother only by Jove, something
which has scarcely happened to me: that is how much she trusts in her
                                                                    beauty.
I shall see that she is disappointed, and I'm not Saturnia unless she   271
is overwhelmed by that Jove of hers and sinks into the Stygian waters.'
With these words, she rose from her throne, hid herself in a bright yellow
                                                                      cloud
and approached Semele's threshold, not removing the cloud until
she had made herself like an old woman by putting white hairs on her
                                                                  temples,
furrowing her skin with wrinkles, bending her body   276
and adopting a tottering gait, and making her voice too an old woman's;
she was just like Beroë, Semele's Epidaurian nurse.
And so, as they struck up conversation, and had talked for a long time,
when they came to the name of Jupiter, she sighed and, 'I want   280
it to be Jupiter,' she said, 'but it all worries me: many men
have got into an innocent bedroom by using the name of a god.
But it isn't enough that he be Jupiter, he must give proof of his love,
if indeed it really is him, and just as he is, just as great, as when he is
                                                                   received
by Juno on high, you must ask him to be just like that, just as great, 285
as he gives you his embrace and, before that, to put on his regalia.'
With such words had Juno moulded Cadmus' unknowing
daughter: she asked Jove for a favour unspecified.
And, 'Choose:' the god said to her, 'you'll not suffer rebuff.
And, that you may believe me the more, let the spirits of Styx' torrent too
be witness; he is a source of fear and a god for the gods.'   291
Happy with her misfortune, all too persuasive and about to perish because
                                                        of the compliance
of her lover, Semele said, 'Just as you are when Saturnia
embraces you, when you enter Venus' compact,
give yourself to me just like that.' The god wanted to stop up her mouth
as she spoke: but her hasty words had already escaped into the air.   296

ingemuit; neque enim non haec optasse, neque ille
non iurasse potest, ergo maestissimus altum
aethera conscendit uultuque sequentia traxit
300 nubila, quis nimbos immixtaque fulgura uentis
addidit et tonitrus et ineuitabile fulmen.
qua tamen usque potest, uires sibi demere temptat
nec, quo centimanum deiecerat igne Typhoea,
nunc armatur eo: nimium feritatis in illo est.
305 est aliud leuius fulmen, cui dextra Cyclopum
saeuitiae flammaeque minus, minus addidit irae:
tela secunda uocant superi; capit illa domumque
intrat Agenoream. corpus mortale tumultus
non tulit aetherios donisque iugalibus arsit.
310 imperfectus adhuc infans genetricis ab aluo
eripitur patrioque tener (si credere dignum est)
insuitur femori maternaque tempora complet.
furtim illum primis Ino matertera cunis
educat; inde datum nymphae Nyseides antris
315 occuluere suis lactisque alimenta dedere.
    dumque ea per terras fatali lege geruntur
tutaque bis geniti sunt incunabula Bacchi,
forte Iouem memorant diffusum nectare curas
seposuisse graues uacuaque agitasse remissos
320 cum Iunone iocos et, 'maior uestra profecto est
quam quae contingit maribus,' dixisse, 'uoluptas.'
illa negat. placuit quae sit sententia docti
quaerere Tiresiae: Venus huic erat utraque nota.
nam duo magnorum uiridi coeuntia silua
325 corpora serpentum baculi uiolauerat ictu,
deque uiro factus (mirabile) femina septem
egerat autumnos; octauo rursus eosdem
uidit et, 'est uestrae si tanta potentia plagae,'
dixit, 'ut auctoris sortem in contraria mutet,
330 nunc quoque uos feriam.' percussis anguibus isdem,
forma prior rediit genetiuaque uenit imago.
arbiter hic igitur sumptus de lite iocosa
dicta Iouis firmat; grauius Saturnia iusto
nec pro materia fertur doluisse suique
335 iudicis aeterna damnauit lumina nocte.
at pater omnipotens (neque enim licet inrita cuiquam
facta dei fecisse deo) pro lumine adempto
scire futura dedit poenamque leuauit honore.

He groaned; for neither could she not have wished it,
nor he not have sworn. And so, very sadly, he climbed up
the high ether and with his expression drew up the mists
that followed him to which he added clouds, and lightning flashes mixed
with winds, and thunderings and the inescapable bolt.   301
And yet, as far as he could, he tried to reduce his strength,
and did not now equip himself with the fire which had hurled down
Typhoeus of the hundred hands: there was too much ferocity in that one.
There was another lighter kind of bolt to which the right hand of the
                                                            Cyclopes
had added less savagery and flame, less anger: 306
they were called his second weapons by the gods; he took them up and
                                                             entered
Agenor's home. Her mortal body could not endure
the ethereal assaults and was set on fire by his marriage gifts.
Her baby, still not fully formed, was snatched from his mother's   310
womb and the delicate child was sewn (if it is to be believed)
into his father's thigh to complete his mother's term.
Ino, his mother's sister, secretly brought him up from his earliest days
in the cradle: afterwards he was given to the Nysaean nymphs who
                                                      concealed him
in their caves and gave him nourishing milk.   315
        And while these things were being done on earth by the law of fate,
and twice born Bacchus was safe in his cradle,
it is the story that Jupiter chanced to be relaxing with his nectar, laying
his heavy cares aside, and to have been exchanging casual
jokes with an idle Juno, and that he had said, 'Your pleasure is,   320
of course, greater than that which comes to males.'
She denied it. They decided to seek the opinion of
learned Tiresias: he had known both Venuses.
For while the bodies of two great serpents had been coupling
in the green wood, he had abused them with his staff,   325
and from a man, he was made (amazingly) into a woman and spent
seven autumns so; in the eighth, he saw the same creatures
again and said, 'If the power of a blow on you is
so great that it changes the lot of its perpetrator into its opposite,
I shall hit you now too.' And when he had struck these same snakes, 330
his earlier form returned and his natural appearance came back.
And so, appointed to arbitrate this jocular dispute,
he confirmed the words of Jove; Saturnia, they say, was upset
more seriously than was fair and out of proportion to the issue, and
she condemned the eyes of their judge to eternal night.   335
But the almighty father (for there is not any god allowed
to nullify the actions of a god) allowed him to know the future,
in place of his eyesight now removed, and lightened his punishment with
                                                      that honour.

ille per Aonias fama celeberrimus urbes
340 inreprehensa dabat populo responsa petenti.
prima fide uocisque ratae temptamina sumpsit
caerula Liriope, quam quondam flumine curuo
implicuit clausaeque suis Cephisos in undis
uim tulit, enixa est utero pulcherrima pleno
345 infantem nymphe, iam tum qui posset amari,
Narcissumque uocat. de quo consultus, an esset
tempora maturae uisurus longa senectae,
fatidicus uates, 'si se non nouerit,' inquit.
uana diu uisa est uox auguris: exitus illam
350 resque probat letique genus nouitasque furoris.
namque ter ad quinos unum Cephisius annum
addiderat poteratque puer iuuenisque uideri;
multi illum iuuenes, multae cupiere puellae;
sed (fuit in tenera tam dura superbia forma)
355 nulli illum iuuenes, nullae tetigere puellae.
aspicit hunc trepidos agitantem in retia ceruos
uocalis nymphe, quae nec reticere loquenti
nec prior ipsa loqui didicit, resonabilis Echo.
corpus adhuc Echo, non uox erat; et tamen usum
360 garrula non alium, quam nunc habet, oris habebat,
reddere de multis ut uerba nouissima posset.
(fecerat hoc Iuno quia, cum deprendere posset
sub Ioue saepe suo nymphas in monte iacentes,
illa deam longo prudens sermone tenebat,
365 dum fugerent nymphae. postquam hoc Saturnia sensit,
'huius,' ait, 'linguae, qua sum delusa, potestas
parua tibi dabitur uocisque breuissimus usus,'
reque minas firmat: tantum haec in fine loquendi
ingeminat uoces auditaque uerba reportat.)
370 ergo ubi Narcissum per deuia rura uagantem
uidit et incaluit, sequitur uestigia furtim,
quoque magis sequitur, flamma propiore calescit,
non aliter quam cum summis circumlita taedis
admotas rapiunt uiuacia sulphura flammas.
375 o quotiens uoluit blandis accedere dictis
et molles adhibere preces! natura repugnat
nec sinit incipiat; sed, quod sinit, illa parata est
exspectare sonos, ad quos sua uerba remittat.
forte puer comitum seductus ab agmine fido
380 dixerat, 'ecquis adest?' et, 'adest,' responderat Echo.

His fame was spread abroad throughout the Aonian cities,
and when the people asked he would give them unblamable responses.   340
The first to engage in a trial of his word and his reliability
was aquamarine Liriope; Cephisos had once caught hold of her
in his winding stream and, when he had confined her in his waves,
he took her violently. She was a most beautiful nymph and bore
from her full womb a baby boy who even then could have been loved,   345
and she called him Narcissus. When consulted about him, whether he
would see the lengthy days of a ripe old age,
the oracular seer said, 'If he does not get to know himself.'
For a long time the augur's word seemed empty: but the outcome and the
                                                            event
confirmed it, as did the nature of his fate and the strangeness of his
                                                            passion.
For when the Cephisian had added one year to three times   351
five, and could seem to be a boy or man,
many men, many girls desired him;
but (there was in his delicate beauty so stiff a pride)
no men, no girls affected him.   355
As he was driving nervous stags into the nets, he was noticed
by a talkative nymph who had learnt neither to keep silent
for a speaker nor to speak first herself, she was sound-repeating Echo.
Echo was still a body, not a voice; and yet the chatterbox
had no other use for her mouth than she has now,   360
that she could return the very last words out of many.
(Juno had done this because often, when she could have caught
nymphs lying under her Jupiter on the mountain,
she would deliberately hold the goddess up with lengthy conversation
until the nymphs could escape. And when Saturnia realized it,   365
'The power of this tongue,' she said, 'by which I have been tricked,
will be rendered slight, and the use of your voice most brief.'
And she confirmed her threats with action: the nymph began only to
                                                            reiterate words
at the ends of speeches, and repeat what she had heard.)
So when, as Narcissus roamed through remote country,   370
she saw him and caught fire, she followed his footsteps secretly,
and the more she followed the closer the flame that fired her,
just as when lively sulphur daubed around
the tops of torches seizes on the flames brought near.
Oh how often did she want to approach him with coaxing words   375
and make soft prayers to him! Her condition fought against it
and did not allow her to begin; but, and it did allow this, she prepared
                                                            herself
to wait for sounds at which she could send back her words.
It happened that the boy, separated from his band of faithful comrades,
had said, 'Is there anybody here?' and, 'Here,' Echo had replied.   380

hic stupet, utque aciem partes dimittit in omnes,
uoce, 'ueni,' magna clamat: uocat illa uocantem.
respicit et rursus nullo ueniente, 'quid,' inquit
'me fugis?' et totidem quot dixit uerba recepit.
385 perstat et alternae deceptus imagine uocis,
'huc coeamus,' ait, nullique libentius umquam
responsura sono, 'coeamus,' rettulit Echo
et uerbis fauet ipsa suis egressaque silua
ibat, ut iniceret sperato bracchia collo.
390 ille fugit fugiensque, 'manus complexibus aufer;
ante,' ait, 'emoriar, quam sit tibi copia nostri.'
rettulit illa nihil nisi, 'sit tibi copia nostri.'
spreta latet siluis pudibundaque frondibus ora
protegit et solis ex illo uiuit in antris;
395 sed tamen haeret amor crescitque dolore repulsae:
attenuant uigiles corpus miserabile curae,
adducitque cutem macies, et in aera sucus
corporis omnis abit; uox tantum atque ossa supersunt:
uox manet; ossa ferunt lapidis traxisse figuram.
400 inde latet siluis nulloque in monte uidetur,
omnibus auditur: sonus est, qui uiuit in illa.

        sic hanc, sic alias undis aut montibus ortas
luserat hic nymphas, sic coetus ante uiriles;
inde manus aliquis despectus ad aethera tollens,
405 'sic amet ipse licet, sic non potiatur amato!'
dixerat. adsensit precibus Rhamnusia iustis.
fons erat inlimis, nitidis argenteus undis,
quem neque pastores neque pastae monte capellae
contigerant aliudue pecus, quem nulla uolucris
410 nec fera turbarat nec lapsus ab arbore ramus.
gramen erat circa, quod proximus umor alebat,
siluaque sole locum passura tepescere nullo.
hic puer, et studio uenandi lassus et aestu,
procubuit faciemque loci fontemque secutus;
415 dumque sitim sedare cupit, sitis altera creuit,
dumque bibit, uisae correptus imagine formae,
spem sine corpore amat, corpus putat esse, quod unda est.
astupet ipse sibi uultuque immotus eodem
haeret, ut e Pario formatum marmore signum.
420 spectat humi positus geminum, sua lumina, sidus
et dignos Baccho, dignos et Apolline crines,

He was stunned and directed his gaze in all directions
shouting, 'Come,' in a loud voice: she called the caller.
He looked round again and when no one came, 'Why,' he said,
'do you flee from me?' And he got back just as many words as he had
          spoken.
He persisted, deceived as he was by the illusion of an answering voice; 385
'Here, let us come together,' he said and Echo, who would never respond
more willingly to any sound, replied, 'Let us come together,'
and she helped her words along by leaving the wood
and coming to throw her arms upon the neck that she had longed for.
He fled and, as he fled, 'Hands off, do not embrace me.   390
I would die,' he said, 'before I would offer myself to you.'
She answered nothing except, 'I would offer myself to you.'
Spurned, she hid in the woods and, in her shame, covered her face
with foliage and lived henceforth in lonely caves;
and yet her love clung to her and grew with the pain of rejection: 395
her cares kept her awake and made her body pitiably thin,
her skin wasted and shrivelled up and all her body's
moisture went off into the air; only her voice and bones were left:
her voice remained; her bones, they say, took on the appearance of stone.
Since then she has hidden in the woods and is never seen on the mountains,
she is heard by all: but it is only sound that lives in her.   401
    So he had toyed with her and so with the other nymphs that were
          sprung
from waves or mountains and so, earlier, with crowds of men;
till one of those he had disdained raised his hands up towards the ether
and said, 'So may he too love, so may he not gain   405
what he has loved!' Rhamnusia assented to this just prayer.
There was a slimeless spring, with shimmering, silvery waters,
which neither shepherds nor goats that graze upon the mountain
had touched, nor any other flock, which no bird
nor wild beast had disturbed, nor any branch fallen from a tree.   410
There was grass around it, nurtured by nearby water,
and a wood that let no sunshine in to overheat the place.
Here the boy, tired from keen hunting and the heat,
had lain down, drawn there by the spring and by the beauty of the place,
and while he wanted to relieve his thirst, another thirst grew in him, 415
and while he drank, he saw a beautiful reflection and was captivated,
he loved a hope without a body, and what he thought was body was but
          water.
He was overwhelmed by himself and, unmoving and holding the same
          expression,
he was fixed there like a statue moulded out of Parian marble.   419
As he lay there on the ground, he gazed at the twin stars that were his
          eyes,
and at his locks that were worthy of Bacchus, and worthy of Apollo too,

impubesque genas et eburnea colla decusque
oris et in niueo mixtum candore ruborem,
cunctaque miratur, quibus est mirabilis ipse.
425 se cupit imprudens et, qui probat, ipse probatur,
dumque petit, petitur, pariterque accendit et ardet.
inrita fallaci quotiens dedit oscula fonti!
in mediis quotiens uisum captantia collum
bracchia mersit aquis nec se deprendit in illis!
430 quid uideat nescit, sed quod uidet uritur illo
atque oculos idem qui decipit incitat error.
credule, quid frustra simulacra fugacia captas?
quod petis est nusquam; quod amas, auertere, perdes.
ista repercussae, quam cernis, imaginis umbra est.
435 nil habet ista sui; tecum uenitque manetque,
tecum discedet, si tu discedere possis.
non illum Cereris, non illum cura quietis
abstrahere inde potest, sed opaca fusus in herba
spectat inexpleto mendacem lumine formam
440 perque oculos perit ipse suos; paulumque leuatus,
ad circumstantes tendens sua bracchia siluas,
'ecquis, io siluae, crudelius,' inquit, 'amauit?
scitis enim et multis latebra opportuna fuistis.
ecquem, cum uestrae tot agantur saecula uitae,
445 qui sic tabuerit, longo meministis in aeuo?
et placet et uideo, sed quod uideoque placetque
non tamen inuenio: tantus tenet error amantem.
quoque magis doleam, nec nos mare separat ingens
nec uia nec montes nec clausis moenia portis:
450 exigua prohibemur aqua! cupit ipse teneri;
nam quotiens liquidis porreximus oscula lymphis,
hic totiens ad me resupino nititur ore.
posse putes tangi; minimum est quod amantibus obstat.
quisquis es, huc exi! quid me, puer unice, fallis
455 quoue petitus abis? certe nec forma nec aetas
est mea, quam fugias; et amarunt me quoque nymphae.
spem mihi nescioquam uultu promittis amico,
cumque ego porrexi tibi bracchia, porrigis ultro;
cum risi, adrides; lacrimas quoque saepe notaui
460 me lacrimante tuas; nutu quoque signa remittis
et, quantum motu formosi suspicor oris,
uerba refers aures non peruenientia nostras.

and at his unbearded cheeks, his ivory-coloured neck and his glorious
face, its blush mingled with a snowy radiance,
and he admired everything for which he was himself admired.   424
Unwittingly, he desired himself and both praised and was himself the
                                                        praised one,
and while he sought, he was being sought, and he was at once both burning
                                                        and igniting.
How many times did he give vain kisses to the deceitful spring!
How many times did he plunge into the middle of the waters arms that
                                                        tried
to clasp the neck that he had seen, but he did not clasp himself in there!
He did not know what he was seeing, but he was on fire at what he saw,
and his eyes were thrilled and misled by the same confusion.   431
Naive one, why do you vainly clasp at fleeting images?
What you seek is nowhere; turn away, and you will lose your beloved.
What you are looking at is a shadow, a reflected image.
It has nothing of its own: it comes and stays with you,   435
with you it will depart, if only you could depart.
No thought of Ceres, no thought of rest could
drag him from there but, stretched out upon the shady grass,
he gazed at the deceiving image with an insatiable gaze
and by his own eyes he was himself undone; then raising himself a little,
he stretched his arms out to the woods that stood around him   441
and said, 'Alas, oh woods, is there anyone who has loved more painfully?
For you know, since many lovers have found in you a ready hiding place.
Is there anyone that you remember in your long lifetime, since you have
                                                        lived
for so many centuries, that has pined away like this?   445
I am delighted by what I see, but what I see and what delights me,
that I cannot find: so much confusion thwarts this lover.
And, to make me grieve the more, there is no vast sea that separates us,
nor a road, nor mountains, nor city walls with closed gates:
we are kept apart by a little bit of water! He too wants to be held;   450
for, whenever I have stretched my lips down to the clear waters,
each time he has strained towards me with upturned mouth.
You would think he could be touched: it is so small a thing that stops our
                                                        love.
Whoever you are, come out here! Why do you deceive me, matchless boy,
when I reach for you, where do you go? Well, at least it's not my beauty,
nor my age that makes you run away; and the nymphs have loved me too.
There is some sort of hope you offer me with your friendly look,   457
and when I stretch my arms to you, you stretch yours back in return.
When I smile, you smile back; and I have often noticed your tears too,
when I have been shedding tears; when I nod too, you return the sign   460
and, as far as I can guess from the movements of your beautiful mouth,
you answer me with words that do not reach my ears.

iste ego sum! sensi, nec me mea fallit imago.
uror amore mei, flammas moueoque feroque.
465   quid faciam? roger anne rogem? quid deinde rogabo?
quod cupio mecum est; inopem me copia fecit.
o utinam a nostro secedere corpore possem!
uotum in amante nouum, uellem quod amamus abesset.
iamque dolor uires adimit, nec tempora uitae
470   longa meae superant, primoque extinguor in aeuo.
nec mihi mors grauis est posituro morte dolores;
hic qui diligitur uellem diuturnior esset.
nunc duo concordes anima moriemur in una.'
dixit et ad faciem rediit male sanus eandem
475   et lacrimis turbauit aquas, obscuraque moto
reddita forma lacu est. quam cum uidisset abire,
'quo refugis? remane nec me, crudelis, amantem
desere;' clamauit, 'liceat, quod tangere non est,
aspicere et misero praebere alimenta furori.'
480   dumque dolet, summa uestem deduxit ab ora
nudaque marmoreis percussit pectora palmis.
pectora traxerunt roseum percussa ruborem,
non aliter quam poma solent, quae candida parte,
parte rubent, aut ut uariis solet uua racemis
485   ducere purpureum nondum matura colorem.
quae simul aspexit liquefacta rursus in unda,
non tulit ulterius sed, ut intabescere flauae
igne leui cerae matutinaeque pruinae
sole tepente solent, sic attenuatus amore
490   liquitur et tecto paulatim carpitur igni;
et neque iam color est mixto candore rubori,
nec uigor et uires et quae modo uisa placebant,
nec corpus remanet, quondam quod amauerat Echo.
quae tamen ut uidit, quamuis irata memorque
495   indoluit, quotiensque puer miserabilis, 'eheu,'
dixerat, haec resonis iterabat uocibus, 'eheu.'
cumque suos manibus percusserat ille lacertos,
haec quoque reddebat sonitum plangoris eundem.
ultima uox solitam fuit haec spectantis in undam:
500   'heu frustra dilecte puer!' totidemque remisit
uerba locus, dictoque uale, 'uale,' inquit et Echo.
ille caput uiridi fessum submisit in herba,
lumina mors clausit domini mirantia formam.
tum quoque se, postquam est inferna sede receptus,
505   in Stygia spectabat aqua. planxere sorores

I am that one! I realize it and my reflection does not deceive me.
I am burning with a love for myself, I both excite the flames and suffer
them.
What am I to do? Am I to be wooed, or do I woo? And then, how shall I
woo?
What I desire is with me: my plenty has made me poor.   466
Oh would that I were able to withdraw from my body;
and, a strange wish in a lover, I should like what I love to be apart.
And now the pain is taking my strength away, my life
has no long time left, I am being cut off in my youth.   470
Death is no burden for me, for in death I shall lay aside this pain:
but I would wish that he that I have adored might live longer.
As it is, the two of us will die in a single breath.'
He spoke and, in his sickness, went back to that same face;   474
with his tears he disturbed the waters and the image that came back to him
from the lake in motion was obscured. And, when he saw that it was gone,
'Where are you fleeing to? Stay, do not, cruel one, abandon me,
your lover,' he cried, 'and let me gaze on what I may not
touch, and so give nourishment to my unhappy passion.'
And while he agonized, he pulled his cloak off by its upper hem   480
and beat his bare breast with his alabaster palms.
His breast took on a rosy blush under the blows,
just as apples will when they are white in one part
and blushing in another, or as, among the many-coloured bunches, a grape
which has not ripened yet will take on a purple colour.   485
And as soon as he saw this in the water, now cleared again,
he could not bear it any longer but, just as yellow wax
will melt before a low fire, or the morning frost
in warm sunshine, so was he wasted and dissolved
by love and slowly consumed by its hidden fire;   490
and he no longer had that fair complexion mingled with a blush,
nor his strength and vigour and those things which, when seen just now,
had pleased him;
and that body was no more, which Echo once had loved.
But, when she saw him, in spite of her anger and her memories,
she was pained for him, and whenever the pitiable boy, 'Alas,'   495
had said, she would repeat with an echoing voice, 'Alas.'
And when he beat his arms and shoulders with his hands,
she too would return the same sound of grief.
His last words were these, as he gazed into the familiar spring,
'Alas, oh boy adored in vain,' and the place returned   500
those very words, and when he had said farewell, 'Farewell,' said Echo too.
He lowered his weary head onto the green grass,
death closed the eyes still admiring the beauty of their lord.
And after he had been received by the place below, even then
he would gaze upon himself in the water of the Styx. His Naiad sisters 505

Naides et sectos fratri posuere capillos,
planxerunt Dryades; plangentibus adsonat Echo.
iamque rogum quassasque faces feretrumque parabant:
nusquam corpus erat; croceum pro corpore florem
510 inueniunt foliis medium cingentibus albis.
        cognita res meritam uati per Achaidas urbes
attulerat famam, nomenque erat auguris ingens.
spernit Echionides tamen hunc ex omnibus unus
contemptor superum Pentheus praesagaque ridet
515 uerba senis tenebrasque et cladem lucis ademptae
obicit. ille mouens albentia tempora canis,
'quam felix esses, si tu quoque luminis huius
orbus,' ait, 'fieres, ne Bacchica sacra uideres.
namque dies aderit, quam non procul auguror esse,
520 qua nouus huc ueniat, proles Semeleia, Liber;
quem nisi templorum fueris dignatus honore,
mille lacer spargere locis et sanguine siluas
foedabis matremque tuam matrisque sorores.
eueniet; neque enim dignabere numen honore,
525 meque sub his tenebris nimium uidisse quereris.'
talia dicentem proturbat Echione natus.
        dicta fides sequitur, responsaque uatis aguntur.
Liber adest, festisque fremunt ululatibus agri;
turba ruit, mixtaeque uiris matresque nurusque
530 uulgusque proceresque ignota ad sacra feruntur.
'quis furor, anguigenae, proles Mauortia, uestras
attonuit mentes?' Pentheus ait, 'aerane tantum
aere repulsa ualent et adunco tibia cornu
et magicae fraudes, ut, quos non bellicus ensis,
535 non tuba terruerit, non strictis agmina telis,
femineae uoces et mota insania uino
obscenique greges et inania tympana uincant?
uosne, senes, mirer, qui longa per aequora uecti
hac Tyron, hac profugos posuistis sede penates,
540 nunc sinitis sine Marte capi? uosne, acrior aetas,
o iuuenes, propiorque meae, quos arma tenere,
non thyrsos, galeaque tegi, non fronde decebat?
este, precor, memores, qua sitis stirpe creati,
illiusque animos, qui multos perdidit unus,
545 sumite serpentis. pro fontibus ille lacuque
interiit: at uos pro fama uincite uestra.

grieved for him and offered their shorn locks for their brother,
the Dryads grieved for him; and Echo resounded to them as they grieved.
They were now preparing a pyre, torches to shake and a bier:
but the body was nowhere; instead of the body they found a flower
with white petals surrounding its yellow centre.   510
      News of the affair had brought the seer deserved fame
throughout the Achaean cities, and the augur's reputation was enormous.
But, Echion's son was alone of all men in despising him,
Pentheus, who was contemptuous of the gods, and he laughed at the old
                                                                      man's
prophetic words and taunted him with his blindness and the misfortune of
                                                                   his loss
of sight. He shook his hoary, grey-haired temples   516
and said, 'How lucky you would be if you too were to be made
bereft of this light, so that you could not see the Bacchic rites.
For a day will come and, according to my auguries, it is not far off
when a new god, Liber, offspring of Semele, will come here;   520
and unless you deem him worthy to be honoured by temples
you will be torn apart and scattered in a thousand places, and with your
                                                                     blood
you will defile the woods, your mother and your mother's sisters.
It will come to pass! For you will not deem the god worthy of honour,
and you will cry out that in this darkness I have seen too much.'   525
As he said such things, Echion's son thrust him aside.
      Confirmation of what he said soon followed, the seer's answers were
                                                                 fulfilled.
Liber had come and the fields rang with the screamings of his festival.
A throng rushed out, and matrons and young women with men mixed in,
the common people and the nobles were borne along to the unknown rites.
'What frenzy, you snake-descended ones, offspring of Mars, has stunned 531
your minds?' said Pentheus. 'Are the clashings of bronze
on bronze so strong, and the flute with its curved bell
and magic tricks, that men who are not frightened by the sword
of war, or by the bugle, or by battle lines with weapons drawn,   535
are conquered by women's voices, by the madness that wine
brings on, by lascivious hordes and by the hollow drums?
Am I to admire you, old men who, having voyaged far across the sea
to set Tyre upon this site here, and here your exiled penates,
are now letting it be taken without a fight? -- or you, of a more active
                                                                      age,
nearer to my own, young men, who should have been holding   541
weapons not thyrsi, and wearing a helmet not leaves?
Remember, I beg you, from what stock you were produced
and take on the spirit of that serpent who, all alone,
destroyed so many men. It was for springs and for a lake   545
that it died: but you must conquer for your renown.

ille dedit leto fortes, uos pellite molles
et patrium retinete decus. si fata uetabant
stare diu Thebas, utinam tormenta uirique
550 moenia diruerent, ferrumque ignisque sonarent:
essemus miseri sine crimine, sorsque querenda,
non celanda foret, lacrimaeque pudore carerent:
at nunc a puero Thebae capientur inermi,
quem neque bella iuuant nec tela nec usus equorum,
555 sed madidus murra crinis mollesque coronae
purpuraque et pictis intextum uestibus aurum.
quem quidem ego actutum (modo uos absistite) cogam
adsumptumque patrem commentaque sacra fateri.
an satis Acrisio est animi contemnere uanum
560 numen et Argolicas uenienti claudere portas,
Penthea terrebit cum totis aduena Thebis?
ite citi,' famulis hoc imperat, 'ite ducemque
attrahite huc uinctum. iussis mora segnis abesto.'
hunc auus, hunc Athamas, hunc cetera turba suorum
565 corripiunt dictis frustraque inhibere laborant.
acrior admonitu est inritaturque retenta
et crescit rabies, moderaminaque ipsa nocebant:
sic ego torrentem, qua nil obstabat eunti,
lenius et modico strepitu decurrere uidi;
570 at quacumque trabes obstructaque saxa tenebant,
spumeus et feruens et ab obice saeuior ibat.
ecce cruentati redeunt et Bacchus ubi esset
quaerenti domino Bacchum uidisse negarunt.
'hunc,' dixere, 'tamen comitem famulumque sacrorum
575 cepimus,' et tradunt, manibus post terga ligatis,
sacra dei quendam Tyrrhena gente secutum.
aspicit hunc Pentheus oculis quos ira tremendos
fecerat et, quamquam poenae uix tempora differt,
'o periture tuaque aliis documenta dature
580 morte,' ait, 'ede tuum nomen nomenque parentum
et patriam morisque noui cur sacra frequentes.'
ille metu uacuus, 'nomen mihi,' dixit, 'Acoetes,
patria Maeonia est, humili de plebe parentes.
non mihi quae duri colerent pater arua iuuenci
585 lanigerosue greges, non ulla armenta reliquit.

It sent brave men to their doom: you must drive out weaklings
and maintain the glory of your fathers. If the fates forbade
that Thebes should stand for long, then I wish that men and catapaults
would smash her walls down, that fire and the sword would resound.   550
Then, we would be unhappy, but free of guilt, our lot would be one to
                                                              lament,
not to conceal, and our tears would be without shame:
but, as it is, Thebes will be captured by an unarmed boy
who enjoys neither wars nor weapons nor the use of horses,
but hair drenched in oil of myrrh, soft garlands   555
and purple and gold woven into the decoration of his clothes.
And I will straightway (just stand aside) compel him
to admit that the story of his father is made up and that his rites are
                                                          fraudulent.
Did Acrisius have courage enough to despise this spurious
divinity and close the Argive gates as he approached,   560
and will Pentheus and all of Thebes be frightened by the stranger?
Go quickly,' this was his command to his attendants, 'go and bind
their leader and bring him here. Do as you are ordered without slothful
                                                              delay.'
      His grandfather spoke to him and rebuked him, so did Athamas and
                                                    so did the rest
of his thronging people, and they strove in vain to hold him back.   565
The advice made him more severe, his fury was provoked
and grew from being held in check, the restraints themselves were
                                                              harmful:
even so have I seen a torrent, where there was nothing to obstruct
its flow, run down quite smoothly with a moderate din;
but wherever logs and rocks clogged it and held it up,   570
it frothed and raged and flowed more violently because of the obstruction.
Look, they returned all bloodied and, when their lord asked them
where Bacchus was, they said they had not seen Bacchus.
'But this man,' they said, 'his companion and the attendant at his rites,
we have captured,' and they handed him over with his hands tied behind
                                                          his back,
a follower of the god's rites from the Tyrrhenian race.   576
      Pentheus inspected him with eyes which anger had made
fearsome and, although he was hardly putting off the time of punishment,
'You, who are going to perish,' he said, 'and by your death provide
others with a warning, give me your name and the name of your parents
and your country, and tell me why you are celebrating the rites of this
                                                        new cult.'
He, quite without fear, said, 'My name is Acoetes,   582
my country is Maeonia and my parents are from the lowly plebs.
My father did not leave me fields or sturdy bullocks
to plough them, or wool-bearing flocks or any herds.   585

pauper et ipse fuit linoque solebat et hamis
decipere et calamo salientes ducere pisces.
ars illi sua census erat; cum traderet artem,
"accipe quas habeo, studii successor et heres,"
590   dixit, "opes." moriensque mihi nihil ille reliquit
praeter aquas; unum hoc possum appellare paternum.
mox ego, ne scopulis haererem semper in isdem,
addidici regimen dextra moderante carinae
flectere et Oleniae sidus pluuiale capellae
595   Taygetenque Hyadasque oculis Arctonque notaui
uentorumque domos et portus puppibus aptos.
forte petens Delon Chiae telluris ad oras
adplicor et dextris adducor litora remis
doque leues saltus udaeque immittor harenae.
600   nox ubi consumpta est (aurora rubescere primo
coeperat), exsurgo laticesque inferre recentes
admoneo monstroque uiam, quae ducat ad undas.
ipse quid aura mihi tumulo promittat ab alto
prospicio comitesque uoco repetoque carinam.
605   "adsumus en," inquit sociorum primus Opheltes,
utque putat, praedam deserto nactus in agro
uirginea puerum ducit per litora forma.
ille mero somnoque grauis titubare uidetur
uixque sequi; specto cultum faciemque gradumque:
610   nil ibi quod credi posset mortale uidebam.
et sensi et dixi sociis, "quod numen in isto
corpore sit, dubito, sed corpore numen in isto est.
quisquis es, o faueas nostrisque laboribus adsis.
his quoque des ueniam." "pro nobis mitte precari"
615   Dictys ait, quo non alius conscendere summas
ocior antemnas prensoque rudente relabi.
hoc Libys, hoc flauus, prorae tutela, Melanthus,
hoc probat Alcimedon et, qui requiemque modumque
uoce dabat remis, animorum hortator Epopeus,
620   hoc omnes alii: praedae tam caeca cupido est.
"non tamen hanc sacro uiolari pondere pinum
perpetiar," dixi; "pars hic mihi maxima iuris,"
inque aditu obsisto. furit audacissimus omni
de numero Lycabas, qui Tusca pulsus ab urbe
625   exilium dira poenam pro caede luebat.
is mihi, dum resto, iuuenali guttura pugno
rupit et excussum misisset in aequora, si non

He was a poor man himself and would trick fish
with hook and line and, as they jumped, use his rod to draw them in.
This skill was his fortune; as he passed the skill to me,
"Receive the wealth I have," he said, "and be the inheritor
and follower of my craft." And at his death he left me nothing   590
except the water; that was the only thing that I can call my father's.
Soon, so that I would not always stick on the same rocks,
I learnt to ply the tiller of a ship and to control it
with my right hand, and I used my eyes to note the rainy star
of the Olenian she-goat, Taygete, the Hyades and Arctos,   595
the homes of the winds and the harbours fit for boats.
As I was making for Delos, I happened to arrive at the shores of the Chian
land and sailed to the beach with skilful oars
and, making an easy leap, I threw myself on the wet sand.
When the night was spent (dawn had just begun   600
to redden), I arose and gave the order to bring fresh
water, and showed the way that led to the spring.
I myself looked out from a high hill to see what the wind
was promising me, then I summoned my companions and made for the ship
                                                                again.
"Look, here we are," said Opheltes, the first of my comrades,   605
as he brought along the shore a boy with a maiden's beauty,
plunder, as he thought, that he had come across in a deserted field.
He, slowed down by pure wine and sleepiness, seemed to stagger
and to find it difficult to follow; I looked at his dress, his face and his
                                                                walk:
I saw nothing there that was conceivably mortal.   610
I realized, and said to my comrades, "What god is in
that body, I am not sure, but in that body, there is a god.
Whoever you are, oh look favourably on us and be with us in our labours.
May you also give pardon to these men." "Drop your prayers for us,"
said Dictys; no other man was quicker than he was to climb   615
the highest yard-arms and to grasp a rope to slide back down again.
His words were applauded by Libys, by the ship's lookout, fair-haired
                                                                Melanthus,
by Alcimedon, and by the one whose voice gave
rest and rhythm to the oarsmen, urging on their spirits, Epopeus,
and by all the rest: so great was their blind greed for plunder.   620
"I still will not allow this boat to be defiled by a holy
cargo," I said; "the greatest authority here is mine,"
and I stood there blocking the gangway. Lycabas, the boldest of all
their number, was enraged; he had been expelled from the Tuscan city
and was paying the penalty of exile for a dreadful killing.   625
While I was resisting him, he smashed his strong young fist
against my throat and would have hurled me overboard into the sea, if I
                                                                had not

haesissem quamuis amens in fune retentus.
impia turba probat factum; tum denique Bacchus
630   (Bacchus enim fuerat), ueluti clamore solutus
sit sopor aque mero redeant in pectora sensus,
"quid facitis? quis clamor?" ait, "qua, dicite, nautae,
huc ope perueni? quo me deferre paratis?"
"pone metum," Proreus, "et quos contingere portus
635   ede uelis," dixit; "terra sistere petita."
"Naxon," ait Liber, "cursus aduertite uestros.
illa mihi domus est, uobis erit hospita tellus."
per mare fallaces perque omnia numina iurant
sic fore meque iubent pictae dare uela carinae.
640   dextera Naxos erat; dextra mihi lintea danti,
"quid facis, o demens? quis te furor," inquit, "Acoetes
pro se quisque tenet "laeuam pete!" maxima nutu
pars mihi significat, pars quid uelit aure susurrat.
obstipui, "capiat" que "aliquis moderamina," dixi
645   meque ministerio scelerisque artisque remoui.
increpor a cunctis, totumque immurmurat agmen;
e quibus Aethalion, "te scilicet omnis in uno
nostra salus posita est," ait et subit ipse meumque
explet opus Naxoque petit diuersa relicta.
650   tum deus inludens, tamquam modo denique fraudem
senserit, e puppi pontum prospectat adunca
et flenti similis, "non haec mihi litora, nautae,
promisistis," ait, "non haec mihi terra rogata est.
quo merui poenam facto? quae gloria uestra est,
655   si puerum iuuenes, si multi fallitis unum?"
iamdudum flebam: lacrimas manus impia nostras
ridet et impellit properantibus aequora remis.
per tibi nunc ipsum (nec enim praesentior illo
est deus) adiuro tam me tibi uera referre
660   quam ueri maiora fide: stetit aequore puppis
haud aliter quam si siccum nauale teneret.
illi admirantes remorum in uerbere perstant
uelaque deducunt geminaque ope currere temptant.
impediunt hederae remos nexuque recuruo
665   serpunt et grauidis distingunt uela corymbis.
ipse racemiferis frontem circumdatus uuis
pampineis agitat uelatam frondibus hastam;
quem circa tigres simulacraque inania lyncum
pictarumque iacent fera corpora pantherarum.

been caught up in a rope and, though stunned, had clung to it.
The impious throng applauded what he had done; then, at last, Bacchus
(for Bacchus it was), as if the shouting had freed him   630
from his drowsiness and, after the pure wine, his senses had come back
                                                into his breast,
said, "What are you doing? What is this shouting? How is it, oh sailors,
tell me, that I have come here? Where are you planning to convey me?"
"Have no fear," said Proreus, "but say what port
you would like to reach: you will be set down in the country that you
                                                        seek."
"Naxos," said Liber, "turn your course there.   636
That is my home, the land will be hospitable to you."
The treacherous men swore by the sea and by all the gods
that it would be so, and they ordered me to hoist the sail on the painted
                                                        ship.
Naxos was on our right: and, as I set the sail toward the right,   640
"What are you doing; you fool? What madness, Acoetes," said
· "Hold to the left." Most of them
signalled to me with nods, some whispered in my ear what they wanted.
I was dumbfounded and said, "Let someone else take the rudder,"
and I detached myself from their criminal service and its contrivances. 645
I was abused by all of them, the whole crew was muttering;
one of them, Aethalion, said, "It's on you alone, I suppose,
that all our safety depends." and he came up and took on
my task himself and made for the opposite direction with Naxos left
                                                        behind.
Then the god, playing with them, as if he had only now at last realized
their deceit, gazed out over the sea from the curved stern   650
and, with feigned tears, said, "These are not the shores, oh sailors,
you promised me, this is not the country that I asked for.
What have I done to deserve this punishment? What glory will you gain
if you, grown men and so many, deceive a solitary boy?"   655
I was already weeping: the impious band laughed at
our tears and struck the sea with hurrying oars.
Now I swear to you by the god himself (for there is no god
more present than he is) that what I am telling you is as true
as it is beyond belief: the ship stopped on the sea   660
just as if it were held in a dry dock.
They were amazed but kept up their beating with the oars,
let down the sail and tried to run with these twin helps.
Ivy entangled the oars, creeping on with twisted
runners to embellish the sail with heavy clusters.   665
He himself had his forehead surrounded with grapes in bunches
as he brandished a spear clothed in vine leaves;
and around him lay the empty images of tigers
and of lynxes and the wild bodies of spotted panthers.

670 exsiluere uiri, siue hoc insania fecit
siue timor, primusque Medon nigrescere toto
corpore et expresso spinae curuamine flecti
incipit; huic Lycabas, "in quae miracula," dixit
"uerteris?" et lati rictus et panda loquenti
675 naris erat squamamque cutis durata trahebat.
at Libys, obstantes dum uult obuertere remos,
in spatium resilire manus breue uidit et illas
iam non esse manus, iam pinnas posse uocari.
alter, ad intortos cupiens dare bracchia funes,
680 bracchia non habuit truncoque repandus in undas
corpore desiluit; falcata nouissima cauda est,
qualia dimidiae sinuantur cornua lunae.
undique dant saltus multaque aspergine rorant
emerguntque iterum redeuntque sub aequora rursus
685 inque chori ludunt speciem lasciuaque iactant
corpora et acceptum patulis mare naribus efflant.
de modo uiginti (tot enim ratis illa ferebat)
restabam solus: pauidum gelidumque trementi
corpore uixque meum firmat deus, "excute," dicens,
690 "corde metum Diamque tene." delatus in illam,
accessi sacris Baccheaque sacra frequento.'
'praebuimus longis,' Pentheus, 'ambagibus aures,'
inquit, 'ut ira mora uires absumere posset.
praecipitem, famuli, rapite hunc cruciataque diris
695 corpora tormentis Stygiae demittite nocti.'
protinus abstractus solidis Tyrrhenus Acoetes
clauditur in tectis; et dum crudelia iussae
instrumenta necis ferrumque ignesque parantur,
sponte sua patuisse fores lapsasque lacertis
700 sponte sua fama est, nullo soluente, catenas.
perstat Echionides nec iam iubet ire, sed ipse
uadit, ubi electus facienda ad sacra Cithaeron
cantibus et clara bacchantum uoce sonabat.
ut fremit acer equus, cum bellicus aere canoro
705 signa dedit tubicen, pugnaeque adsumit amorem,
Penthea sic ictus longis ululatibus aether
mouit, et audito clamore recanduit ira.
monte fere medio est, cingentibus ultima siluis,
purus ab arboribus, spectabilis undique campus.
710 hic oculis illum cernentem sacra profanis
prima uidet, prima est insano concita cursu,

The men jumped up, perhaps madness made them,   670
perhaps fear; Medon was the first whose whole body
began to grow black and to be bent with a marked curving
of the spine; to him Lycabas said, "What wonder are you
being turned into?" But, as he spoke, his mouth gaped wide, his nose
was rounded and his skin began to harden and to take on scales.   675
But Libys, while he was trying to twist the resisting oars away,
saw his hands shrink to a smaller size, and that now
they were hands no longer, now he can call them fins.
Another wanted to set his arms to work on the entangled ropes,
but he had no arms and, with a limbless body and flattened muzzle,   680
he leapt backwards into the waves: the very last part of his tail was curved
like the sinuous horns of the half moon.
They leapt in from every side, they were drenched with much spray,
and they emerged again and returned once more under the sea,
and they sported as if in a dance, and they tossed their playful   685
bodies, and took in and breathed out the sea through their broad noses.
Out of twenty just before (for that was the number the boat was carrying)
I alone was left: cold with fear, my body trembling,
and hardly in possession of myself, I was encouraged by the god saying,
                                                            "Shake off
the fear in your heart and hold the course for Dia." When I had been
                                                    conveyed there,
I joined the rites and celebrate the rites of Bacchus."'   691
      'We have given our ears to your long ramblings,' Pentheus
said, 'so that our anger could exhaust its strength in the delay.
Attendants, seize him instantly, torture his body
with grim torments and send him down to the Stygian night.'   695
Immediately, Tyrrhenian Acoetes was dragged off and shut away
in a secure place; and while they were preparing the cruel instruments
to bring about his death as ordered, the iron and the fires,
of their own accord the doors opened and the chains slipped   699
of their own accord from his arms, so the story goes, with no man to
                                                        release them.
      Echion's son persisted and did not any longer order others to go, but
                                                            proceeded
himself to where Cithaeron, chosen for the performance of the rites,
was resounding with the bacchants' songs and their clear voices.
As a spirited horse snorts when in war he hears the bugler's
signal on the sounding bronze and is inspired with a love of battle,   705
even so was Pentheus moved by the lengthy screamings striking
upon the ether and, as he heard their shouts, his anger glowed hot again.
About half way up the mountain side, there is, its edges surrounded
by woods, a plain free of trees and visible from every side.
Here, as he gazed upon the rites with sacrilegious eyes,   710
the first to see him, the first to be provoked into a mad charge,

prima suum misso uiolauit Penthea thyrso
mater et, 'o geminae,' clamauit, 'adeste, sorores!
ille aper, in nostris errat qui maximus agris,
715   ille mihi feriendus aper.' ruit omnis in unum
turba furens; cunctae coeunt fremituque sequuntur
iam trepidum, iam uerba minus uiolenta loquentem,
iam se damnantem, iam se peccasse fatentem.
saucius ille tamen, 'fer opem, matertera!' dixit,
720   'Autonoes moueant animos Actaeonis umbrae.'
illa quis Actaeon nescit dextramque precantis
abstulit; Inoo lacerata est altera raptu.
non habet infelix quae matri bracchia tendat,
trunca sed ostendens dereptis uulnera membris,
725   'aspice, mater!' ait. uisis ululauit Agaue
collaque iactauit mouitque per aera crinem
auulsumque caput digitis complexa cruentis
clamat, 'io comites, opus hoc uictoria nostra est.'
non citius frondes autumni frigore tactas
730   iamque male haerentes alta rapit arbore uentus,
quam sunt membra uiri manibus derepta nefandis.
     talibus exemplis monitae noua sacra frequentant
turaque dant sanctasque colunt Ismenides aras.

the first to throw a thyrsus at her Pentheus and wound him was
his mother and, 'Come here,' she cried, 'my sisters, both of you!
That great boar straying in our fields,
that boar is mine to strike.' The whole throng rushed   715
frenziedly on him alone; they all came together and he was noisily
                                                    pursued by them,
now terrified, now speaking less violent words,
now condemning himself, now admitting that he had sinned.
But, when he was wounded, he said, 'Aunt, help me!
May Autonoë's spirit be moved by Actaeon's shades.'   720
But she did not know who Actaeon was, and, as he prayed to her,
she pulled his right hand off while Ino snatched and tore his other hand.
The unhappy man had no arms to stretch out to his mother,
but, showing her the mutilated wounds where his limbs had been struck off,
he said, 'Look, mother!' Agaue saw them and screamed   725
and tossed her neck and moved her hair through the air
and wrenched his head off and embraced it with her bloody fingers
crying, 'Io, my companions, this deed is a victory for us.'
No more swiftly does the wind snatch from a tall tree the autumn leaves,
when they have been touched by the cold and are already scarcely clinging
                                                                  on,
than were the man's limbs torn apart by their abominable hands.   731
    With such examples to warn them, the Ismenides celebrated
the new rites, and gave them incense and worshipped at their holy altars.

LIBER IV

At non Alcithoe Minyeias orgia censet
accipienda dei, sed adhuc temeraria Bacchum
progeniem negat esse Iouis sociasque sorores
impietatis habet. festum celebrare sacerdos
5   immunesque operum famulas dominasque suorum
pectora pelle tegi, crinales soluere uittas,
serta coma, manibus frondentes sumere thyrsos
iusserat et saeuam laesi fore numinis iram
uaticinatus erat: parent matresque nurusque
10   telasque calathosque infectaque pensa reponunt
turaque dant Bacchumque uocant Bromiumque Lyaeumque
ignigenamque satumque iterum solumque bimatrem;
additur his Nyseus indetonsusque Thyoneus
et cum Lenaeo genialis consitor uuae
15   Nycteliusque Eleleusque parens et Iacchus et Euhan
et quae praeterea per Graias plurima gentes
nomina, Liber, habes; tibi enim inconsumpta iuuenta est,
tu puer aeternus, tu formosissimus alto
conspiceris caelo; tibi, cum sine cornibus adstas,
20   uirgineum caput est; Oriens tibi uictus adusque
decolor extremo qua tingitur India Gange.
Penthea tu, uenerande, bipenniferumque Lycurgum
sacrilegos mactas Tyrrhenaque mittis in aequor
corpora; tu biiugum pictis insignia frenis
25   colla premis lyncum; Bacchae Satyrique sequuntur,
quique senex ferula titubantes ebrius artus
sustinet et pando non fortiter haeret asello.
quacumque ingrederis, clamor iuuenalis et una
femineae uoces impulsaque tympana palmis
30   concauaque aera sonant longoque foramine buxus.
'placatus mitisque,' rogant Ismenides 'adsis,'
iussaque sacra colunt; solae Minyeides intus
intempestiua turbantes festa Minerua
aut ducunt lanas, aut stamina pollice uersant,
35   aut haerent telae famulasque laboribus urgent;
e quibus una leui deducens pollice filum,
'dum cessant aliae commentaque sacra frequentant,
nos quoque, quas Pallas, melior dea, detinet,' inquit,
'utile opus manuum uario sermone leuemus

BOOK IV

But it was not the judgement of Alcithoe, daughter of Minyas, that
                the god's
orgies should be accepted; she still recklessly denied
that Bacchus was Jove's offspring and she had sisters
as allies in this impiety. The priest had ordained that a feast day
be observed and that the housemaids and their ladies be released   5
from their work, cover their breasts with skins, undo the band
on their hair and set a garland in their locks and a leafy thyrsus
in their hands, and he prophesied fierce anger from the god
if he were slighted: the matrons and young women obeyed
and put away their looms, their baskets and their unfinished weaving   10
and gave incense and called on Bacchus and Bromius and Lyaeus,
the fire-born one, the sown again, and the only twice-mothered one;
and they added Nyseus to these and the unbarbered Thyoneus,
and the planter of the joyous grape together with Lenaeus,
Nyctelius, father Eleleus, Iacchus and Euhan   15
and the very many names you have besides, oh Liber,
throughout the Greek tribes; for inexhaustible youth is yours,
you are the eternal boy, you are revealed as the most handsome
in high heaven; when you stand there without your horns, yours
is the head of a maiden; you have conquered the East as far as   20
where swarthy India is moistened by the remote Ganges.
Pentheus and Lycurgus of the double axe were slain for their sacrilege
by you, whom we adore; you threw the bodies of the Tyrrhenians
into the sea; you weigh down the necks of double yoked lynxes,
glorious in their decorated harnesses; Bacchae and Satyrs follow you,   25
so does the drunken old man who props up his staggering limbs
with a stick and clings insecurely to his sway-backed ass.
Wherever you come, there is the sound of youthful shouting,
together with women's voices, the beating of palms on drums,
hollow brazen cymbals and the boxwood flute with its long stop.   30
    'Be with us in mercy and gentleness,' asked the Ismenides,
and observed the rites that had been ordered; only the Minyeides, staying
                in
to spoil the feast day with untimely service to Minerva,
were either spinning wool, or using their thumbs to twist the strands,
or staying close to the loom and keeping their maidservants at their tasks;
one of them, as she was drawing off a thread with her nimble thumb,   36
said, 'While the other women are idle and celebrating spurious rites,
let us who are kept here by Pallas, a better goddess,
lighten the useful work of our hands with tales of every kind,

40 perque uices aliquid, quod tempora longa uideri
  non sinat, in medium uacuas referamus ad aures.'
  dicta probant primamque iubent narrare sorores;
  illa quid e multis referat (nam plurima norat)
  cogitat et dubia est, de te, Babylonia, narret,
45 Derceti, quam uersa squamis uelantibus artus
  stagna Palaestini credunt motasse figura,
  an magis ut sumptis illius filia pennis
  extremos albis in turribus egerit annos,
  Nais an ut cantu nimiumque potentibus herbis
50 uerterit in tacitos iuuenalia corpora pisces
  donec idem passa est, an, quae poma alba ferebat,
  ut nunc nigra ferat contactu sanguinis arbor.
  hoc placet; haec quoniam uulgaris fabula non est,
  talibus orsa modis lana sua fila sequente:
55 'Pyramus et Thisbe, iuuenum pulcherrimus alter,
  altera, quas Oriens habuit, praelata puellis,
  contiguas tenuere domos, ubi dicitur altam
  coctilibus muris cinxisse Semiramis urbem.
  notitiam primosque gradus uicinia fecit;
60 tempore creuit amor; taedae quoque iure coissent,
  sed uetuere patres; quod non potuere uetare,
  ex aequo captis ardebant mentibus ambo.
  conscius omnis abest; nutu signisque loquuntur,
  quoque magis tegitur, tectus magis aestuat ignis.
65 fissus erat tenui rima, quam duxerat olim
  cum fieret, paries domui communis utrique.
  id uitium nulli per saecula longa notatum
  (quid non sentit amor?) primi uidistis amantes
  et uocis fecistis iter, tutaeque per illud
70 murmure blanditiae minimo transire solebant.
  saepe, ubi constiterant hinc Thisbe, Pyramus illinc,
  inque uices fuerat captatus anhelitus oris,
  "inuide," dicebant, "paries, quid amantibus obstas?
  quantum erat ut sineres toto nos corpore iungi,
75 aut, hoc si nimium est, uel ad oscula danda pateres?
  nec sumus ingrati, tibi nos debere fatemur
  quod datus est uerbis ad amicas transitus aures."
   talia diuersa nequiquam sede locuti
  sub noctem dixere, "uale," partique dedere
80 oscula quisque suae non peruenientia contra.
  postera nocturnos aurora remouerat ignes

taking turns to relate to all our ready ears something   40
which will not allow the time to seem so long.'
Her sisters approved her words and asked her to be the first to tell a
                                                                  story;
she thought about which of many (for she knew very many) she should
                                                                  relate
and she wondered if she should tell about you, Dercetis
of Babylon, who, the Palestinians believe, changed her shape   45
and covered her limbs in scales and disturbed the ponds,
or rather how her daughter put on wings
and spent her last years in whitened towers,
or how a Naiad used an incantation and herbs of excessive power
to turn the bodies of young men into silent fish   50
until she suffered the same thing, or how a tree, which used to bear
white fruit, now, from being touched by blood, bears black.
She decided on this one; since this tale was not well known
she started thus while the wool was following its threads:
'Pyramus and Thisbe, one the most handsome of young men,   55
the other pre-eminent among the girls of the East,
lived in adjacent houses in the lofty city which, it is said,
Semiramis had ringed with walls of baked bricks.
Their nearness made for acquaintance and first approaches;
love grew with time; they would have joined in lawful marriage too,   60
but their fathers forbade it; but, and this could not be forbidden,
both burned equally in their captivated hearts.
No one was there to share their secret, they used nods and signs for
                                                                  speech,
and the more that it was hidden, the more their hidden fire blazed up.
There was a split in the party wall of the two houses   65
along a crack which had been caused long ago when it was being built.
This fault, which no one had noticed in many a long year,
(what does love not sense?) was first seen by you lovers,
and you made it a path for words, and safely through it
in the lowest of whispers, your endearments crossed.   70
Often, when Thisbe had taken her place on one side and Pyramus on the
                                                                  other,
and they had in turns caught the sighs that they mouthed,
"Jealous wall," they used to say, "why do you obstruct lovers?
What would it be for you to let us embrace with all our body,
or, if that is too much, for you at least to open up and let us kiss? 75
We are not ungrateful, we admit that it is to you we owe it
that our words have been given a passage to loving ears."
    After speaking in vain like this from their separate positions,
at nightfall they said, "Good-bye," and each of them gave
to their own side kisses which did not get through.   80
The next dawn had dispersed the fires of the night

solque pruinosas radiis siccauerat herbas:
ad solitum coiere locum. tum murmure paruo
multa prius questi, statuunt ut nocte silenti
85   fallere custodes foribusque excedere temptent,
cumque domo exierint, urbis quoque tecta relinquant,
neue sit errandum lato spatiantibus aruo,
conueniant ad busta Nini lateantque sub umbra
arboris: arbor ibi niueis uberrima pomis,
90   ardua morus, erat, gelido contermina fonti.
pacta placent; et lux, tarde discedere uisa,
praecipitatur aquis, et aquis nox exit ab isdem.
callida per tenebras uersato cardine Thisbe
egreditur fallitque suos adopertaque uultum
95   peruenit ad tumulum dictaque sub arbore sedit.
audacem faciebat amor: uenit ecce recenti
caede leaena boum spumantes oblita rictus
depositura sitim uicini fontis in unda;
quam procul ad lunae radios Babylonia Thisbe
100   uidit et obscurum timido pede fugit in antrum,
dumque fugit, tergo uelamina lapsa reliquit.
ut lea saeua sitim multa compescuit unda,
dum redit in siluas, inuentos forte sine ipsa
ore cruentato tenues laniauit amictus.
105   serius egressus uestigia uidit in alto
puluere certa ferae totoque expalluit ore
Pyramus; ut uero uestem quoque sanguine tinctam
repperit, "una duos," inquit, "nox perdet amantes,
e quibus illa fuit longa dignissima uita,
110   nostra nocens anima est. ego te, miseranda, peremi,
in loca plena metus qui iussi nocte uenires
nec prior huc ueni. nostrum diuellite corpus
et scelerata fero consumite uiscera morsu,
o quicumque sub hac habitatis rupe leones:
115   sed timidi est optare necem." uelamina Thisbes
tollit et ad pactae secum fert arboris umbram
utque dedit notae lacrimas, dedit oscula uesti,
"accipe nunc," inquit, "nostri quoque sanguinis haustus."
quoque erat accinctus, demisit in ilia ferrum,
120   nec mora, feruenti moriens e uulnere traxit.
ut iacuit resupinus humo, cruor emicat alte,
non aliter quam cum uitiato fistula plumbo
scinditur et tenues stridente foramine longe

and the sun's rays had dried the frosty grass:
they met at their usual place. Then, in a low whisper,
after much complaining, they decided that in the silence of the night
they would slip past their guards and try to get out through the doors,   85
and, when they had escaped the house, that they would leave the city and
its buildings too,
and, in case they should get lost as they wandered in the extensive
countryside,
that they would meet at Ninus' tomb and hide in the shadow
of a tree: there was a tree there most luxuriant with snowy fruit,
a tall mulberry, close up against a cool spring.   90
They approved this plan; and the sunlight, which had seemed slow to
depart,
rushed down into the waters, and from the same waters there came the
night.
Skilfully in the darkness Thisbe turned the door hinge
and emerged, she slipped past the household and, with her face covered,
arrived at the burial mound and sat, as they had said, beneath the tree. 95
Love made her bold. Look, there came a lioness,
jaws foaming and smeared with the blood from freshly slaughtered cattle,
to relieve her thirst in the water of the spring nearby;
Babylonian Thisbe saw her from afar by the moon's
rays and fled on timid feet into a dark cave,   100
and, as she fled, her shawl slipped from her back and was left behind.
When the lioness had eased her fierce thirst with much water,
and as she was returning to the woods, she chanced to find the thin
garment without its owner and she tore at it with her bloody mouth.
Later there emerged, to see in the deep dust   105
the clear tracks of the beast and to grow pale in all his face,
Pyramus; but when he found her clothing too all drenched
in blood, "One night," he said, "will destroy two lovers;
of the two of us, she most deserved a long life;
mine was the guilty soul. I have struck you down, oh piteous one,   110
I who told you to come by night into this fearful place,
and did not come here before you. Rend my body apart
and devour with your fierce bite my sinful bowels,
oh whatever lions you are that live by this rock:
but it is a timid man that only prays for death." He picked up Thisbe's 115
shawl and took it with him to the shadow of the tree they had agreed on,
and when he had given tears and given kisses to the familiar clothing,
"Take now," he said, "a draught of my blood too."
And he plunged the sword that he was girded with into his side
and, without delay, as he was dying, drew it from the boiling wound.   120
As he lay face up upon the earth, blood spurted high,
just as when a pipe with faulty lead
bursts and hissing through the hole there is a long thin

eiaculatur aquas atque ictibus aera rumpit.
125   arborei fetus aspergine caedis in atram
uertuntur faciem, madefactaque sanguine radix
purpureo tingit pendentia mora colore.
      ecce metu nondum posito, ne fallat amantem,
illa redit iuuenemque oculis animoque requirit,
130   quantaque uitarit narrare pericula gestit;
utque locum et uisa cognoscit in arbore formam,
sic facit incertam pomi color: haeret, an haec sit.
dum dubitat, tremebunda uidet pulsare cruentum
membra solum retroque pedem tulit oraque buxo
135   pallidiora gerens exhorruit aequoris instar,
quod tremit, exigua cum summum stringitur aura.
sed postquam remorata suos cognouit amores,
percutit indignos claro plangore lacertos
et laniata comas amplexaque corpus amatum
140   uulnera suppleuit lacrimis fletumque cruori
miscuit et gelidis in uultibus oscula figens,
"Pyrame," clamauit, "quis te mihi casus ademit?
Pyrame, responde! tua te, carissime, Thisbe
nominat: exaudi uultusque attolle iacentes."
145   ad nomen Thisbes oculos iam morte grauatos
Pyramus erexit uisaque recondidit illa.
quae postquam uestemque suam cognouit et ense
uidit ebur uacuum, "tua te manus," inquit, "amorque
perdidit, infelix. est et mihi fortis in unum
150   hoc manus, est et amor: dabit hic in uulnera uires.
persequar extinctum letique miserrima dicar
causa comesque tui; quique a me morte reuelli,
heu, sola poteras, poteris nec morte reuelli.
hoc tamen amborum uerbis estote rogati,
155   o multum miseri, meus illiusque parentes,
ut quos certus amor, quos hora nouissima iunxit,
componi tumulo non inuideatis eodem.
at tu, quae ramis arbor miserabile corpus
nunc tegis unius, mox es tectura duorum,
160   signa tene caedis pullosque et luctibus aptos
semper habe fetus, gemini monimenta cruoris."
dixit et aptato pectus mucrone sub imum
incubuit ferro, quod adhuc a caede tepebat.
uota tamen tetigere deos, tetigere parentes:

jet of water which cleaves the air with its impact.
The tree's fruits were changed in appearance and made dark   125
by the spattering of the blood, and the root, soaked with blood,
tinged the hanging mulberries with a purple colour.
     Look, though she had not yet laid aside her fear, still, so as not to
                                        disappoint her lover,
she returned to search for the young man with her eyes and with her
                                                        heart,
and she was itching to tell him what great dangers she had eluded.   130
And although she recognized the place and the shape of the tree that she
                                                    had seen,
yet the colour of the fruit made her uncertain: she was stuck as to
                                        whether this was it.
While she was hesitating, she tremblingly saw a body writhing
on the bloody ground and she drew back shuddering,
with a face paler than boxwood, like the sea   135
that is ruffled when a slight breeze skims across its surface.
But after a pause when she had recognized her love,
she struck her blameless arms with a loud blow,
tore at her hair, embraced the body that she loved,
filled his wounds with tears and mixed her weeping   140
with his blood and, planting kisses on his cold face,
"Pyramus," she cried, "what misfortune has taken you from me?
Pyramus, answer! It is your Thisbe, dearest, who
is calling you: listen to me, lift up your drooping head."
At Thisbe's name, Pyramus raised his eyes that were by now   145
heavy with death, he saw her and closed them again.
And after she had recognized her clothing and had seen
his ivory empty of its sword, "Your hand," she said, "and love
have destroyed you, unhappy one. But I too have a hand strong   149
for this one thing, and I have love too: it will give the strength to wound.
I shall follow you into extinction and I shall be called the most wretched
                                                        cause
and companion of your death; and you, who could have been torn from me
by death, alas, alone, cannot now be torn from me even by death.
But this you must be asked by the words of both of us,
oh most wretched parents, mine and his,   155
not to begrudge that those that a sure love, those that their last hour·
joined be laid to rest in the same mound.
But you, oh tree, whose branches cover now
one pitiable body, and soon will cover two,
keep the marks of the killing and always have sombre   160
fruits fit for griefs, memorials of a double act of bloodshed."
She spoke, and, with its point fitted against the bottom of her breast
she fell upon his sword which was still warm from his killing.
But her prayers touched the gods and touched the parents:

165   nam color in pomo est, ubi permaturuit, ater,
          quodque rogis superest, una requiescit in urna.'
             desierat, mediumque fuit breue tempus, et orsa est
          dicere Leuconoe; uocem tenuere sorores.
          'hunc quoque, siderea qui temperat omnia luce,
170   cepit amor Solem; Solis referemus amores.
          primus adulterium Veneris cum Marte putatur
          hic uidisse deus; uidet hic deus omnia primus.
          indoluit facto Iunonigenaeque marito
          furta tori furtique locum monstrauit. at illi
175   et mens et quod opus fabrilis dextra tenebat
          excidit: extemplo graciles ex aere catenas
          retiaque et laqueos, quae lumina fallere possent,
          elimat (non illud opus tenuissima uincant
          stamina, non summo quae pendet aranea tigno),
180   utque leues tactus momentaque parua sequantur
          efficit et lecto circumdata collocat apte.
          ut uenere torum coniunx et adulter in unum,
          arte uiri uinclisque noua ratione paratis
          in mediis ambo deprensi amplexibus haerent.
185   Lemnius extemplo ualuas patefecit eburnas
          immisitque deos: illi iacuere ligati
          turpiter, atque aliquis de dis non tristibus optat
          sic fieri turpis; superi risere, diuque
          haec fuit in toto notissima fabula caelo.
190   exigit indicii memorem Cythereia poenam
          inque uices illum, tectos qui laesit amores,
          laedit amore pari. quid nunc, Hyperione nate,
          forma colorque tibi radiataque lumina prosunt?
          nempe tuis omnes qui terras ignibus uris,
195   ureris igne nouo, quique omnia cernere debes,
          Leucothoen spectas et uirgine figis in una
          quos mundo debes oculos. modo surgis Eoo
          temperius caelo, modo serius incidis undis
          spectandique mora brumales porrigis horas.
200   deficis interdum, uitiumque in lumina mentis
          transit, et obscurus mortalia pectora terres.
          nec, tibi quod lunae terris propioris imago
          obstiterit, palles: facit hunc amor iste colorem.
          diligis hanc unam, nec te Clymeneque Rhodosque
205   nec tenet Aeaeae genetrix pulcherrima Circes,
          quaeque tuos Clytie, quamuis despecta, petebat

for the colour in the fruit, when it has ripened, is black,   165
and what remained from the pyres rests in a single urn.'
     She had stopped, and there was a brief interval; then Leuconoe
began to speak; her sisters held their tongues.
'Even this Sun, who regulates all things with his starry
light, was caught by love: I shall tell the loves of the Sun.   170
It is thought that he was the first god to see Venus'
adultery with Mars: this is the god who is first to see everything.
He was pained by the deed and showed to the Juno-born
husband the violation of his marriage bed and the place of that violation.
                                                                   But he
lost both his mind and the task that his craftsman's hand   175
was holding: immediately he fashioned slender chains
from bronze and nets and snares which could deceive
the eye (the finest strands could not outdo
that work, nor the spider's web that hangs from the highest beam),
and he made them so that they would yield to a light touch and small 180
movements and he placed them skilfully around the bed.
When the wife and the adulterer had come to the same couch,
the husband's skill and his chains prepared in novel style
held them both fixed in the middle of their embrace.
Immediately, the Lemnian opened up his ivory doors   185
and let the gods in: they were lying there bound
shamefully, and one of the unabashed gods was saying he would like
to be put to shame like that: the gods laughed and for a long time
this was the best known tale in the whole of heaven.
     Cythereia exacted a punishment to keep the informer in remembrance
hurting him in his turn with an equal love   191
for hurting her hidden love. What good to you, son of Hyperion,
were your beauty and colour now, or your radiant light.
For, as we know, you, who can burn all the lands with your fires,
were being burnt by a new fire, and you, who ought to look at all things,
were gazing at Leucothoe and fixing on one maiden   196
eyes which ought to have been on the world. Sometimes you rose from the
                                                                       dawn
sky too early, sometimes you set beneath the waves too late
and the delay while you gazed upon her stretched out the hours of the
                                                                winter's day.
From time to time, your light failed as the fault in your mind passed   200
to your rays and your darkness frightened mortal hearts.
And it was not because the shadow of the moon too near was blocking off
                                                                   the lands
from you that you went dim: it was love that made you that colour.
You loved her alone and were taken neither by Clymene nor by Rhodos,
nor by Aeaean Circe's most beautiful mother,   205
nor by Clytie who, though you despised her, wanted

concubitus ipsoque illo graue uulnus habebat
tempore: Leucothoe multarum obliuia fecit,
gentis odoriferae quam formosissima partu
210 edidit Eurynome; sed postquam filia creuit,
quam mater cunctas, tam matrem filia uicit.
rexit Achaemenias urbes pater Orchamus isque
septimus a prisco numeratur origine Belo.
axe sub Hesperio sunt pascua Solis equorum:
215 ambrosiam pro gramine habent; ea fessa diurnis
membra ministeriis nutrit reparatque labori.
dumque ibi quadripedes caelestia pabula carpunt
noxque uicem peragit, thalamos deus intrat amatos
uersus in Eurynomes faciem genetricis et inter
220 bis sex Leucothoen famulas ad lumina cernit
leuia uersato ducentem stamina fuso.
ergo ubi ceu mater carae dedit oscula natae,
"res," ait, "arcana est: famulae, discedite, neue
eripite arbitrium matri secreta loquendi."
225 paruerant, thalamoque deus sine teste relicto,
"ille ego sum," dixit, "qui longum metior annum,
omnia qui uideo, per quem uidet omnia tellus,
mundi oculus: mihi, crede, places." pauet illa metuque
et colus et fusus digitis cecidere remissis.
230 ipse timor decuit, nec longius ille moratus
in ueram rediit speciem solitumque nitorem.
at uirgo, quamuis inopino territa uisu,
uicta nitore dei posita uim passa querella est.
   inuidit Clytie (neque enim moderatus in illa
235 Solis amor fuerat) stimulataque paelicis ira
uulgat adulterium diffamatumque parenti
indicat; ille ferox immansuetusque precantem
tendentemque manus ad lumina Solis et, "ille
uim tulit inuitae," dicentem defodit alta
240 crudus humo tumulumque super grauis addit harenae.
dissipat hunc radiis Hyperione natus iterque
dat tibi, qua possis defossos promere uultus;
nec tu iam poteras enectum pondere terrae
tollere, nympha, caput corpusque exsangue iacebas.
245 nil illo fertur uolucrum moderator equorum
post Phaethonteos uidisse dolentius ignes.

to sleep with you and felt deeply wounded by you at that very
time: Leucothoe brought forgetfulness of many girls;
Eurynome, the loveliest from the perfume-bearing race,
had given birth to her; but, when the daughter had grown up,   210
the daughter surpassed the mother by as much as the mother had all
                                                              others.
Orchamus, her father, reigned over the Achaemenian cities, and he
was counted seventh in line from ancient Belus, their founder.
Under the Western sky are the pastures of the Sun's horses:
they have ambrosia instead of grass; that is what feeds their limbs, 215
tired from the tasks of the day, and refreshes them for work.
And while the steeds were browsing on the heavenly fodder there
and night had taken up her turn, the god entered the beloved bedroom,
having been turned into the likeness of Eurynome, her mother, and in the
                                                              lamplight
beheld Leucothoe among her twice six housemaids   220
drawing the light strand from the turning spindle.
Then he gave her a kiss as a mother does to her dear daughter
and said, "This is a private matter; depart, housemaids, and don't
deprive a mother of her right to tell her secrets."
They obeyed and the god, now that the bedroom had been left without a
                                                              witness,
said, "I am the one who measures the long year,   226
who sees all things, through whom the earth sees all things,
the world's eye: you delight me, do believe it." She panicked and, in her
                                                              fright,
let both the distaff and the spindle fall from her limp fingers.
Fear itself became her, and delaying no longer   230
he returned to his true likeness and his usual radiance.
But the maiden, though terrified by the unexpected sight,
was overwhelmed by the god's radiance and suffered his violence without
                                                              complaint.

     Clytie was jealous, for her love of the Sun
had not been restrained and, with her anger at the wench aroused,   235
she broadcast the adultery and informed the girl's father
of the story she had spread; he was fierce and intractable to his daughter's
                                                              pleas
and, as she stretched her hands up to the Sun's light saying, "It was he
that took me violently against my will," he savagely buried her
deep in the ground and piled a heavy mound of sand upon her.   240
Hyperion's son scattered it with his rays and gave
you a way through which you could bring out your buried face.
But, oh nymph, you could not raise your head
killed by the weight of the earth and you lay there, a bloodless body.
They say that that driver of swift horses had seen   245
nothing more painful since Phaethon's fires.

ille quidem gelidos radiorum uiribus artus
si queat in uiuum temptat reuocare calorem,
sed quoniam tantis fatum conatibus obstat
250 nectare odorato sparsit corpusque locumque,
multaque praequestus, "tanges tamen aethera," dixit.
protinus imbutum caelesti nectare corpus
delicuit terramque suo madefecit odore,
uirgaque per glaebas sensim radicibus actis
255 turea surrexit tumulumque cacumine rupit.
    at Clytien, quamuis amor excusare dolorem
indiciumque dolor poterat, non amplius auctor
lucis adit Venerisque modum sibi fecit in illa.
tabuit ex illo dementer amoribus usa
260 nympharum impatiens et sub Ioue nocte dieque
sedit humo nuda nudis incompta capillis.
perque nouem luces expers undaeque cibique
rore mero lacrimisque suis ieiunia pauit,
nec se mouit humo: tantum spectabat euntis
265 ora dei uultusque suos flectebat ad illum.
membra ferunt haesisse solo, partemque coloris
luridus exsangues pallor conuertit in herbas;
est in parte rubor, uiolaeque simillimus ora
flos tegit. illa suum, quamuis radice tenetur,
270 uertitur ad Solem mutataque seruat amorem.'
    dixerat, et factum mirabile ceperat aures;
pars fieri potuisse negant, pars omnia ueros
posse deos memorant; sed non est Bacchus in illis.
    poscitur Alcithoe, postquam siluere sorores.
275 quae radio stantis percurrens stamina telae,
'uulgatos taceo,' dixit, 'pastoris amores
Daphnidis Idaei, quem nymphe paelicis ira
contulit in saxum: tantus dolor urit amantes,
nec loquor ut quondam naturae iure nouato
280 ambiguus fuerit modo uir, modo femina Sithon.
te quoque, nunc adamas, quondam fidissime paruo,
Celmi, Ioui largoque satos Curetas ab imbri
et Crocon in paruos uersum cum Smilace flores
praetereo, dulcique animos nouitate tenebo.
285 unde sit infamis, quare male fortibus undis
Salmacis eneruet tactosque remolliat artus,
discite. causa latet, uis est notissima fontis.
Mercurio puerum diua Cythereide natum
Naides Idaeis enutriuere sub antris,
290 cuius erat facies in qua materque paterque

He tried, in case he could use the strength of his rays
to restore her chilled limbs to warm life,
but since fate opposed so great an enterprise
he sprinkled perfumed nectar on the body and on the place   250
and, after many precomplaints, he said, "But you will touch the ether."
Immediately the body, drenched in heavenly nectar,
melted away and soaked the earth with its perfume
and throughout the plot there gradually rose up, driven by its roots,
a sprig of incense breaking through the mound with its tip.   255
     But Clytie, though love could have excused her spite,
and spite her turning informer, was approached no more
by the source of light, who brought his Venus with her to an end.
From then on she wasted away, for she had loved insanely;
she could not endure the nymphs and sat night and day   260
beneath Jove's sky on the bare earth, bare headed, her hair uncombed.
And for nine days, without food or water,
she fed her hunger on just dew and tears,
and she did not move from the ground: she merely gazed at the
                             countenance
of the god as he went by and turned her face towards him.   265
They say her limbs stuck to the ground and a ghastly pallor
turned part of her complexion into a bloodless plant,
but there was a ruddy part, and a flower, very like the violet,
covered her face. Though held by a root, she turned
towards her Sun and, though transformed, she kept her love.'   270
     She had spoken, and their ears were captivated by the amazing event.
Some said it could not have happened, some pointed out that true gods
could do anything; but Bacchus was not one of them.
     They called for Alcithoe after her sisters had fallen silent.
And as she ran through the warp with the shuttle of the standing loom, 275
'I am silent,' she said, 'about the well-known loves of Daphnis,
the shepherd of Ida, who was turned into a rock by a nymph
angered by his wench: such is the spite that burns in lovers,
and I am not speaking about how, by a change in the law of nature,
equivocal Sithon was sometimes a man, sometimes a woman.   280
You too, Celmis, now a block of adamant but once most faithful
to the young Jove, and the Curetes, born from a heavy shower,
and Crocos who, with Smilax, was turned into tiny flowers,
I pass over these, but I shall hold your attention with a charming novelty.
Why Salmacis is thought ill of, how the evil strength   285
of its waters enfeebles and softens the limbs they touch
you must learn. The cause is obscure, but the power of the spring is most
                             famous.
There was a boy born to Mercury and the goddess of Cythera
and cared for by the Naiads in the caves of Ida;
his was a face in which both mother and father   290

cognosci possent; nomen quoque traxit ab illis.
is tria cum primum fecit quinquennia, montes
deseruit patrios Idaque altrice relicta
ignotis errare locis, ignota uidere
295   flumina gaudebat, studio minuente laborem.
ille etiam Lycias urbes Lyciaeque propinquos
Caras adit: uidet hic stagnum lucentis ad imum
usque solum lymphae. non illic canna palustris
nec steriles uluae nec acuta cuspide iunci:
300   perspicuus liquor est, stagni tamen ultima uiuo
caespite cinguntur semperque uirentibus herbis.
nympha colit, sed nec uenatibus apta nec arcus
flectere quae soleat nec quae contendere cursu,
solaque Naiadum celeri non nota Dianae.
305   saepe suas illi fama est dixisse sorores,
"Salmaci, uel iaculum uel pictas sume pharetras,
et tua cum duris uenatibus otia misce."
nec iaculum sumit nec pictas illa pharetras,
nec sua cum duris uenatibus otia miscet;
310   sed modo fonte suo formosos perluit artus,
saepe Cytoriaco deducit pectine crines
et quid se deceat spectatas consulit undas;
nunc perlucenti circumdata corpus amictu
mollibus aut foliis aut mollibus incubat herbis;
315   saepe legit flores. et tum quoque forte legebat,
cum puerum uidit uisumque optauit habere.
nec tamen ante adiit, etsi properabat adire,
quam se composuit, quam circumspexit amictus
et finxit uultum et meruit formosa uideri.
320   tum sic orsa loqui: "puer o dignissime credi
esse deus, seu tu deus es, potes esse Cupido,
siue es mortalis, qui te genuere, beati
et frater felix et fortunata profecto,
si qua tibi soror est, et quae dedit ubera nutrix.
325   sed longe cunctis longeque beatior illis,
si qua tibi sponsa est, si quam dignabere taeda.
haec tibi siue aliqua est, mea sit furtiua uoluptas,
seu nulla est, ego sim, thalamumque ineamus eundem."
Nais ab his tacuit; pueri rubor ora notauit
330   (nescit enim quid amor) sed et erubuisse decebat.
hic color aprica pendentibus arbore pomis
aut ebori tincto est aut sub candore rubenti,
cum frustra resonant aera auxiliaria, lunae.

could be recognized; and he took his name from them.
As soon as he had lived three times five years, he left
his father's mountains and abandoned Ida where he had been brought up
and began to enjoy wandering in unfamiliar places and seeing
unfamiliar rivers with a zeal that made light of toil.   295
He even went to the Lycian cities and to the Lycians' neighbours,
the Carians: here he saw a pond of water
gleaming all the way to the bottom. There was no marsh reed there,
nor barren sedge, nor rushes with pointed tips:
the water was clear, but the edge of the pond was surrounded   300
by a fresh lawn, with grass that was always green.
A nymph lived there, not one that was good at hunting or used
to bending a bow or competing in a chase,
and the only one of the Naiads unknown to swift Diana.
The story is that her sisters had often said to her,   305
"Salmacis, take up the javelin or the painted quiver
and vary your leisure with a strenuous hunt."
She did not take up the javelin, nor the painted quiver
nor did she vary her leisure with a strenuous hunt;
but sometimes she washed her beautiful limbs in her spring   310
and often she drew her hair out with a Cytorian comb
and gazed into the waters to see what would become her;
and then she wrapped her body in a shining dress
or lay down on the soft leaves or on the soft grass;
often she picked flowers. And then too she happened to be picking them
when she saw the boy and, on seeing him, she wanted to possess him.   316
But she did not approach him, though she was eager to approach him,
till she had composed herself, till she had inspected her dress
and arranged her expression and achieved a beautiful appearance.
This was how she then began to speak: "Oh boy, most worthy to be thought
a god or, if you are a god, you could be Cupid,   321
but if you are a mortal, blest are those who gave you birth,
your brother is a lucky man and, if you have a sister,
she is fortunate too and so is the nurse who gave the breast to you.
But far, far more blest than all of them is that girl,   325
if there is one, that is engaged to you, if you think that there is any that
                                deserves the wedding torch.
If you have someone, let mine be a secret pleasure,
but if you have no one, let me be her and let us go into the marriage bed
                                                together."
With this, the Naiad fell silent and a blush appeared on the boy's cheek
(for he did not know what love was) but even to blush became him.   330
He was the colour of apples hanging from a sun drenched tree,
or of stained ivory or of the moon grown red
in the midst of her brightness while the relieving bronze sounds out in
                                                vain.

poscenti nymphae sine fine sororia saltem
335   oscula iamque manus ad eburnea colla ferenti,
"desinis? an fugio tecumque," ait, "ista relinquo?"
Salmacis extimuit, "loca" que "haec tibi libera trado,
hospes," ait simulatque gradu discedere uerso,
tum quoque respiciens, fruticumque recondita silua
340   delituit flexuque genu submisit; at ille,
scilicet ut uacuis et inobseruatus in herbis,
huc it et hinc illuc et in adludentibus undis
summa pedum taloque tenus uestigia tingit;
nec mora, temperie blandarum captus aquarum
345   mollia de tenero uelamina corpore ponit.
tum uero placuit, nudaeque cupidine formae
Salmacis exarsit; flagrant quoque lumina nymphae,
non aliter quam cum puro nitidissimus orbe
opposita speculi referitur imagine Phoebus,
350   uixque moram patitur, uix iam sua gaudia differt,
iam cupit amplecti, iam se male continet amens.
ille cauis uelox applauso corpore palmis
desilit in latices alternaque bracchia ducens
in liquidis translucet aquis, ut eburnea si quis
355   signa tegat claro uel candida lilia uitro.
"uicimus et meus est," exclamat Nais, et omni
ueste procul iacta mediis immittitur undis
pugnantemque tenet luctantiaque oscula carpit
subiectatque manus inuitaque pectora tangit
360   et nunc hac iuueni, nunc circumfunditur illac.
denique nitentem contra elabique uolentem
implicat, ut serpens quam regia sustinet ales
sublimemque rapit (pendens caput illa pedesque
alligat et cauda spatiantes implicat alas),
365   utue solent hederae longos intexere truncos,
utque sub aequoribus deprensum polypus hostem
continet ex omni dimissis parte flagellis.
perstat Atlantiades sperataque gaudia nymphae
denegat: illa premit commissaque corpore toto
370   sicut inhaerebat, "pugnes licet, improbe," dixit,
"non tamen effugies. ita di iubeatis, et istum
nulla dies a me nec me diducat ab isto."
uota suos habuere deos: nam mixta duorum
corpora iunguntur faciesque inducitur illis
375.   una; uelut, si quis conducat cortice ramos,

The nymph was endlessly demanding sisterly kisses
at least, and was already putting her hands on his ivory-coloured neck, 335
when he said, "Will you stop? Or shall I run away and leave all this and
                                                        you?"
Salmacis was terrified and said, "I give you this place
freely, stranger," and she turned on her heel and pretended to depart,
but even then she looked back and, hiding in a forest of bushes,
concealed herself by crouching down, knees bent; but he,   340
supposing that he was unobserved on the deserted grass,
went here and there and everywhere dipping just the tips of his feet,
then up to his ankles, into the playful waters;
and there was no delay before he was captivated by the sweet and
                                                temperate waters
and took the soft clothing from his delicate body.   345
Then indeed he gave pleasure and Salmacis burned with desire
for his naked beauty: and the nymph's eyes were aflame too,
just as when Phoebus' orb, clear and at its brightest,
is reflected in the image of a mirror facing it.
She could scarcely bear delay, scarcely put off her pleasure,   350
now she wanted to embrace him, now in her madness she could hardly
                                                contain herself.
He swiftly jumped down into the waters slapping his body
with hollowed palms and, plying his arms in turn,
he gleamed through the transparent waters just like an ivory statue
or white lilies if someone encases them in clear glass.   355
"I have won, and he is mine," cried out the Naiad, and she threw
all her clothing well away from her and rushed into the middle of the
                                                waters
and held him as he fought against her, violently snatching kisses
and bringing her hands up under him and touching his unwilling breast;
and now she draped herself around the youth this way and that.   360
At last, though he struggled against her in his desire to get away,
she entwined herself around him like a snake picked up by the king of birds
and snatched aloft (as she hangs from him she binds his head
and feet and entwines her tail around his spreading wings),
or like ivy which likes to weave its way up tall tree trunks,   365
or like an octopus catching and holding its enemy
beneath the sea by spreading its tentacles in all directions.
Atlas' great-grandson resisted and refused the nymph the pleasures
that she hoped for; but she pressed on and, touching him with all her body
as she clung to him, "Though you fight me, you rascal," she said,   370
"you still will not escape. Oh gods may you so order it, and let
no day take him away from me or me from him."
Her prayers were granted by the gods: for their two bodies
were mingled and joined, and they put on the appearance
of one; just as, if someone puts branches through a tree's bark,   375

crescendo iungi pariterque adolescere cernit,
sic, ubi complexu coierunt membra tenaci,
nec duo sunt sed forma duplex, nec femina dici
nec puer ut possit, neutrumque et utrumque uidentur.
380 ergo ubi se liquidas, quo uir descenderat, undas
semimarem fecisse uidet mollitaque in illis
membra, manus tendens, sed iam non uoce uirili
Hermaphroditus ait; "nato date munera uestro,
et pater et genetrix, amborum nomen habenti:
385 quisquis in hos fontes uir uenerit, exeat inde
semiuir et tactis subito mollescat in undis."
motus uterque parens nati rata uerba biformis
fecit et incesto fontem medicamine tinxit.'
 finis erat dictis, et adhuc Minyeia proles
390 urget opus spernitque deum festumque profanat,
tympana cum subito non apparentia raucis
obstrepuere sonis et adunco tibia cornu
tinnulaque aera sonant et olent murraeque crocique,
resque fide maior, coepere uirescere telae
395 inque hederae faciem pendens frondescere uestis.
pars abit in uites et, quae modo fila fuerunt,
palmite mutantur; de stamine pampinus exit;
purpura fulgorem pictis accommodat uuis.
iamque dies exactus erat tempusque subibat,
400 quod tu nec tenebras nec possis dicere lucem
sed cum luce tamen dubiae confinia noctis.
tecta repente quati pinguesque ardere uidentur
lampades et rutilis conlucere ignibus aedes
falsaque saeuarum simulacra ululare ferarum.
405 fumida iamdudum latitant per tecta sorores
diuersaeque locis ignes ac lumina uitant;
dumque petunt tenebras, paruos membrana per artus
porrigitur tenuique includit bracchia penna.
nec qua perdiderint ueterem ratione figuram
410 scire sinunt tenebrae. non illas pluma leuauit:
sustinuere tamen se perlucentibus alis.
conataeque loqui minimam et pro corpore uocem
emittunt peraguntque leues stridore querellas,
tectaque, non siluas celebrant lucemque perosae
415 nocte uolant seroque tenent a uespere nomen.
 tum uero totis Bacchi memorabile Thebis
nomen erat, magnasque noui matertera uires
narrat ubique dei, de totque sororibus expers

he sees them joined as they grow and maturing together,
so, when their bodies had come together in a clinging embrace,
they were not two, but they had a dual form that could be said to be
neither woman nor boy, they seemed to be neither and both,   379
    And so, when he saw that the transparent waters, to which he had
gone down
a man, had made him a half-male, and that his limbs had been made soft
in them, Hermaphroditus stretched out his hands and said,
but no longer with a man's voice, "Grant your son a favour,
oh father and mother too, for my name comes from both of you:
whoever comes into this spring a man, let him come out from here   385
a half-man, softened immediately he touches the waters."
Both his parents were moved and fulfilled the words of their two-formed
son by infecting the spring with an unholy drug.'
    That was the end of her words, and still Minyas' offspring
were driving on with their work and scorning the god and profaning his
feast day,
when suddenly they were confronted by the raucous din   391
of invisible drums and a flute of curved horn,
and clashing cymbals sounded and there was the smell of myrrh and
saffron,
and, an event beyond belief, their looms began to grow green
and the hanging cloth sprouted leaves to look like ivy.   395
Part of it turned into vines and what had just been threads
were changed into tendrils; a vine branch came from the warp,
and the purple lent its sheen to painted grapes.
And now the day was ended and that time was approaching
which you could call neither dark nor daylight   400
but the uncertain boundary of night and day.
Suddenly the house began to shake and the oil-filled lamps
to blaze and the rooms to shine with ruddy fires
and false images of savage beasts to howl.
The sisters were already hiding in the smoke-filled house   405
in various places to avoid the fires and lights.
And while they were seeking the darkness, a film spread over
their slender limbs and encased their arms in a thin wing.
But the darkness did not let them know how
they had lost their former shape. No feather lifted them up: 410
and yet they supported themselves on transparent wings.
And when they tried to speak, they produced a very small voice,
just like their bodies, and uttered light, high-pitched complaints.
They frequent houses not forests and, hating the light,
they fly by night and take their name from the evening.   415
    Then indeed in all of Thebes they began to tell of
Bacchus' name and his aunt spoke everywhere
of the new god's strength, for she alone of so many sisters

una doloris erat, nisi quem fecere sorores.
420   aspicit hanc natis thalamoque Athamantis habentem
sublimes animos et alumno numine Iuno
nec tulit et secum, 'potuit de paelice natus
uertere Maeonios pelagoque immergere nautas
et laceranda suae nati dare uiscera matri
425   et triplices operire nouis Minyeides alis:
nil poterit Iuno nisi inultos flere dolores?
idque mihi satis est? haec una potentia nostra est?
ipse docet quid agam (fas est et ab hoste doceri)
quidque furor ualeat Penthea caede satisque
430   ac super ostendit. cur non stimuletur eatque
per cognata suis exempla furoribus Ino?'
       est uia decliuis, funesta nubila taxo;
ducit ad infernas per muta silentia sedes.
Styx nebulas exhalat iners, umbraeque recentes
435   descendunt illac simulacraque functa sepulcris.
pallor hiempsque tenent late loca senta, nouique,
qua sit iter, manes, Stygiam quod ducat ad urbem,
ignorant, ubi sit nigri fera regia Ditis.
mille capax aditus et apertas undique portas
440   urbs habet, utque fretum de tota flumina terra,
sic omnes animas locus accipit ille nec ulli
exiguus populo est turbamue accedere sentit.
errant exsangues sine corpore et ossibus umbrae,
parsque forum celebrant, pars imi tecta tyranni,
445   pars aliquas artes, antiquae imitamina uitae,
exercent, aliam partem sua poena coercet.
       sustinet ire illuc caelesti sede relicta
(tantum odiis iraeque dabat) Saturnia Iuno.
quo simul intrauit sacroque a corpore pressum
450   ingemuit limen, tria Cerberus extulit ora
et tres latratus simul edidit. illa sorores
Nocte uocat genitas, graue et implacabile numen.
carceris ante fores clausas adamante sedebant
deque suis atros pectebant crinibus angues.
455   quam simul agnorunt inter caliginis umbras,
surrexere deae. Sedes Scelerata uocatur.
uiscera praebebat Tityos lanianda nouemque
iugeribus distractus erat; tibi, Tantale, nullae
deprenduntur aquae, quaeque imminet, effugit arbor;
460   aut petis aut urges rediturum, Sisyphe, saxum;

was free of sorrow, except that caused by her sisters.
Juno noticed that her children, her marriage to Athamas   420
and her divine foster-child had made her spirit proud
and she could not endure it, but said to herself, 'The wench's son could
transform Maeonian sailors and plunge them into the sea,
and give a mother her son's bowels to tear at,
and cover up Minyas' three daughters in strange new wings: 425
can Juno do nothing but weep at her unavenged griefs?
Is that enough for me? Is this my only power?
He himself has taught me what to do (it is right to learn from an enemy)
and in Pentheus' slaughter he has shown more than enough
what frenzy can achieve. Why shouldn't Ino be lashed   430
by her own frenzies into following the examples of her relatives?"
        There is a downward path, shaded by funereal yew;
it leads through a hushed silence to the place below.
The sluggish Styx breathes mists, and the fresh shades
descend that way with the ghosts who have experienced the tomb.   435
The place is drear everywhere, gripped by gloom and cold, and the new
spirits do not know where the path is that leads to the Stygian
city, or where is the wild palace of black Dis.
It is an extensive city with a thousand entrances
and open gates on every side, and as the sea receives rivers   440
from all the land so that place takes every soul and is not too small
for any people nor does it feel that a crowd is being added to it.
The bloodless shades wander without bodies or bones,
some throng the forum. others the house of the underworld's king,
some practise their skills in imitation of their former   445
lives, others submit to their punishment.
        Saturnian Juno left her seat in heaven to endure
the journey to that place (so much was she giving in to hatred and to
                                                          anger).
As soon as she had entered, and the threshold had groaned beneath the
                                                          weight
of her sacred body, Cerberus lifted his three mouths up   450
and gave three barks together. She called out to
the sisters that were born to Night, those grim and implacable divinities.
They were sitting in front of the prison doors, which were closed with
                                                          adamant,
and from their hair they were combing the black snakes out.
As soon as they recognized her in the shadowy darkness,   455
the goddesses rose up; it is called the Accursed Place.
Tityos was offering his bowels to be ripped at, stretched out
as he was over nine acres; Tantalus, you could not catch hold
of any of the water, and the branch that hung above eluded you;   459
you, Sisyphus, were either pushing your rock up, though it would return, or
                                                          going after it;

uoluitur Ixion et se sequiturque fugitque;
molirique suis letum patruelibus ausae
adsiduae repetunt, quas perdant, Belides undas.
    quos omnes acie postquam Saturnia torua
465   uidit et ante omnes Ixiona, rursus ab illo
Sisyphon aspiciens, 'cur hic e fratribus,' inquit,
'perpetuas patitur poenas, Athamanta superbum
regia diues habet, qui me cum coniuge semper
spreuit?' et exponit causas odiique uiaeque
470   quidque uelit: quod uellet erat ne regia Cadmi
staret, et in facinus traherent Athamanta furores.
imperium, promissa, preces confundit in unum
sollicitatque deas. sic haec Iunone locuta,
Tisiphone canos ut erat turbata capillos
475   mouit et obstantes reiecit ab ore colubras
atque ita, 'non longis opus est ambagibus:' inquit,
'facta puta quaecumque iubes. inamabile regnum
desere teque refer caeli melioris ad auras.'
laeta redit Iuno, quam caelum intrare parantem
480   roratis lustrauit aquis Thaumantias Iris.
nec mora, Tisiphone madefactam sanguine sumit
importuna facem fluidoque cruore rubentem
induitur pallam tortoque incingitur angue
egrediturque domo; Luctus comitatur euntem
485   et Pauor et Terror trepidoque Insania uultu.
limine constiterat; postes tremuisse feruntur
Aeolii pallorque fores infecit acernas
Solque locum fugit. monstris exterrita coniunx,
territus est Athamas, tectoque exire parabant:
490   obstitit infelix aditumque obsedit Erinys,
nexaque uipereis distendens bracchia nodis
caesariem excussit; motae sonuere colubrae,
parsque iacent umeris, pars circum pectora lapsae
sibila dant saniemque uomunt linguisque coruscant.
495   inde duos mediis abrumpit crinibus angues
pestiferaque manu raptos immisit; at illi
Inoosque sinus Athamanteosque pererrant
inspirantque graues animas: nec uulnera membris
ulla ferunt, mens est, quae diros sentiat ictus.
500   attulerat secum liquidi quoque monstra ueneni,
oris Cerberei spumas et uirus Echidnae
erroresque uagos caecaeque obliuia mentis
et scelus et lacrimas rabiemque et caedis amorem,
omnia trita simul, quae sanguine mixta recenti
505   coxerat aere cauo, uiridi uersata cicuta.

Ixion was spun around both pursuing and fleeing himself;
and, for having dared to engineer their cousins' deaths,
the Belides went continuously back to get the water they had lost.
       When Saturnia had looked at all of them with a grim
gaze and, above all, at Ixion, she turned from him to look   465
at Sisyphus again and said, 'Why is it that of the brothers it is he
that suffers eternal punishment, while proud Athamas
is living in a rich palace and he, together with his wife, has always
scorned me?' And she explained the reasons for her hatred and for her
                                                                      journey
and what she wanted: what she wanted was that Cadmus' palace   470
should not stand and that Athamas should be driven by frenzy into crime.
She mixed commands, promises and prayers to one end
as she beset the goddesses. When Juno had spoken thus,
Tisiphone shook her hoary locks, disshevelled
as they were, and pushed back the snakes that were in her face   475
and said, 'You have no need to ramble on at length:
consider done whatever you command. Leave the loveless
kingdom and take yourself back to the better air of heaven.'
Juno returned joyfully and, as she prepared to enter heaven,
Thaumantian Iris purified her with sprinkled waters.   480
Without delay, Tisiphone the relentless, took up her torch
that was drenched in blood, put on a cloak flowing
red with blood and girt up by a twisted snake,
and emerged from her house; Grief accompanied her as she went
and so did Fear and Fright and Madness with her terrified expression. 485
At the threshold she stopped; they say that Aeolus' doorposts
trembled, that the maple doors took on a pallor,
and that the Sun fled from his place. The portents terrified his wife,
they terrified Athamas, and they prepared to leave the house:
but the cheerless Erinys stood in the way and blocked their path   490
and, stretching out arms that were wrapped in the coils of a viper,
she shook her locks of hair; at that movement the snakes made a sound.
Some lay on her shoulders, others had slipped around her breasts,
giving hisses and spewing pus as their tongues flicked in and out.
Then she seized and broke off two snakes from the middle   495
of her hair and threw them with her baleful hand. But they
slid across the breasts of Ino and of Athamas
exhaling their oppressive breath: they inflicted
no physical injuries, it was their minds that felt the dreadful blows.
She had brought with her wondrous poisonous liquids too,   500
froth from the mouth of Cerberus and the venom of Echidna,
wayward ramblings of the mind and blind forgetfulness,
crime, tears, savagery and the love of slaughter,
all ground together; she had mixed them with fresh blood   504
and cooked them in a bronze cauldron, stirring them with green hemlock.

dumque pauent illi, uergit furiale uenenum
pectus in amborum praecordiaque intima mouit.
tum face iactata per eundem saepius orbem
consequitur motis uelociter ignibus ignes.
510   sic uictrix iussique potens ad inania magni
regna redit Ditis sumptumque recingitur anguem.
      protinus Aeolides media furibundus in aula
clamat, 'io, comites, his retia tendite siluis!
hic modo cum gemina uisa est mihi prole leaena,'
515   utque ferae sequitur uestigia coniugis amens
deque sinu matris ridentem et parua Learchum
bracchia tendentem rapit et bis terque per auras
more rotat fundae rigidoque infantia saxo
discutit ora ferox. tum denique concita mater,
520   seu dolor hoc fecit seu sparsum causa uenenum,
exululat passisque fugit male sana capillis
teque ferens paruum nudis, Melicerta, lacertis,
'euhoe Bacche,' sonat. Bacchi sub nomine Iuno
risit et, 'hos usus praestet tibi,' dixit, 'alumnus.'
525   imminet aequoribus scopulus; pars ima cauatur
fluctibus et tectas defendit ab imbribus undas,
summa riget frontemque in apertum porrigit aequor.
occupat hunc (uires insania fecerat) Ino
seque super pontum nullo tardata timore
530   mittit onusque suum; percussa recanduit unda.
at Venus immeritae neptis miserata labores
sic patruo blandita suo est: 'o numen aquarum,
proxima cui caelo cessit, Neptune, potestas,
magna quidem posco, sed tu miserere meorum,
535   iactari quos cernis in Ionio immenso
et dis adde tuis. aliqua et mihi gratia ponto est,
si tamen in medio quondam concreta profundo
spuma fui Graiumque manet mihi nomen ab illa.'
adnuit oranti Neptunus et abstulit illis
540   quod mortale fuit maiestatemque uerendam
imposuit nomenque simul faciemque nouauit
Leucothoeque deum cum matre Palaemona dixit.
      Sidoniae comites, quantum ualuere secutae,
signa pedum primo uidere nouissima saxo;
545   nec dubium de morte ratae, Cadmeida palmis
deplanxere domum, scissae cum ueste capillos,

And while they trembled, she poured the maddening poison
into their breasts, and moved them to the bottom of their hearts.
Then she spun her torch again and again round the same orbit
and produced fires from the swiftly moving fire.
So, victorious, with her orders discharged, she returned to the empty   510
kingdom of great Dis and unfastened the snake she had put on.
    Immediately, the son of Aeolus, though in the middle of his halls,
                                              frenziedly
shouted out, 'Tally ho, my companions, stretch your nets here in the
                                              woods!
I have just seen a lioness here with a pair of cubs.'
And in his madness, he followed his wife's tracks as if she were a wild
                                              beast.
Learchus was laughing and stretching his little arms out,   516
but he snatched him from his mother's breast and spun him like a sling
                                              shot
two or three times through the air and dashed the child's face
ferociously against the solid rock. Then at last the mother was aroused,
perhaps it was her grief, perhaps the poison sprinkled on her was the
                                             cause,
but she howled out and fled insanely, her hair all flowing loose,   521
carrying you, little Melicertes, in her bare arms
and crying, 'Euhoe, Bacchus.' At the name of Bacchus, Juno
laughed and said, 'May your foster-son ever confer such benefits upon you.'
There was a cliff overhanging the sea; its lowest part was hollowed out
by the billows, and it protected the waves it covered from the rainstorms;
its top was solid and its headland stretched over the open sea.
Ino (madness had given her the strength) climbed to this place
and, with no fear to hold her back, threw herself and her burden
over the sea. The water went white at the point of impact.   530
But Venus pitied her grand-daughter and her undeserved sufferings
and coaxed her uncle thus: 'Oh god of the waters,
Neptune, to whom befell the power next to heaven's,
I ask, indeed, for much; but pity my family
as you see them tossed on the vast Ionian,   535
and add them to your deities. I have some credit with the sea
if indeed I once was foam condensing
in the divine deep, for I still keep my name in Greek from that.'
Neptune assented to her prayer with a nod and removed from them
what was mortal, and conferred a dread majesty   540
upon them and changed both their names and their likenesses,
calling him, as god, Palaemon, and his mother, Leucothoe.
    Her Sidonian companions had followed her, as far as they were able,
and had seen her very last footprints at the edge of the rock;   544
thinking there was no doubt about her death, they pounded with their hands
in lamentation for the house of Cadmus, tearing at their hair and at their
                                              clothes,

utque parum iustae nimiumque in paelice saeuae
inuidiam fecere deae. conuicia Iuno
non tulit et, 'faciam uos ipsas maxima,' dixit,
550   'saeuitiae monimenta meae.' res dicta secuta est.
nam quae praecipue fuerat pia, 'persequar,' inquit,
'in freta reginam,' saltumque datura moueri
haud usquam potuit scopuloque adfixa cohaesit;
altera, dum solito temptat plangore ferire
555   pectora, temptatos sensit riguisse lacertos;
illa, manus ut forte tetenderat in maris undas,
saxea facta manus in easdem porrigit undas;
huius, ut arreptum laniabat uertice crinem,
duratos subito digitos in crine uideres;
560   quo quaeque in gestu deprensa est, haesit in illo.
pars uolucres factae, quae nunc quoque gurgite in illo
aequora destringunt summis Ismenides alis.
        nescit Agenorides natam paruumque nepotem
aequoris esse deos; luctu serieque malorum
565   uictus et ostentis, quae plurima uiderat, exit
conditor urbe sua, tamquam fortuna locorum,
non sua se premeret; longisque erroribus actus
contigit Illyricos profuga cum coniuge fines.
iamque malis annisque graues, dum prima retractant
570   fata domus releguntque suos sermone labores,
'num sacer ille mea traiectus cuspide serpens,'
Cadmus ait, 'fuerat, tum cum Sidone profectus
uipereos sparsi per humum, noua semina, dentes?
quem si cura deum tam certa uindicat ira,
575   ipse, precor, serpens in longam porrigar aluum.'
dixit et, ut serpens, in longam tenditur aluum
durataeque cuti squamas increscere sentit
nigraque caeruleis uariari corpora guttis;
in pectusque cadit pronus, commissaque in unum
580   paulatim tereti tenuantur acumine crura.
bracchia iam restant; quae restant bracchia tendit,
et lacrimis per adhuc humana fluentibus ora,
'accede, o coniunx, accede, miserrima,' dixit,
'dumque aliquid superest de me, me tange manumque
585   accipe, dum manus est, dum non totum occupat anguis.'
        ille quidem uult plura loqui, sed lingua repente
in partes est fissa duas, nec uerba loquenti
sufficiunt, quotiensque aliquos parat edere questus,
sibilat; hanc illi uocem natura reliquit.
590   nuda manu feriens exclamat pectora coniunx,
'Cadme, mane, teque, infelix, his exue monstris.

and they were angry with the goddess for being quite unjust
and too cruel to the wench; Juno could not bear
these insults and said, 'I shall make you yourselves into the greatest
memorials of my cruelty.' The word was followed by the deed.   550
For the one who had been most dutiful said, 'I shall follow
my queen into the sea,' but as she was set to make her leap she became
immovable in every way and was stuck fixed to the cliff;
another tried to strike herself with the usual breast
beating till she sensed her arms were stiffening as she tried them;   555
that one, just as she happened to be, stretching her hands out to the sea's
                                                                                                   waves,
was made stone and held her hands out to the same waves;
you would see the fingers of this other one, as she tore and plucked
at the hair on her head, suddenly harden in her hair;
in whatever action each was seized, that was the one she was stuck in. 560
Some became birds, and even now on that part of the sea
the Ismenides skim the waters with the tips of their wings.
            Agenor's son did not know his daughter and his small grandson
were gods of the sea; sorrow and a train of ills
had overcome him as had the very many prodigies he had seen, and he left
the city he had founded as if it were the bad luck of the place   566
and not his own that oppressed him; wandering far, he made his way
till he touched in at the Illyrian borders, a fugitive with his wife.
And now, weighed down by ills and years, they were recalling the first
events of their house and recounting their sufferings in conversation;   570
'Was that indeed a sacred serpent that my spear transfixed
then,' said Cadmus, 'when I had left Sidon
and scattered the viper's teeth, strange seeds, upon the ground?
But if it is the gods' concern to avenge it with such sure anger,   574
may I myself, I pray, be a serpent stretched out at length upon my belly.
He spoke and, as a serpent, he was stretched out at length upon his belly.
He felt his skin hardening and scales growing on it,
and his black body being varied with blue-green spots;
and he fell down flat on his breast while his legs were slowly
joined in one and tapered to a smooth point.   580
His arms remained yet, and he stretched out the arms that remained
and, with tears flowing down his face that was human still,
'Approach me, oh wife, approach me, most unhappy one,' he said,
'and while there is something left of me, touch me and take
my hand, while it is a hand, and the snake has not seized the whole of me.'
            Of course he wanted to say more, but suddenly his tongue   586
was split into two parts; and, when he wanted to speak, the words
were not there and, each time he prepared to utter some complaint,
he hissed; that was the sort of speech nature had left him.
His wife struck her bare breasts with her hand and shouted out,   590
'Cadmus, wait, unhappy man, strip off this monstrous form.

Cadme, quid hoc? ubi pes? ubi sunt umerique manusque
et color et facies et, dum loquor, omnia? cur non
me quoque, caelestes, in eandem uertitis anguem?'
595 dixerat; ille suae lambebat coniugis ora
inque sinus caros, ueluti cognosceret, ibat
et dabat amplexus adsuetaque colla petebat.
quisquis adest (aderant comites) terretur; at illa
lubrica permulcet cristati colla draconis,
600 et subito duo sunt iunctoque uolumine serpunt,
donec in adpositi nemoris subiere latebras.
nunc quoque nec fugiunt hominem nec uulnere laedunt,
quidque prius fuerint, placidi meminere dracones.
   sed tamen ambobus uersae solacia formae
605 magna nepos dederat, quem debellata colebat
India, quem positis celebrabat Achaia templis.
solus Abantiades ab origine cretus eadem
Acrisius superest, qui moenibus arceat urbis
Argolicae contraque deum ferat arma genusque
610 non putet esse Iouis; neque enim Iouis esse putabat
Persea, quem pluuio Danae conceperat auro.
mox tamen Acrisium (tanta est praesentia ueri)
tam uiolasse deum quam non agnosse nepotem
paenitet; impositus iam caelo est alter, at alter
615 uiperei referens spolium memorabile monstri
aera carpebat tenerum stridentibus alis.
cumque super Libycas uictor penderet harenas,
Gorgonei capitis guttae cecidere cruentae,
quas humus exceptas uarios animauit in angues;
620 unde frequens illa est infestaque terra colubris.
   inde per immensum uentis discordibus actus
nunc huc, nunc illuc exemplo nubis aquosae
fertur et ex alto seductas aethere longe
despectat terras totumque superuolat orbem.
625 ter gelidas Arctos, ter Cancri bracchia uidit,
saepe sub occasus, saepe est ablatus in ortus;
iamque cadente die ueritus se credere nocti
constitit Hesperio, regnis Atlantis, in orbe
exiguamque petit requiem, dum Lucifer ignes
630 euocet Aurorae, currus Aurora diurnos.
   hic hominum cunctis ingenti corpore praestans
Iapetionides Atlas fuit; ultima tellus

Cadmus, what is this? Where is your foot? Where are your shoulders and
your hands,
your complexion and your face and, even as I speak, everything? Why do
you not,
oh heavenly ones, turn me too into a snake like that?'
She had spoken; but he began to lick his wife's face   595
and go into her bosom as one who knew it
and give her an embrace and seek out her familiar neck.
Whoever was there (their companions were there) was terrified; but she
caressed the glistening neck of the crested snake
and suddenly there were two of them creeping along with coils entwined,
until they went down to a lair in the copse nearby.   601
Even now, they neither flee from man nor hurt or injure him
and, as peaceful snakes, they remember what they were before.
      But their grandson had given them both great
solace for the change in their appearance; he had conquered India   605
and was worshipped there, he was honoured in Achaea by the setting up of
temples.
Acrisius, son of Abas, who was sprung from that same stock,
was the only one left to keep him from the walls of his city,
Argos, to take up arms against the god, and not
to think that he was from Jove's race; nor did he think that Perseus   610
was Jove's, the one that Danaë had conceived in a shower of gold.
But soon Acrisius (such is the power of truth)
regretted outraging a god as much as not acknowledging
his grandson; one had now been set in heaven, but the other
was bringing back the memorable spoils of the snaky monster   615
and pressing through the gentle air with whirring wings.
And while he hung victorious over the Libyan sands
drops of blood from the Gorgon's head fell down
and the ground received them and breathed life into them as snakes of
various kinds.
And so it is that that land is densely snake-infested.   620
      From there he was driven through immeasurable space by the
discordant winds
and borne now here, now there, in the manner of a watery
cloud as, from high ether, he looked down upon the lands
so far removed from him and flew over all the world.
Three times he saw the cold Bears, three times the Crab's arms,   625
often he was borne away beneath the West and often to the East;
and now, as day fell, afraid to entrust himself to the night,
he stopped in the West of the world, at Atlas' kingdom,
to seek a little rest till Lucifer called up
the fires of Dawn and Dawn the chariot that brings the day.   630
      Here, surpassing all mankind with his huge body,
was Atlas, son of Iapetus; the farthest end of the earth

rege sub hoc et pontus erat, qui Solis anhelis
aequora subdit equis et fessos excipit axes.
635 mille greges illi totidemque armenta per herbas
errabant, et humum uicinia nulla premebant.
arboreae frondes auro radiante nitentes
ex auro ramos, ex auro poma tegebant.
'hospes,' ait Perseus illi, 'seu gloria tangit
640 te generis magni, generis mihi Iuppiter auctor;
siue es mirator rerum, mirabere nostras.
hospitium requiemque peto.' memor ille uestustae
sortis erat (Themis hanc dederat Parnasia sortem):
'tempus, Atla, ueniet, tua quo spoliabitur auro
645 arbor et hunc praedae titulum Ioue natus habebit.'
id metuens solidis pomaria clauserat Atlas
moenibus et uasto dederat seruanda draconi
arcebatque suis externos finibus omnes.
huic quoque, 'uade procul, ne longe gloria rerum
650 quam mentiris,' ait, 'longe tibi Iuppiter absit.'
uimque minis addit manibusque expellere temptat
cunctantem et placidis miscentem fortia dictis.
uiribus inferior (quis enim par esset Atlantis
uiribus?), 'at quoniam parui tibi gratia nostra est,
655 accipe munus,' ait, laeuaque a parte Medusae
ipse retro uersus squalentia protulit ora.
quantus erat, mons factus Atlas: nam barba comaeque
in siluas abeunt, iuga sunt umerique manusque,
quod caput ante fuit, summo est in monte cacumen,
660 ossa lapis fiunt. tum partes altus in omnes
creuit in immensum (sic, di, statuistis) et omne
cum tot sideribus caelum requieuit in illo.
clauserat Hippotades aeterno carcere uentos,
admonitorque operum caelo clarissimus alto
665 Lucifer ortus erat: pennis ligat ille resumptis
parte ab utraque pedes teloque accingitur unco
et liquidum motis talaribus aera findit.
gentibus innumeris circumque infraque relictis,
Aethiopum populos Cepheaque conspicit arua.
670 illic immeritam maternae pendere linguae
Andromedan poenas iniustus iusserat Ammon.
quam simul ad duras religatam bracchia cautes
uidit Abantiades (nisi quod leuis aura capillos
mouerat et tepido manabant lumina fletu,
675 marmoreum ratus esset opus), trahit inscius ignes
et stupet et uisae correptus imagine formae

was under this king and so was the sea which puts its waters beneath
the panting horses of the Sun and receives his tired axles.
A thousand flocks and as many herds roamed through   635
his grasslands and he had no neighbours pressing in upon his land.
The foliage of his trees, gleaming with radiant gold,
covered branches of gold and fruit of gold.
'Stranger,' said Perseus to him, 'if the glory of high
birth affects you, the instigator of my birth was Jove;   640
but if you are an admirer of deeds, you will admire mine.
I seek hospitality and rest.' But the other was mindful of an ancient
oracle (Themis of Parnassus had given him this oracle):
'Atlas, a time will come when your tree will be despoiled
of its gold and a son of Jove will take the credit for the plunder.' 645
    In fear of this, Atlas had shut his orchard up with solid
walls and had given it to a huge snake to guard
and kept all outsiders away from his borders.
To this one too he said, 'Move off, and far, in case you are
badly let down by the deeds you lied about and badly by Jove too.'   650
And he added violence to his threats using his hands to try and drive him
                                                                  off,
while he lingered there mixing strong words with peaceful ones.
He was inferior in strength (for who would be equal to Atlas'
strength?),'But, since my good will means little to you,
take this gift,' he said, and from his left hand side, turning   655
back himself, he held out Medusa's foul face.
Atlas became a mountain, as big as he had been: for his beard and hair
changed into woods, his shoulders and his hands were the slopes;
what had been his head before was the summit at the mountain top,
and his bones became rock. Then, raised up in all directions,   660
he grew immeasurably (for so, oh gods, you decided) and all
the sky together with so many stars rested upon him.
    Hippotes' son had shut the winds up in their everlasting prison
and Lucifer had risen, the brightest star in the lofty sky,
to remind men of their work: he took up his wings again   665
and bound them to his feet and girded himself with his curved sword
and cleaved the air with the motion of his winged sandals.
Leaving countless races around him and below him,
he caught sight of Ethiopia's peoples and of Cepheus' fields.
There unjust Ammon had ordered that Andromeda   670
pay an undeserved penalty for her mother's tongue.
As soon as Abas' descendant had seen her tied by the arms
to the hard cliffs (but for a light breeze which had moved
her hair and her eyes flowing with warm tears,   674
he would have thought she was a work of marble), he unconsciously took
                                                                 fire,
he was stunned and overwhelmed by the beauty of the vision he had seen

paene suas quatere est oblitus in aere pennas.
ut stetit, 'o,' dixit, 'non istis digna catenis,
sed quibus inter se cupidi iunguntur amantes,
680 pande requirenti nomen terraeque tuumque
et cur uincla geras.' primo silet illa nec audet
appellare uirum uirgo, manibusque modestos
celasset uultus, si non religata fuisset;
lumina, quod potuit, lacrimis impleuit obortis.
685 saepius instanti, sua ne delicta fateri
nolle uideretur, nomen terraeque suumque,
quantaque maternae fuerit fiducia formae,
indicat; et nondum memoratis omnibus unda
insonuit, ueniensque immenso belua ponto
690 imminet et latum sub pectore possidet aequor.
conclamat uirgo; genitor lugubris et una
mater adest, ambo miseri, sed iustius illa,
nec secum auxilium, sed dignos tempore fletus
plangoremque ferunt uinctoque in corpore adhaerent,
695 cum sic hospes ait: 'lacrimarum longa manere
tempora uos poterunt, ad opem breuis hora ferendam est.
hanc ego si peterem Perseus Ioue natus et illa,
quam clausam impleuit fecundo Iuppiter auro,
Gorgonis anguicomae Perseus superator et alis
700 aetherias ausus iactatis ire per auras,
praeferrer cunctis certe gener; addere tantis
dotibus et meritum, faueant modo numina, tempto.
ut mea sit seruata mea uirtute paciscor.'
accipiunt legem (quis enim dubitaret?) et orant
705 promittuntque super regnum dotale parentes.
ecce uelut nauis praefixo concita rostro
sulcat aquas iuuenum sudantibus acta lacertis,
sic fera, dimotis impulsu pectoris undis;
tantum aberat scopulis, quantum Balearica torto
710 funda potest plumbo medii transmittere caeli,
cum subito iuuenis pedibus tellure repulsa
arduus in nubes abiit; ut in aequore summo
umbra uiri uisa est, uisam fera saeuit in umbram.
utque Iouis praepes, uacuo cum uidit in aruo
715 praebentem Phoebo liuentia terga draconem,
occupat auersum, neu saeua retorqueat ora,
squamigeris auidos figit ceruicibus ungues,
sic celeri missus praeceps per inane uolatu
terga ferae pressit dextroque frementis in armo

and he almost forgot to flap his wings in the air.
As he stood there, 'Oh,' he said, 'you do not deserve those chains
but the sort that eager lovers are joined to one another by;
reveal to me, for I am asking you, your name and this land's   680
and why you are wearing fetters.' At first she was silent and did not dare,
a virgin, to address a man, and she would have modestly concealed
her face behind her hands, if she had not been tied up.
But, and that she could do, she filled her eyes with tears as they welled up.
He pressed her more and more and, in case it seemed there were misdeeds
                                                                    of hers
she was unwilling to admit, she told him her name and the land's   686
and how great her mother's confidence had been in her own beauty,
and, although she had still not mentioned everything, the water
resounded and a monster came up from the vast sea
looming over her and encompassing the wide ocean beneath its breast. 690
       The maiden screamed; her sorrowful father was there   691
together with her mother, both wretched, but she more justly,
and they brought no help with them, just tears befitting
the moment and breast beating, and they clung to her fettered body.
Thus then did the stranger speak, 'You can have   695
a long time left for tears, the hour for bringing help is brief.
If I sought her as the Perseus born to Jupiter and to her
whom Jupiter made pregnant with fertile gold, though she was shut away,
or as the Perseus who overcame the Gorgon with the snaky hair and dared
to go through airy breezes on beating wings,   700
I would certainly be preferred to anyone as son-in-law; but I am trying to
                                                                     add
to such endowments a deserving service, if only the gods look favourably
                                                                    on me.
My proposal is that she be mine if she is rescued by my courage.'
The parents accepted the terms (for who would hesitate?) and begged him
to do it, promising their kingdom as a dowry besides.   705
Look, just as a swift ship, with a beak fixed to her prow,
ploughs through the waters driven by the sweating arms of her men,
so was the wild beast as it pushed its breast against the parting waves;
it was as far from the cliffs as a Balearic sling
can traverse the intervening sky with its spinning lead,   710
when suddenly the young man pushed off from the ground with his feet
and went high up into the clouds; when his shadow could be seen
on the surface of the sea, the wild beast saw the shadow and savaged it.
And as the swift bird of Jove, when in an empty field it sees
a snake displaying its livid back to Phoebus   715
seizes it from behind and, in case it twists back with its savage mouth,
fixes its eager claws into its scaly neck,
so, sending himself headlong through the void in swift flight,
Inachus' descendant attacked the wild beast's back and, as it roared,

720 Inachides ferrum curuo tenus abdidit hamo.
uulnere laesa graui modo se sublimis in auras
attollit, modo subdit aquis, modo more ferocis
uersat apri, quem turba canum circumsona terret;
ille auidos morsus uelocibus effugit alis,
725 quaque patet, nunc terga cauis super obsita conchis,
nunc laterum costas, nunc qua tenuissima cauda
desinit in piscem, falcato uerberat ense.
belua puniceo mixtos cum sanguine fluctus
ore uomit; maduere graues aspergine pennae;
730 nec bibulis ultra Perseus talaribus ausus
credere conspexit scopulum, qui uertice summo
stantibus exstat aquis, operitur ab aequore moto.
nixus eo rupisque tenens iuga prima sinistra
ter quater exegit repetita per ilia ferrum.
735 litora cum plausu clamor superasque deorum
impleuere domos; gaudent generumque salutant
auxiliumque domus seruatoremque fatentur
Cassiope Cepheusque pater; resoluta catenis
incedit uirgo, pretiumque et causa laboris.
740 ipse manus hausta uictrices abluit unda;
anguiferumque caput dura ne laedat harena,
mollit humum foliis natasque sub aequore uirgas
sternit et imponit Phorcynidos ora Medusae.
uirga recens bibulaque etiamnunc uiua medulla
745 uim rapuit monstri tactuque induruit huius
percepitque nouum ramis et fronde rigorem.
at pelagi nymphae factum mirabile temptant
pluribus in uirgis et idem contingere gaudent
seminaque ex illis iterant iactata per undas;
750 nunc quoque curaliis eadem natura remansit,
duritiam tacto capiant ut ab aere, quodque
uimen in aequore erat fiat super aequora saxum.
dis tribus ille focos totidem de caespite ponit,
laeuum Mercurio, dextrum tibi, bellica uirgo;
755 ara Iouis media est. mactatur uacca Mineruae,
alipedi uitulus, taurus tibi, summe deorum.
protinus Andromedan et tanti praemia facti
indotata rapit; taedas Hymenaeus Amorque
praecutiunt, largis satiantur odoribus ignes,
760 sertaque dependent tectis et ubique lyraeque
tibiaque et cantus, animi felicia laeti
argumenta, sonant; reseratis aurea ualuis

buried his sword up to its curved hook into the right shoulder.   720
In pain from the deep wound, it first raised itself high
into the air, then it sank beneath the waters, then it turned just like
a fierce boar terrified by a noisy pack of dogs all round;
Perseus used his swift wings to escape its eager bite
and, wherever there was an opening, now on its back smothered with
                                                            hollow shells,
now at the ribs in its sides, now where the thinnest part of its tail   726
gave way to fish, he beat at it with his curved sword.
The monster spewed out sea water from its mouth mixed
with crimson blood; his wings grew wet and heavy from the spray;
and Perseus no longer dared to trust his drenched   730
sandals but caught sight of a cliff which, at its very top,
stood out from the waters when they were still but was covered by the
                                                            sea in motion.
Leaning on this and grasping the rock's main ridges with his left hand,
he drove his sword three or four times through its guts, attacking again
                                                            and again.
         Shouting and applause filled the shores and the houses   735
of the gods above. Cassiope and father Cepheus
rejoiced to greet their son-in-law acknowledging him
as the helper and saviour of their house; freed from her chains,
the maiden advanced, the reward and the reason for his efforts.
He himself drew water to wash his conquering hands;   740
and in case he hurt the snake-bearing head on the hard sand,
he made the ground soft with leaves, strewed sprays of seaweed
on it, and laid the face of Medusa, daughter of Phorcus, there.
The sprays were fresh, still then alive with absorbent tissue,
and they sucked in the monster's power and hardened at its touch,   745
acquiring a strange stiffness in its branches and its leaves.
And the sea nymphs tried out this amazing fact
on more sprays and were delighted that the same thing happened,
and they repeated it by throwing seeds from them throughout the waves;
even now, the property of coral has remained the same,   750
it takes on hardness when it is touched by air, and what
was, in the sea, a twig becomes, above the sea, a rock.
         He set up three turf altars to as many gods,
on the left one to Mercury, on the right one to you, oh warrior maiden,
and the altar inbetween for Jove. A cow was sacrificed to Minerva,   755
a calf to the wing-footed one and a bull to you, the greatest of the gods.
Immediately he took Andromeda without a dowry, his reward
for so great a deed; Hymenaeus and Love shook the torches
before them, the fires were filled with spreading perfumes,
garlands hung from the roof, and everywhere there sounded   760
lyres and the flute and singing, the happy proof
of a joyful soul; they unbarred the double doors and the whole

atria tota patent, pulchroque instructa paratu
Cepheni proceres ineunt conuiuia regis.

765   postquam epulis functi generosi munere Bacchi
diffudere animos, cultusque genusque locorum

767   quaerit Lyncides moresque animumque uirorum.
769   qui simul edocuit, 'nunc, o fortissime,' dixit,
770   'fare, precor, Perseu, quanta uirtute quibusque
artibus abstuleris crinita draconibus ora.'

narrat Agenorides gelido sub Atlante iacentem
esse locum solidae tutum munimine molis;
cuius in introitu geminas habitasse sorores

775   Phorcidas, unius partitas luminis usum;
id se sollerti furtim, dum traditur, astu
supposita cepisse manu perque abdita longe
deuiaque et siluis horrentia saxa fragosis
Gorgoneas tetigisse domos passimque per agros

780   perque uias uidisse hominum simulacra ferarumque
in silicem ex ipsis uisa conuersa Medusa.
se tamen horrendae clipei, quem laeua gerebat,
aere repercussae formam aspexisse Medusae;
dumque grauis somnus colubrasque ipsamque tenebat,

785   eripuisse caput collo, pennisque fugacem
Pegason et fratrem matris de sanguine natos.
addidit et longi non falsa pericula cursus,
quae freta, quas terras sub se uidisset ab alto
et quae iactatis tetigisset sidera pennis.

790   ante exspectatum tacuit tamen; excipit unus
ex numero procerum quaerens cur sola sororum
gesserit alternis immixtos crinibus angues.

hospes ait, 'quoniam scitaris digna relatu,
accipe quaesiti causam. clarissima forma

795   multorumque fuit spes inuidiosa procorum
illa, neque in tota conspectior ulla capillis
pars fuit; inueni, qui se uidisse referret.
hanc pelagi rector templo uitiasse Mineruae
dicitur: auersa est et castos aegide uùltus

800   nata Iouis texit, neue hoc impune fuisset,
Gorgoneum crinem turpes mutauit in hydros.
nunc quoque, ut attonitos formidine terreat hostes,
pectore in aduerso, quos fecit, sustinet angues.'

hall lay open, as the Cephenian nobles came into
the beautifully laid out banquet of their king.
    When the feast was over and the gift of high-born Bacchus   765
had relaxed their minds, Lynceus' descendant asked about the farming
and the sort of lands there and about the customs and the character of
                                                 the men;
and the one who answered him said, 'Oh bravest man,   769
now tell us, Perseus, I beseech you, with what courage and with what   770
tricks you made off with the head with snakes for hair.'
    Agenor's descendant told them of a place that lay below
cold Atlas, safely protected by its solid mass,
and that at its entrance lived twin sisters,
Phorcus' daughters, who shared the use of a single eye;   775
this he had taken secretly, while it was being passed, by the clever
and cunning interposing of his hand; then, through remote and deeply
hidden places and through rocks covered by rough woods
he had reached the Gorgons' homes where, here and there throughout the
                                                 fields
and throughout the paths, he saw statues of men and of wild beasts   780
turned from their true selves into stone by the sight of Medusa.
But he had seen the dreadful aspect of Medusa reflected
in the brazen shield he carried in his left hand;
and while a heavy sleep gripped the snakes and their mistress,
he wrenched her head from her neck, and out of their mother's blood   785
were born fleet-winged Pegasus and his brother.
He added, without a lie, the dangers of his journey,
what seas, what lands he had seen beneath him from on high,
and what stars he had reached on his beating wings.
    But he fell silent before they expected; one from the group   790
of nobles seized on his words to ask why she alone of the sisters
had snakes mixed alternately with her hair.
    The stranger said, 'Since what you want to know is worth the telling,
hear the reason for what you asked about. The brightest beauty
and the jealous hope of many nobles is what   795
she was; and in the whole of her there was no other part more striking
than her hair; I found a man who told me he had seen it.
The ruler of the sea deflowered her in the temple of Minerva,
so they say: Jove's daughter turned away and covered
her chaste face with the aegis and, lest this go unpunished,   800
she changed the Gorgon's hair into foul water-snakes.
Even now, to stun her enemies with fear and terrify them,
she keeps the snakes she made on the front of her breast.

COMMENTARY

1-4   *Prologue*
A very brief prologue for a very long poem.

1   shapes changed: *mutatas...formas,* a translation of the Greek word, *metamorphoses,* and an immediate introduction to the key feature of the work. Lee (16-8) and Otis (1966) 346-8; (1970) 375-7 provide a basic survey of what little we know of Ovid's indebtedness to his Hellenistic predecessors in this *genre.*

2   Oh gods: not, as is more usual, the Muses, but the various gods who effected the metamorphoses.

4   continuous song: the starting point for any discussion of this phrase must be the beginning of the first fragment of Callimachus' *Aetia* (Trypanis's translation):

> *I know that the Telchines,*
> *who are ignorant and no friends*
> *of the Muse, grumble at*
> *my poetry, because I did*
> *not accomplish one continuous*
> *poem of many thousands*
> *of lines...*

Callimachus was a third century Greek poet whose celebrated preoccupation with form was taken up by Roman poets at least as early as the time of Catullus. Wilkinson (152-3) believes that the *Aetia* was intended as a 'continuous song', Otis (46) does not; there can be no doubt, however, that Ovid, like Virgil before him, had started his poetic career in the short poem tradition and, also like Virgil, had intended to bring it to a climax with a *magnum opus* of epic length, though graced with the chief characteristics of the Hellenistic short poem. The notion of a single theme on which to hang a series of stories is not original to Ovid, but he became by far the most famous and influential of the classical examples; Boccaccio and Chaucer, perhaps the most important of the later exponents of this method, were much in his debt. For an urbane and polished analysis of the whole issue, see Wilkinson, 'The World of the Metamorphoses' in Herescu (231-44). See also Hollis xi-xv.

5-75   *The Creation*
Otis (1966) 348-9; (1970) 377-8 conveniently traces the antecedents of this section. Stoic ideas and terminology rub shoulders with Epicurean terms, but Ovid is no original thinker. Wilkinson (213-4) analyses Ovid's

philosophy, such as it is, but it is as a poet that he writes, a poet deeply versed in the treatment afforded creation by a wide variety of his poetic predecessors, from the traditional epic poet, Apollonius of Rhodes (1.496ff.) to a modern didactic poet such as Lucretius (5.416-508) and from the youthful Virgil (*Ecl.* 6.31ff.) to the mature master (*Aen.* 1.740-6). Ovid himself had tried the subject earlier (*Ars. Am.* 2.456ff., *Fast.* 1.103ff., 5.11ff.). Milton's treatment of the theme (*P.L.* 7) includes many echoes of Ovid's lines as discussed in some detail by Lee.

5-15   sea...sea: *mare...pontus*; see on 1.291-2.

7   Chaos: a familiar 'technical term' of Greek cosmology, originally indicating the gap that opened up between heaven and earth (Hesiod *Theog.* 116), but eventually, probably under Stoic influence, developing into something approaching its modern meaning, as clearly intended here. See Kirk and Raven (1957) 26-32; (1983) 36-41 for a full discussion.

9   seeds of...things: *semina rerum*, Lucretius' primary term for 'atoms'. Lucretius' great poem on Epicureanism, a masterpiece of the didactic *genre*, had a profound influence on Latin hexameter poetry, notably on the work of Virgil and Ovid. Here, Ovid not only introduces into a Stoic account of creation a phrase indelibly associated with Rome's most forceful Epicurean, but he changes its reference from Epicurean atoms to the elements, discussed in more detail a little further on (1.15-31) and much more clearly at *Fast.* 1.103-11.

10   Titan: according to Hesiod (*Theog.* 371-2), the Titan, Hyperion, was the father of the Sun, the Moon and Dawn. Hence Cicero (*Arat.* 589) uses *Titan* for the sun, followed by Virgil, (*Aen.* 4.119), Ovid, Seneca and others extensively. Chaucer (*Troilus and Criseyde* 3.1464) introduced the usage to English; but Shakespeare's 'Titan's fiery wheels' (*Romeo and Juliet* 2.3.4.) is, perhaps, more reminiscent of Ovid.

11   Phoebe: Catullus 34 is the most familiar authority for the association of Diana, Lucina and the moon. Thus, Virgil (*Georg.* 1.431) can use *Phoebe* for the moon, since Diana is, of course, the sister of Phoebus Apollo. Readers who would prefer this note in more elevated language should consult Shakespeare's *Love's Labour's Lost* (4.2.39):

> *What is Dictynna?*
> *A title to Phoebe, to Luna, to the moon.*

or Chaucer (*Troilus and Criseyde* 4.1591):

> *Er Phebus suster, Lucina the shene.*

12-13   Anaximander seems to have originated the notion that the earth was at the centre of things and held there by some sort of equilibrium. In spite of the development of rival theories, including the heliocentric view of Aristarchus of Samos, this remained the prevailing intellectual opinion throughout antiquity and beyond.

12 Earth: *Tellus;* probably personified in view of the proximity of Titan, Phoebe and Amphitrite; it is clear, however, that the personification ceases by line 15.

13 Amphitrite: the use of this sea goddess's name for the sea is Homeric (*Od.* 3.91) and seems to have been introduced into Latin by Catullus (64.11) perhaps from a Hellenistic source. See also the note on 2.268.

16 unstable: the normal meaning of *instabilis.* Here, however, Ovid coins a new word *innabilis,* 'unswimmable', thus humorously substituting or adding a new meaning for *instabilis,* 'that cannot be stood on'. Such a meaning for the word was not, in fact, wholly new, but it would be far from obvious here without *innabilis.* Comic effects from new coinages are not infrequent in Ovid.

19 the cold were: i.e. the cold elements were etc.

21 God, or more kindly Nature: Latin *et* (normally 'and') can, as here, introduce a synonym. That the terms are synonymous is a Stoic commonplace as in Seneca (*Ben.* 4.7.1): 'For what is Nature other than God and the Divine Reason?'
    more kindly: i.e. than the Chaos before.

22-3 The sky, *caelo,* of line 22 (i.e. ether and air) is subdivided in line 23 where the same word, *caelum,* is used to mean only the ether, excluding the air. The idea is further developed at 1.26ff. where it is important to remember the association of ether and fire. For a fuller discussion of ether see the note on 1.67.
    the lands...the waves: i.e. the elements, earth and water.

30 circling: *circumfluus,* perhaps another of Ovid's coinages; this is its earliest extant appearance. Milton (*P.L.* 7.270) borrowed it for his description of the second day of Creation (261-75) whose more obvious debt to *Genesis* tends to conceal its very real debt to this section of the *Metamorphoses.*

31 disk: the word *orbis* can mean either 'sphere', as it clearly does four lines later, or 'disk'. Here it must have a different sense from that of line 35 or the whole of lines 32-5 will have no meaning. That the world is a disk floating on and/or surrounded by water is an ancient notion familiar from Homer and Thales. Here Ovid tries to reconcile the disk floating on water with the sphere poised in equilibrium (12-3) by assuming that the latter developed from the former. He was, however, no cosmologist and at 1.187 and 2.7 he reverts unselfconsciously to the more primitive picture. The repetition of *orbis* in two different senses, which the translation does not reflect, may be an attempt to conceal the conceptual confusion.

32   whichever of the gods he was: the same philosophical concept as at line 21. For most of the work it is Jupiter and the Olympians who rule, but it was agreed by both the primitive cosmologies and the sophisticated philosophical systems that the Olympians, if they existed at all, were products not instigators of Creation.

33   divided...divided: *secuit sectam;*   Ovid juxtaposes two parts of the same word in a way characteristic of Latin, and a favourite trick of Ovid's. See 1.141-4, 167, 386, 402, 720; 2.7, 216, 280-1, 313, 322, 492, 494, 579, 796; 3.60, 95, 98, 382, 390, 417, 424-6, 446; 4.64, 89, 256-7, 261, 316 etc. The device is now alien to English but it was not always so. Consider Shakespeare's 'love is not love that alters when it alteration finds'. (*Sonnet* 116).

37   surround the shores of the encircled earth: pleonasm is another rhetorical trick now largely out of favour.

45-51   Here the world is undoubtedly a sphere divided into five zones, one, an uninhabitable torrid zone around the equator, two uninhabitable cold zones around each pole and two inhabitable temperate zones on each side of the torrid zone, between it and the cold zones. The notion is familiar from Virgil (*Georg.* 1.233-8), to whom Ovid clearly owes much here, and [Tibullus] (4.1.151-68). We shall meet the idea again at 2.129. It probably originated with Eratosthenes and was later taken up by the Stoics (Diog. Laert. 7.83.155) and later became a commonplace. Compare Thomas Carew's *Mediocrity in Love Rejected:*

> *Give me more love or more disdain;*
> *The torrid or the frozen zone*
> *Bring equal ease unto my pain;*
> *The temperate affords me none.*

56   Note that in this 'scientific' section it is the wind, not Jupiter, that causes thunderbolts and contrast, for instance, 1.154-5.

57   The Maker of the world: *mundi Fabricator; fabricator* is the basic Latin word for a craftsman, corresponding to the Greek *demiourgos,* the word used by Plato, and then by the Stoics, for the creator of the world. It is, accordingly, yet another term, and a particularly Stoic one, for the creator god first encountered at 1.21.

58   by these: i.e. by the winds. Clearer in the Latin than in English.

Latin's richer and more precise pronouns create many such problems for a translator. See also 2.103.

62   the mountain range beneath the morning rays: somewhere far to the East clearly, but speculation as to whether the Himalayas or the Hindu Kush or some other range is intended is to attribute to Ovid a greater geographical expertise than is plausible.

64   and the Seven Oxen: *Septemque Triones,* the seven stars that make up the Great Bear, hence 'the North'. See also 2.514-30.

67   ether: *aether,* in Homer, the word refers to heaven, but in Classical Greek it came to mean the upper air, as here. I have translated it as 'ether' throughout but all thoughts of laughing gas or radio waves must be cleared from the mind; think rather of the English derivative 'ethereal'. The concept was alluded to at 1.22-3 though the word was not used; see the note there.

71-3   the stars...the stars: *sidera...astra.* The repetition in the English is unavoidable, we do not have two distinct basic words for 'star'. See also the note on 1.157-8.

73   and: *-que;* some commentators take this *-que* as explanatory, as at 1.21, others assume that two different ideas are intended, perhaps the fixed stars and the planets as suggested by Lee.
heaven's floor: Lee compares Shakespeare (*Merchant of Venice* 5.1.58-9):

> Sit, Jessica: look how the floor of heaven
> Is thick inlaid with patins of bright gold.

76   *The Creation of Man*
Editors of the *Metamorphoses* and of *Paradise Lost* are rightly struck by the debt owed to this passage by Milton (*P.L.* 7.505-8):

> There wanted yet the Master work, the end
> Of all yet done; a Creature who not prone
> And Brute as other Creatures, but endu'd
> With Sanctity of Reason...

78-83   The presentation of alternative hypotheses is characteristic of serious intellectual writing in antiquity. It is noticeable first, perhaps, in Herodotus and, among Latin poets, is particularly marked in Lucretius as, of course, it should be in a true follower of Epicurus; see, for instance, *Letters to Pythocles* 87 (Geer's translation):

> If one accepts one explanation
> and rejects another that is equally
> in agreement with the evidence,

> it is clear that he is altogether
> rejecting science and taking refuge
> in myth.

Ovid's is not, of course, a scientific treatise, but it is an imitation of one.

78   divine seed: Cleanthes, Zeno's successor as head of the Stoic school, seems to have introduced the notion of a divine origin for man into Stoic dogma. His famous *Hymn to Zeus*, most conveniently available in the *Oxford Book of Greek Verse*, expresses the idea very poetically and it recurs throughout Stoic literature. St. Paul (*Acts* 17.28) was the first of a long line of Christians to try to use this Stoic belief as a bridge to Christianity when he quoted, without naming him, the Stoic poet, Aratus (*Phaen.* 4-5).

79   universal Craftsman: *Opifex rerum; opifex*, a synonym for *fabricator*, see the note on 1.57.

80-3   According to Hesiod (*Works and Days* 47-58) and Aeschylus (*P.V.*), men received fire from Prometheus, they were not created by him; Plato (*Protagoras* 320D-322A) attributes more of a role to Prometheus and his brother Epimetheus, but even he essentially restricts them to equipping animals and men with their various characteristics. That God created man in his own image from earth is an idea familiar from *Genesis* (1.26-7; 2.7), but the idea is also present in Hesiod (*Theog.* 570-93, *Works and Days* 70ff.) and Plato's *Protagoras.*

82   the son of Iapetus: i.e. Prometheus; see the note on 4.632.

84   prone: i.e. with the body horizontal, not erect. 'So Ovid expresses an old Socratic fancy already Latinized by Cicero.' Wilkinson (214) referring to *de Legibus* 1.26, *de Nat. Deorum* 2.140 and Xenophon *Mem.* 1.4.11. The notion is frequently exploited by Ovid in his descriptions of humans turning into beasts and the reverse process.

88   unknown: i.e. hitherto unknown.

89-150   *The Ages of Man*
That man has degenerated from a primitive innocence is an idea familiar to us from *Genesis* 3, though there there are only two stages. Our earliest extant Greek version is Hesiod's (*Works and Days* 109-201) where there are four degenerating ages of Gold, Silver, Bronze and Iron, though the inclusion of a fifth age of Heroes between the Bronze and Iron ages, and better than either, suggests there has been tampering with a much older story. Aratus (*Phaen.* 96-136) has three ages, Gold, Silver and Bronze, and Tibullus (1.3.35-50) two, an 'Eden' ruled by Saturn and a

'Fall' ruled by Jupiter. Virgil's picture (*Georg.* 1.125-46) is similar to that of Tibullus but more obliquely presented. All these passages have much in common, especially in their list of evils not practised in the age of innocence. There is very little in the Ovidian version that cannot be found in one or other of these passages. For a full discussion of the idea see H. C. Baldry, 'Who invented the Golden Age?', *CQ* n.s. 2 (1952) 83ff.

92   fixed bronze: Roman laws were published by being inscribed in tablets. See also the note on 1.171-5.

94   felled pines: a striking way to emphasise the commonplace that navigation is essentially sinful. The conceit is familiar from Catullus 4.10-12. The imagery seems more dead at 2.184 and 3.621 where *pinus* has been rendered 'boat'.

102   uninjured: the word emphasises the commonplace that agriculture is sinful; compare 1.94.

106   Jupiter's tree was the oak, and acorn eating was supposed to have been the practice of primitive man, see Herodotus 1.66.

107-12   'Five of these six beautiful hexameters have their sense completed at line-ending; this helps to build up the impression of peace and composure.' Lee. End stop lines, the norm in elegiacs, Ovid's medium before he attempted the *Metamorphoses*, are certainly less common in developed hexameter writing.

111   nectar: properly the drink of the gods, as at 3.318; 4.250-2, but sometimes used, as surely here, to mean wine; in Virgil's Golden Age (*Georg.* 1.132), the rivers certainly ran with wine.

112   green holm-oak: the *ilex* (holm-oak) is an evergreen.

113   Saturn: identified with Zeus' predecessor, Kronos. Gransden (36-8) has a sensitive discussion of the differences between the Virgilian concept of the Saturnian age and the traditional Greek one revived here by Ovid.

113-27   The treatment of the Silver and Bronze ages is relatively perfunctory; Ovid's chief interest is in the ages of Gold and Iron which are notable for the presence or absence of traditionally sinful activities.

126   dreadful arms: *horrida...arma*, presumably the source of Milton's 'horrid arms' (*P.L.* 2.63) since the phrase is not Virgilian.

133   them: i.e. the winds.

133-4   which...mountains: see 1.94 and the note there.

138   bowels of the earth: quite literally, *uiscera terrae:*

> *And that it was great pity, so it was,*
> *This villainous saltpetre should be digg'd*
> *Out of the bowels of the harmless earth.*

Shakespeare 1 King Henry IV 1.3.59-61

> *Men also...*
> *Ransacked the Centre and with impious hands*
> *Rifled the bowels of their mother Earth*
> *for Treasures better hid.*

Milton P.L. 1.685-8

141-4   iron...iron, had emerged;   there emerged...guest...host: *ferrum ferroque...prodierat;   prodit...hospes ab hospite;* it is not possible to achieve this triple repetition in English since there is no English word that covers both meanings of *hospes*, though 'guest' and 'host' are ultimately derived by the etymologists from *hostis*. See also the note on 1.33.

142   fights with both: i.e. uses both bribery (gold) and violence (iron).

145   no father-in-law from his son-in-law: less cumbersome in Latin, *non socer a genero;* even before their civil war, the juxtaposition of these two words inevitably meant Caesar and Pompey (Catullus 29.24). By Ovid's time, readers are more likely to remember the phrase from Virgil's parade of Roman heroes (*Aen.* 6.830-1).

147   stepmothers: *nouercae,* a word with exactly the same overtones as its English equivalent, e.g. Horace *Epodes* 5.9.

148 The son, who is looking forward to inheriting his father's wealth, is consulting the stars in the hope that they will bring him an indication of his father's early death.

149   Piety: *Pietas* is untranslatable because it conveys a range of qualities, such as dutiful devotion to the gods, family and country, that we would not see as a single coherent virtue. I have used 'piety' generally for the word (and 'pious' for *pius*) but it is important to clear the mind of images of pale virgins on their knees and consider rather Virgil's Aeneas who is always presented as the authentic example of *pietas.*

    the Astraean Virgin: Aratus (*Phaen.* 96-136) was not sure whether the maiden, Justice, was the daughter of Astraeus or not, but he knows that she dwelt freely with men during the Golden Age, retired to the hills during the Silver Age and fled earth altogether when the Bronze Age came and is now to be seen in heaven as the constellation *Virgo*. Thus Dryden can celebrate the Restoration with his *Astraea Redux*, 'the Astraean returned'.

151-62   *The Battle of the Giants*

According to Homer (*Od.* 11.305-20), it was Otus and Ephialtes who piled up the Thessalian mountains in an attempt to conquer heaven. According to Hesiod (*Theog.* 389-96, 629-735), it was the Titans who fought against heaven; he mentions the Giants (*Theog.* 185) only to identify them as born from the blood of Uranus (see note on line 162). In Virgil's *Georgics* (1.278-83), it was the Titans (Coeus, Iapetus and Typhoeus) who piled up the mountains to attack heaven. For further confusion see 1.183-4 and the notes there. The battle was a favourite theme of ancient artists; the most influential of these representations was surely the Pergamene frieze fully discussed by Martin Robertson, *A History of Greek Art* (Cambridge, 1975) 539ff., but the index of that magnificent work under 'Gigantomachy' will lead to a wealth of other representations including some which reflect the confusion between Titans and Giants alluded to above. The Pergamene frieze was so extensively copied in the Hellenistic and Roman worlds that it is extremely likely that Ovid himself would have seen such a representation. In the *Amores* (2.1.11-20), Ovid humorously pretended that he had unsuccessfully attempted a major poem on the subject, something that Propertius (2.1.19-20) had already 'refused' to do. Horace (*Odes* 3.4.42-64) used the story to illustrate a moral point, while Ovid later returned briefly to the theme (*Fasti* 1.307; 3.441). Frazer's Loeb edition of Apollodorus (vol. 2, 318-26) has an appendix on similar tales in Amerindian folk lore.

154-5   In Homer, Propertius and elsewhere in Ovid, Ossa was piled on Olympus and, as the proverb has it, Pelion on Ossa. In Virgil, however, Ossa was piled on Pelion and Olympus on Ossa; here, however, Pelion is again piled on Ossa but Olympus seems to be at the top. In Horace, Pelion is on Olympus and Ossa is not mentioned.

157-8   **blood...blood:** *sanguine...cruorem.* There are not two distinct basic words for 'blood' in English; 'gore' is a possible rendering for *cruorem* here (or for *caedis* at 4.126) but it is a far more outlandish word than either of Ovid's.

162   Ovid assumes that his audience knows that the Giants were born from the blood Uranus shed when his son, Saturn, cut off his father's genitals. See the note on lines 151-62.

163-252   The Council of the Gods and the story of Lycaon.
A council of the gods is an essential feature of a serious epic poem,
almost invariably near its beginning. The first book of the *Iliad* ends
with one, the *Odyssey* starts with one as does its fifth book, a fact
frequently cited in support of the hypothesis that *Odyssey* 1-4, the
Telemachy, is a separate epic poem attached to the beginning of the
true *Odyssey.* There is a divine council in the first book of the *Aeneid*
(223ff.). These councils are not, of course, restricted to the beginning
of epics, but they do usually (though not in *Iliad* 1) introduce a note
of high seriousness. In Ovid's case, naturally, there is a deliberate policy
of undercutting such expectations. See also the note on 4.432-80.

164   **Lycaon:** Greek for 'Wolf man'. What we know of the history of
the legend is complex and most conveniently presented by Frazer on
Apollodorus 3.8.1-2. Ovid suppresses any doubts about Lycaon's guilt
and, by substituting a Molossian hostage (1.227) for his children (or
by choosing such a version), he lays the emphasis on public sin rather
than private, family guilt, a subject he was keeping for later. The were-
wolf still holds a fascination for many people as it clearly did in antiquity.
As late as the second century A.D., Pausanias (8.2.1; 8.38.7) was able
to trace associated rites.

168   **There is a way:** *est uia;* a characteristic ekphrasis of a type that
goes back to Homer (e.g. *Il.* 6.152-5) when the narration is interrupted
to set a scene. Usually, but not always, it begins with *est*, 'there is'.
Compare Virgil *Aen.* 4.480-3 and Austin's notes and 8.597 and Gransden's
note. He also aptly compares Shakespeare's 'There is a willow grows
aslant a brook...' (*Hamlet* 4.7.167).

171-5   It is very Virgilian to introduce purely Roman concepts where
they might seem inappropriate. In book 4 of the *Aeneid*, for instance,
Dido's foundation of her city is full of Roman assumptions and termino-
logy. But, whereas Virgil never loses dignity that way (indeed his method
can enhance the impression he clearly intends, that Roman history
is the unfolding of a divine plan), Ovid is clearly and deliberately seeking
bathos. The obvious Virgilian comparison with this passage is *Aeneid*
8.337-69 where Evander's tour of his primitive settlement implicitly
evokes comparison with the mature Rome of Virgil's time and thereby
gives heightened significance to both. Ovid's deliberately crude and
explicit comparison, by contrast, pokes fun both at divine and human
pretensions. See also 1.92 and the notes on 1.173-5, 382, 576; 3.111-4,
531, 539, 583.

173-6   **the common gods (*plebs*)...Penates...Palatine:** note, again, the
aggressive use of very Roman terminology. Every Roman home had
a shrine to the household gods, *penates.* The Palatine was the poshest

quarter of Rome.

179-80   According to Homer (*Il.* 1.528-30), Zeus' nod shook only Olympus and in this he was followed by Virgil (*Aen.* 9.106); it was Catullus (64.204-6) who had introduced the notion that all the universe shakes. Curiously enough, Horace (*Od.* 3.1.7-8) had also juxtaposed Jupiter's nod and his triumph over the Giants.

179   **three times or four:** see the note on 2.49.

183   **snake-footed:** Apollodorus (1.6.1) supports this idea and Ovid himself repeats it in his *Tristia* (4.7.17). The notion clearly had some currency or Pausanias (8.29.3) would not have contradicted it, nor would it have affected the plastic representation of the Giants in later antiquity. This, however, does seem to be the earliest extant evidence for the idea.

184   **hundred arms:** we first meet a hundred-handed one in Homer (*Il.* 1.402-4) where he is identified as Briareus to the gods and Aegaeon to men. In Hesiod (*Theog.* 149-50), there is mention of three hundred-handed ones, Cottus, Briareus and Gy(g)es, and a hundred-handed Gyges is twice mentioned by Horace (*Od.* 2.17.4; 3.4.69). While the hundred-handed certainly attacked heaven, only here, it seems, are they associated with the Giants or with piling up mountains. At 3.304, Typhoeus, otherwise a Titan, is called hundred-handed.

187   **Nereus:** see the note on 2.268.

188-9   That the gods swear by Styx and that their oath is unbreakable is a commonplace first encountered in Homer (*Il.* 15.37-8 etc.). See also 2.44-6 and 3.288-90 and the notes there.

192   **the Nymphs:** even in Homer this word can refer either to any attractive young woman (*Il.* 9.560) or, as here, to semi-divine creatures who haunt woods and streams (*Il.* 20.8).

193   **Fauns:** rustic demi-gods. Faunus was a Roman figure, later identified with the Greek Pan.
   Satyrs: goat-footed demi-gods of wild places. Rubens's *Two Satyrs* gives a fair impression of their appearance in antiquity. They are frequently associated with Bacchus and proverbially ugly as Shakespeare (*Hamlet* 1.2.139-40) reminds us:
> So excellent a king; that was to this,
> Hyperion to a Satyr.

   Silvanus: a Roman god of forests (*siluae*) sometimes, as here, found in the plural and thought of as a group of gods.

200-6   The extended simile, perhaps the most characteristic feature of high epic style, is familiar to all readers of Homer and Virgil. There is, however, more to this simile than that. In the *Iliad* (2.144-9), Homer compares the troops aroused by Thersites' speech to a storm, and it is only the intervention of the skilful Odysseus that calms them. That simile is reversed in the *Aeneid* (1.148-56) where Neptune's calming of a storm at sea is likened to the intervention of a man of great 'piety' (see the note on line 149) whose authority enables him to calm a mob that is quite out of control. It may or may not be the case that there Virgil intended us to think of Augustus; if he did, the reference is certainly subtly managed. In this pastiche of Virgil (both similes are the first of their respective poems and both stress the role of 'piety'), the reference to Augustus is both explicit and grotesque. The absurdities of this section are, of course, to be linked with those at lines 171-6 and are well discussed by Otis 98-101 and (1970 only) 360-1.

201   Caesar's blood: i.e. the assassination of Julius Caesar, obvious both from the immediate context and from the fact that the *Metamorphoses* ends with that assassination. There is no merit in the suggestion sometimes made that the reference is to one or other of the various attempts made on Augustus' life.

205-8   Some feel that the repetition here is too clumsy even for Ovid and excise line 207.

221   mocked their pious prayers: even without the Virgilian colouring and the allusion back to 'piety', this phrase would conjure up a frisson of anticipation of punishment. See the note on 1.149.

223   doubtable: *dubitabile*, probably an Ovidian coinage.

227   hostage: Jupiter was the patron god of hostages; see also the note on line 164.

228-9   boiled part...and roasted part: Procne (6.645-6) cooked her son in the same way. When Aeneas' men were preparing their first meal after the shipwreck (*Aen.* 1.212-3), Virgil tells us that spits were prepared and water boiled. According to the ancient commentator, Servius, the water was for washing, but the two Ovidian passages tell against him.

234   from the man himself: that the metamorphosis reveals a truth about the victim is not uncommon; compare 1.414-5, 2.485, 832; 3.203, 503-5; 4.270 etc. Hollis (xx) discusses this feature in some detail and relates it to Homer *Od.* 10.239-4 (Lattimore's translation):
   and they took on the look of pigs, with their heads and voices
   and bristles of pigs, but the minds within them stayed as they had been
   before.

For a different perspective on this point, see Galinsky 45ff.

253-312   *The Flood*

This is the earliest extant account of the story of Deucalion and Pyrrha though it was clearly a familiar story. Hesiod (but only in his fragments) and Pindar (*Ol.* 9.64-7) refer to it as do Virgil (*Ecl.* 6.41) and Horace (*Odes* 1.2.6): Horace, indeed, has a vignette on the after effects of the flood which is clearly picked up by Ovid (see the note on line 296). Flood myths are, of course, a commonplace of primitive cultures and there has been much speculation on the connexion, if any, between this myth and the Mesopotamian versions familiar to us from *Genesis* 6-9. On this point, the words of W. G. Lambert and A. R. Millard (*Atra-Hasis, The Babylonian Story of the Flood* (Oxford, 1969) 24-5) are worth quoting:

> The Greco-Roman flood story with Deucalion and Pyrrha as its heroes is not certainly related at all. Unfortunately it is only known from late sources, the fullest form is that in Ovid's **Metamorphoses...** If one could trace back this story it might of course have antecedents more closely resembling its Mesopotamian counterpart, but in its known forms there is no certain connection.

256   that it was in the fates: the Stoics took from Heracleitus the view that the world would eventually be consumed by fire. (Lee aptly quotes *2 Timothy* 3.10 and see the note on 1.78). Readers may also be tempted to think of the far more imminent conflagration to be caused by Phaethon (2.210-318). The Homeric view, that Zeus is theoretically capable of overturning fate, but only at the cost of disturbing the whole order of the universe to his own eventual loss (see *Iliad* 16.433-49), has developed into the simpler view that the fates are immovable even by the gods (see *Met.* 15.807.14).

259   The OED recognizes 'Cyclops' as a plural as well as a singular and it is rhythmically useful here. For their role here, see Hesiod *Theog.* 139-41.

260   the opposite punishment: Otis (91-2) makes much of the balance between a panel culminating in a Flood and another (that of Phaethon) in a Fire. As he points out, this line reinforces the importance of the contrast between fire and water.

264   sent out...flew out: *emittitque...euolat;* the repeated 'out' is an attempt to reproduce the repeated prefix *e-*, which does, of course, carry that sense.

271   drew up the waters: that the rainbow drank up water was a commonplace; see, for instance, Virgil *Georg.* 380-1.

275   his aquamarine brother: i.e. Neptune, see Homer *Il.* 15.184-93. The adjective *caeruleus*, 'aquamarine', indicates a dark blue-green and is a standard epithet for water divinities, compare Virgil *Georg.* 4.388.

279-85   raise the starting gate and give completely free rein...have their head...unbridled course...left the course: note how Ovid sustains the horse racing imagery.

285-7   The rhythm of these lines is very swift and catches the rush of the waters excellently. The translation attempts to produce a similar effect.

289   undemolished: *indeiecta*, apparently another Ovidian coinage.

291-2   sea...sea...sea: *mare...pontus...ponto*; essentially the same problem was discussed in the note on 1.71-3; here, admittedly, *pontus* is not a basic Latin word but a Greek borrowing with a rather poetic register. However, there is no equivalent borrowing into English. See also Mayer on Lucan 8.198.

292   the sea was everything: perhaps borrowed from Virgil *Ecl.* 8.58.

296   a fish at the very top of an elm tree: borrowed from Horace *Od.* 1.2.9.

308-9   sea...sea's: *mare...ponti*, see on lines 291-2.

313-415   Deucalion and Pyrrha
For the antecedents of this myth, see the note on lines 253-312.

316   two peaks: the mistaken belief that Parnassus' two peaks are its summit occurs elsewhere (e.g. 2.221, Lucan 3.173; 5.72, Statius *Theb.* 1.63-4). It seems to have arisen from a misunderstanding of Sophocles *Antigone* 1126 which alludes to the two lower peaks well beneath the real summit, Lycoreia. The topography is well discussed in Smith's *Dictionary of Greek and Roman Geography* s.v. 'Delphi' p. 764.

320   Corycian nymphs: the Corycian cave on Mt Parnassus was celebrated for its sanctity and for its nymphs. Herod. 8.36, Aesch. *Eum.* 22ff., Soph. *Ant.* 1126-7, Eur. *Bacch.* 556-9.

321   **Themis:** According to Aeschylus (*Eum.* 2-8), the oracle was held first by Earth, then by Themis, then by Phoebe and then by Apollo.

325-6   This striking effect is discussed by Rand (80-2) where he relates it to liturgical influence. It is, in any case, a favourite Ovidian trick. See 1.361-2, 481-2, 635-6; 2.82-3; 3.611-2; 4.152-3, 306-9, 575-6 etc.

330-1   **sea...sea:** *maris...pelagi;* the remarks about *pontus* in the note on 1.291-2 apply also to *pelagi* here.

331   **the marine ruler:** i.e. Neptune.

332   **Triton:** son of Poseidon and Amphitrite and a ruler of the sea. (Hes. *Theog.* 930-2). 'Hear you this Triton of the minnows?' Shakespeare *Coriolanus* 3.1.133.

333   **murex:** a shell-fish used in the production of purple dye.

334-5   **sounding conch-shell...hollow horn:** the same instrument, of course. Lee quotes Spenser: 'Triton blowing loud his wreathed horne' (*Colin Clout's Come Home Again* 245) and Wordsworth (*Miscellaneous Sonnets* 1.33):

> Have sight of Proteus rising from the sea,
> Or hear old Triton blow his wreathed horn.

338   **each Phoebus:** *Phoebus*, 'bright', 'shining', is an epithet both of Apollo and, as here, of *Sol*, the Sun. This is, therefore a way of saying both East and West, both the rising and the setting sun.

343   compare line 292.

351   **sister:** *soror*, the ordinary word for 'sister' here bears an extended meaning; Deucalion and Pyrrha were first cousins being the children of the brothers, Prometheus and Epimetheus; see 1.390.

361-2   See the note on 1.325-6.

367-8   **the heavenly power:** *caeleste numen:* a vague term not found elsewhere in the *Metamorphoses*, but it does occur in the *Fasti* (6.23) and at *Pont.* 2.1.27; 2.8.15 etc. There seems no particular point in its use here, the reference is, presumably, to Themis (see 1.321 and 379).

369   The Cephisus flows West to East some twelve miles North of Delphi and eventually flows into Lake Copais, from which the water is discharged in various directions through a number of underground channels. This fact may have given rise to the theory, recorded by Pausanias (10.8.10), that the river was also connected to the Castalian spring on Mt Parnassus. According to Pausanias, the people of Lilaea, a small town on the Cephisus about twelve miles due North of Delphi, used to throw cakes into their river which reappeared in the Castalian spring. Since it is clear that the Castalian spring is what Ovid has in mind here, we must assume either that he is alluding to a story like the one Pausanias was to encounter, or that his geography is confused. See also the note on 3.19.

373   goddess's: i.e. Themis'.

377-8   If...if: a very common prayer formula; see, for instance, Homer *Il.* 1.39-40. Virgil presents a very similar prayer at *Aen.* 2.689-90 where Austin rightly points out that the *si* (if) 'expresses confidence, not doubt'. The formula recurs at *Met.* 3.263-5.

382   veil your heads: Romans covered their heads for sacrifice (Lucr. 5.1198 and see Bailey; Virg. *Aen.* 3.405 and see Williams; Ov. *Fast.* 3.363), Greeks sacrificed bare headed. It is characteristic of Ovid, and of Roman writers in general, to impose Roman customs on non-Romans. See also the note on 1.171-5.

    undo your robes' girding: knots of all kinds are antipathetic to magic. Dido lets her hair down, removes one shoe and undoes her cincture before she begins the ritual that ends in her suicide (Virg. *Aen.* 4.511-8) and, later in the *Metamorphoses* (7.182-3), Medea makes similar preparations before beginning her magic.

383 Ancient oracles were notoriously obscure. Consider the meaning of the English phrase, 'a Delphic response'.

390 See the note on 1.351.

392   holy: *pia*; see the note on 1.149. Here, of course, 'pious' is an absolutely impossible translation, but this line illustrates the point that the range of *pius* and *pietas* is very wide.

395   Titania: Pyrrha, the daughter of Epimetheus, son of the Titan, Iapetus.

402-9   softened...softened...gentler...bent: *mollirique...mollitaque... mitior...flectique*; these words pick up 'softened' *remollescunt* (377), 'gentlest' *mitissima* (380) and 'bent aside' *flectitur* (378), as Fränkel (77) points out.

410   vein: *uena*; in both Latin and English the word has both meanings.

410-5   Another example of a change that reveals the truth; see the note at 1.234 and compare the use of 'the same' *eodem* (410) with the triple repetition of that word at lines 238-9.

411-2   the rocks...took on the likeness of men: Apollodorus (1.7.2), in telling this story, derives the Greek word *laos* (people) from *laas* (stone). In Pindar's version, however, the word used for 'stone' is *lithinos*.

416-51   The Python
The conflict between Apollo and a snake is one of the most fundamental of Greek myths. Sometimes the snake is female (*Homeric Hymn* 3.300-1, Ap. Rhod. 2.701ff.), sometimes male (Eur. *I.T.* 1245-51, Callim. *Hymn* 2.97-102); sometimes Apollo is a baby (Euripides), sometimes a youth (Apollonius). The myth is also frequently depicted on ancient vases. For a full discussion see J. E. Fontenrose *Python, a Study of Delphic Myth and its Origins* (Berkeley, 1959), a work which includes a full discussion, together with illustrations, of the artistic tradition.

419   seeds of things: *semina rerum*; see the note on 1.9. Here, however, the phrase is used in a straightforward non-Lucretian way, although the passage as a whole clearly owes much to Lucretius' account of the origin of life (5.795-800).

422   In antiquity the Nile had seven mouths (Catullus 11.7-8, Virg. *Aen.* 6.800).

424   the ethereal star: i.e. the sun. Virgil also uses the word *sidus* for 'sun' (*Aen.* 12.451).

426-9   This extraordinary passage owes something to Lucretius 2.871-2 and 5.797-848 where the account of spontaneous generation from earth is continued with speculation on a variety of monsters that earth must have produced in the same way. The ultimate origin for these ideas is, no doubt, Empedocles (Kirk and Raven (1957) 336-8; (1983) 303-5). More immediately interesting, however, are the observations of Diodorus Siculus (1.10.4-7, Oldfather's translation):

> In general, they say that if in the flood
> which occurred in the time of Deucalion
> most living things were destroyed, it is
> probable that the inhabitants of southern
> Egypt survived rather than any others,
> since their country is rainless for the most
> part; or if, as some maintain, the destruction
> of living things was complete and the earth
> then brought forth again new forms of
> animals, nevertheless, even on such a

> *supposition the first genesis of living things fittingly attaches to this country...for, whenever the river has begun to recede and the sun has thoroughly dried the surface of the slime, living animals, they say, take shape, some of them fully formed, but some only half so and still actually united with the very earth.*

432 And though fire fights water: another philosophical commonplace. Its origin seems to be in the thought of Anaximander who postulated the interaction of heat and moisture, the sun on mud, as the source of all life and was followed in this by Aristotle. See Kirk and Raven (1957) 141-2; (1983) 141-2; W.K.C. Guthrie *A History of Greek Philosophy* I, (Cambridge, 1967) 92-3.

433 a discordant concord: *discors concordia*; the oxymoron is also present in Horace (*Epp.* 1.12.19) in connexion with Empedocles whose doctrines of Strife and Love and their productive conflict are also, perhaps, relevant here. See Kirk and Raven (1957) 327-332; (1983) 289-94.

441 the archer god: *deus arquitenens*; the standard Latin translation of the Greek *toxophoros* which is used of Apollo as early as the *Homeric Hymns* (3.13) and enters Latin with Naevius.

442 red or yellow deer: *dammis capreisque*; *capra* is the Latin for a 'nanny-goat' (French *chevre*) but *caprea* is the Latin for the red deer (French *chevreuil*), *cervus capreus* in modern zoological terminology. Golding, but not some modern translators, avoids the trap of attributing something as undignified as goat hunting to Apollo.

448-9 with hand or foot or wheel: i.e. in the boxing, running or chariot-racing competitions.

449 a sprig of oak: this idea is merely an Òvidian invention to carry us into the next story, the creation of the laurel.

452-567 *Apollo and Daphne*
The mood now changes from an apparent seriousness to an overt lightness, from an almost philosophical analysis of the origin of the world and its moral weaknesses to a cheerful romp through Greek mythology.

The pre-Ovidian history of the Daphne myth is most conveniently available in Otis (1966) 350ff.; (1970) 379ff. Previously, Daphne had been the daughter of the Arcadian Ladon (or of Amyclas) and had been saved from the unwanted attentions of Apollo not by her father but by Earth, her mother, who either substitutes a laurel for her or transforms her into one. Ovid completely excludes the mother (547 is an obviously crude attempt by an interpolator to re-introduce her) and moves the scene to Thessaly and to a new father, Peneus. This change is at least partly due to Ovid's desire to link Daphne's story with that of Io, and thus to juxtapose two contrasting victims of passion, both daughters of great river gods, Peneus and Inachus (568-85). As usual, it is Ovid's version which becomes standard almost immediately, for although in the next generation Statius can still allude to Ladon as 'almost Apollo's father-in-law' (*Theb.* 4.289-90), even he elsewhere refers to Daphne as Thessalian (*Silv.* 1.2.131). Milton's 'sweet Grove of Daphne by Orontes' (*P.L.* 4.273-4) is something of a mystery.

It is instructive to contrast the direct simplicity of Ovid's plot with that of Parthenius: Daphne, daughter of Amyclas, spent her days hunting with her hounds in Laconia and elsewhere in the Peloponnese. Leucippus fell in love with her and pursued her by disguising himself as a girl joining her in the hunt. Daphne became very fond of her new friend and thus inflamed jealous feelings in Apollo who was also in love with her. The god, therefore, inspired in Daphne a desire to go bathing with her maidens and the disguised Leucippus. When he refused to undress, the girls tore his clothes off and, perceiving his treachery, killed him with their spears. Thereupon Apollo began to chase Daphne but she prayed to Zeus who transformed her into a laurel.

In the Renaissance, the legend is a favourite of poets, painters and sculptors. Indeed, when in 1594 Ottavio Rinuccini wrote the libretto for what was to be regarded as the first opera (long since lost) it was the Daphne story he chose. Some measure of the popularity of the theme can be gained from the casual reference to it in Shakespeare's *Taming of the Shrew* (Induction 2.49-60):

> *Dost thou love pictures? we will fetch thee straight*
> *Adonis painted by a running brook...*
> *We'll show thee Io...*
> *Or Daphne roaming through a thorny wood,*
> *Scratching her legs, that one shall swear she bleeds;*
> *And at that sight shall sad Apollo weep,*
> *So workmanly the blood and tears are drawn.*

Here too Daphne and Io are juxtaposed.

Of the paintings we actually possess, the most charming is perhaps that of Antonio Pollaiuolo (reproduced in Wilkinson's *Ovid Recalled*) in which Apollo is embracing a Daphne each of whose arms has become a fully developed laurel tree growing aloft from her shoulders and scarcely smaller than the rest of her. Bernini's magnificent statue in which Apollo is about to catch Daphne whose feet and hands are just beginning to become laurel is, perhaps, the most accomplished of the plastic representations.

452 **first:** but not last. There were Clymene (1.751ff.), Coronis (2.543ff.), Leucothoe (4.196ff.), Isse (6.122), Dryope (9.331ff.), Chione (11.301ff.), and the Sibyl (14.130ff.). This does not include his boy loves, e.g. Hyacinth (10.162ff.) or other notorious examples not alluded to in the *Metamorphoses*, e.g. Cassandra.

453 **Cupid:** Greek Eros, sexual love. Not, however, the great cosmic force of early Greek speculation (Hesiod, *Theogony* 120 etc.), the driving force of the world's creation, but the sportive and mischievous boy of poetry and art from classical times to the present day. Squabbling amongst gods was, of course, a fruitful source of comedy from Homer on.
This episode owes something to the trick played on Apollo by the infant Hermes *(Hom. Hymn* 4.17ff.).

456 **and:** it is impossible in translation to do justice to this Ovidian trick of including the suffix *-que* "and" that connects *dixerat* ("he had said") to *uiderat* "he had seen" inside the direct quotation.

461 **Be you:** an attempt to render the mock solemn archaism, *esto.* Cupid's torch is a commonplace, (10.312, *Tib.* 2.1.82, *Prop.* 3.16.16).

469 **This routs...brings it on:** the translation has attempted neither the alliteration, nor the pithiness of *fugat hoc, facit illud amorem.* Cupid's two kinds of arrow are to be found in Euripides *I.A.* 548. Spenser *(Faerie Queene* III.11.36.6-7) recasts the imagery entirely:
> *...he Cupid thrild thee Apollo with a leaden dart,*
> *to loue faire **Daphne**, which thee loued lesse.*

470-1 This repetitive parallelism is a favourite Ovidian device, though it immediately gives way to two lines where there is deliberate structural variation.

476 **Phoebe:** Artemis to the Greeks, Diana in Rome, the sister of Phoebus Apollo, goddess of hunting and virginity. Ovid frequently exploits the ironies possible in juxtaposing real hunting and the hunt enjoyed by lovers. The story of Actaeon (3.198ff.) is perhaps the most striking example. Euripides' *Hippolytus* explores the theme fully while Virgil's *Aeneid* has a most subtle use of the twin themes in his treatment of Dido and Aeneas.

481-2 Compare 325-6 and the note there for this typically Ovidian device.

486-7 See Callimachus, *Hymn to Artemis* 6, of which this is essentially a translation.

491   Ovid cannot resist the idea of the god of oracles not only consulting them but being deceived by them, cf. 1.524; 2.618 and the note there.

492-4   The extended simile, that favourite device of high style from Homer on, (see the note on 1.200-6) is deliciously inappropriate for this absurd episode. Stubble burning, which is widely regarded as a novelty in Britain, has in fact a very long history. See, for example, Virgil, *Georgics* 1.85.

504   The translation attempts to preserve the breathless rhythm of the Latin. No linguistic knowledge is required to hear the panting pursuer in *nymphe, precor, Penei, mane*.

511   I shall...more moderately: 'Few but Ovid would have thought of this incongruous idea.' Lee.

512-22   This section is based on Theocritus' eleventh Idyll where the hideous Cyclops, Polyphemus, pursues just as unsuccessfully the lovely Galatea. There, however, the list of advantages claimed by the unhappy Polyphemus are extremely modest and thus increase the pathos. This reminiscence of the ill-favoured but honest Polyphemus adds a special piquancy to the scene before us.   The places listed were all sacred to Apollo. For Virgil's adaptation of the Theocritean Idyll, see *Eclogue* 2.19ff.

518   It was from the infant Hermes (Mercury) that Apollo received the lyre in return for the cattle he had stolen. See *Homeric Hymn* 4.17-502.

521   A commonplace at least as early as Aeschylus *Eum.* 62.

523-4   Compare line 491.

525-6   leaving him and his unfinished words: Ovid enjoys such zeugmas; see the note on 2.312-3.

527-9   Winds...breezes...breath: *uenti...flamina...aura.*   Ovid enjoys strings of synonyms.

533   A Gallic hound is probably a greyhound. The simile is closely based on one of Virgil's most famous (*Aen.* 12.794ff.). It is characteristic of Ovid that in this slight tale he should thus allude to the final pursuit of Turnus by Aeneas, the very climax of the *Aeneid*. See also the note on 4.362-9. Commentators point out that the huntress Daphne has now explicitly become the hunted. See also the note on 3.111-4.

536   Both Golding and some other translators 'improve' the original by giving us a male hound pursuing a female hare. Ovid, in fact, gives us two male animals.

542   Hom. *Il.* 23.765 (Lattimore's translation): 'Great Odysseus was breathing on the back of the head of Aias.'

548-52   Spenser's moral position (*Amoretti* 28.10-13) is entirely different:
> *Proud Daphne scorning Phoebus lovely fyre,*
> *on the Thessalian shore from him did flie:*
> *for which the gods in theyr revengefull yre*
> *did her transforme into a laurell tree.*

The repetition of 'her' in the translation is fortuitous and represents no such repetition in the Latin.

551   *uelox pigris*, a typical juxtaposition of two words of opposite meaning to achieve a striking effect. 'quick is stuck' is an attempt at the same effect but does not achieve the tightness that only an inflected language can give.

552   **radiance:** *nitor.* The allusion is, of course, to the sheen on the evergreen leaves of the laurel.

557-65   An aetiological passage to 'explain' the importance of the laurel in various contexts. The association of the laurel with Apollo is a commonplace but here Ovid, as so often, brings in anachronistic Roman associations (see the note on 1.171-5). Roman generals in triumph wore laurel, two laurel trees stood on either side of Augustus' door which was itself crowned by the oak-wreath granted for saving citizens' lives. As we read in Augustus' *Res Gestae* (34.2):
> *By a Senatorial decree, I was called Augustus*
> *and my door posts were wreathed with laurel and*
> *the civic crown was placed above my door.*

See also Austin on Virgil *Aen.* 6.772.

559-60   **you...you...you...you...:**   *te...te...te...tu...;* this repetition is characteristic of ancient hymns directed from a mortal to a god (see Callimachus *Hymn* 1.6-9; Lucretius 1.6-8; Catullus 34.13-17; Virgil *Aen.* 8.293-9 etc.) though here the roles are reversed. The effect is to give a mock solemnity to the passage. The repetition of 'you' in the two previous lines is quite unconnected arising, as it does, from the need to express personal pronouns in English in many cases where they are naturally absent in Latin.

566   **Paean:** according to Homer (*Il.* 5.401), Paean was the physician of the gods; in Sophocles (*O.T.* 154), *Paean* is an epithet of Apollo who had always been seen, from Homer on (*Il.* 1.8-67), as the bringer and healer of disease. Here the word is used simply for Apollo.

568-746   Io
The sources for the Io story and its relationship to the Daphne story
are discussed at length by Otis (1966) 350ff.; (1970) 379ff. We are told
by a number of our ancient sources (most conveniently collected in
Evelyn-White's Loeb edition of Hesiod, pp. 270-3) that the story of
Io was told by Hesiod. Herodotus begins his *Histories* with a number
of rationalized versions of the myth, and the similar Europa myth,
and speculation on how far these stories lay behind the long standing
animosity between the Greeks and their Eastern neighbours. Bovine
Io has a large part to play in Aeschylus' *Prometheus Vinctus* also, but
it is probably on the lost *Io* of Calvus (a friend of Catullus delightfully
addressed by him in two of his poems, 14 and 53) that Ovid relied most.
Otis offers a complex account of borrowings between the related themes
of Daphne, Io, Europa and Callisto. Suffice it to say here that the
Io story is in many ways a repeat of the Daphne story, except that
the one concentrates on the chase, the other on the conquest and its
consequences. Both are obviously humorous in Ovid, though, especially
in the case of Io, Ovid's sources seem to have been far from humorous.
When he was younger, Ovid had treated the subject more conventionally
(*Her.* 14.85-108), but many phrases used there recur here.

568-73   There is a copse...: another typical ekphrasis, see the note
on 1.168.

569   Tempe: this valley was regarded in antiquity as the supreme
example of natural beauty, to such an extent that the word *Tempe*
came to refer to any beautiful valley (e.g. Virg. *Georg.* 2.469, Hor.
Od. 3.124 and, indeed, Ovid himself at *Fast.* 4.477 and *Am.* 1.1.15).
According to Smith's *Dictionary of Greek and Roman Geography* (s.v.
'Tempe' 1124):

> the scenery is distinguished rather by savage
> grandeur than by the sylvan beauty which
> Aelian [V.H. 3.1] and others attribute to
> it.

This seems, however, to be a fairer criticism of, for example, Catullus
64.285-6 than of Ovid, perhaps because Ovid was writing after Livy's
very prosaic description of the famous valley (44.6). English writers
are not immune to the charms of the spot; consider Sidney (*Sonnet*
74):

> I never drank of Aganippe well,
> Nor ever did in shade of Tempe sit.

Peneus: Daphne's father who provides the link with the Io story;
see the note on lines 452-567.

576   he gave laws: *iura dabat;* the very same phrase is used by Virgil (*Aen.* 1.293) at the climax of Jupiter's prediction of the supreme role Rome will have to play in the history of the world. It is a very Roman expression with deep associations characteristically played with here by Ovid. See also the note on 1.171-5.

578   not knowing...: Ovid squeezes everything he can out of the Daphne story.

579-83   Sperchios...Inachus: these are all rivers of Thessaly eventually discharging into the Northern Aegean, except for the Aeas (an Illyrian river that discharges into the Adriatic) and the Inachus (an Argive river from the South-eastern part of the Peloponnese); a pedant might feel that Inachus' absence from an assembly of the rivers of Northern Greece was unsurprising.

580   old man Apidanus: river gods are always old. Compare Virgil *Aen.* 8.31-2, 540 etc., Macaulay's 'Oh Tiber! father Tiber!' from *Horatius* which is, of course, a deliberate classical borrowing, and 'Old Father Thames' or 'Ol' man river' (of the Mississippi) which, presumably, are not.

587   the worse: i.e. that she was nowhere.

591   A typical Ovidianism. Compare 1.597; 2.703; 9.782. It has an obviously comic effect as well as speeding up the narrative.

595   common: *de plebe;* compare the note on 1.173-6.

597   See the note on line 591.

600   Note the speed of this line and the obvious contrast with the long drawn out and unsuccessful pursuit of Daphne by Apollo. This is the first of many successful rapes in the *Metamorphoses*. For a full and detailed discussion of the topic together with direction to other discussions see Leo Curran, 'Rape and Rape Victims in the *Metamorphoses*', *Arethusa* 11 (1978) 213-41.

    modesty: *pudorem; pudor,* 'shame', 'sense of modesty', is an important Roman concept. Dido, in Virgil's *Aeneid* (4.27), swears that she would rather be swallowed by the earth than disobey the rules of *pudor*; twenty-eight lines later, however, she ignores *pudor* to give way to her feelings for Aeneas. Similarly here, the word recurs eighteen lines later in a classic conflict with *amor*, 'love', though there it must be rendered 'shame'. One of the reasons why we require two different words is that there is no longer a universal assumption that a girl's loss of virginity outside marriage brings shame upon her, regardless of the circumstances. The old fashioned expression, 'she has lost her virtue', reflects something of the attitude. See also 1.129.

606   The most well known catalogue of these deceits is to be found in Homer's *Iliad* (14.315-28) where, in a hilarious passage, Zeus tells Hera (Lattimore's translation):

> For never before has love for any goddess or woman
> so melted about the heart inside of me, broken it to submission,
> as now: not that time when I loved the wife of Ixion
> who bore me Perithoos, equal of the gods in counsel,
> not when I loved Akrisios' daughter, sweet-stepping Danae,
> who bore Perseus to me, pre-eminent among all men,
> etc. etc.

The marital infidelities of Zeus/Jupiter were, of course, proverbial.

615   **Jupiter lied:** see the note on 1.736.

616   **born from earth:** *e terra genitam;   terrae filius,* 'son of earth', was a proverbial expression for a 'nobody'.

617   **surrender:** *addicere,* a technical legal term for transferring ownership from one party to another.

618-9   **shame...love:** *pudor...amor;* such contrasts are of the very essence of ancient rhetoric, there is a striking elaboration of the theme at 7.72-3; see also 3.205, *Her.* 15.121, *Am.* 1.2.32.

620   Juno was Jupiter's sister and wife; Homer puts it with quiet dignity: 'He [Zeus] addressed Hera, his sister and wife' (*Il.* 16.432) and Virgil puts the same phrase into the mouth of Juno (*Aen.* 1.47). Ovid, however, cannot resist undercutting the idea either, as here, with an elaborate circumlocution or, even more strikingly, as at 3.265-6.

622   **wench:** this is the word I have consistently used to render *paelex.* The word's basic meaning, to quote the *Oxford Latin Dictionary*,   is: 'A mistress installed as a rival or in addition to a wife'. In Ovid, however, the word seems frequently to have a jocular connotation, as here, and only sometimes a pejorative one, as at 4.235, 277. While 'wench' does not necessarily carry the connotation of 'mistress', it does cover the range from cheerful ribaldry to moral disapprobation.

624   **Argus:** the story is as old as Aeschylus (*P.V.* 568, *Supp.* 291-310) and may even be as old as Homer, though Hermes' Homeric epithet, traditionally rendered 'Slayer of Argus' (*Il.* 2.103 etc.), may properly mean 'bright appearing' and the story could have arisen to explain the false interpretation. Moschus (*Europa* 44-57) describes a representation of Argus and Io on Europa's basket and this is imitated by Virgil (*Aen.* 7.789-92). Arestor was traditionally his father.

625-7 This picture has, of course, frequently proved irresistible to those seeking a name for a newspaper.

632-4 grass...grassy: *herba...gramen;* see the note on 1.71-3 for a similar situation.

633 unhappy one: *infelix,* very much the *mot juste* in Latin love poetry for the unhappy lover.

635-6 See the notes on 1.325-6 and 2.487.

643 the sisters: i.e. the Naiads.

645 Old Inachus: *senior...Inachus;* see the note on 1.580.

651-3 Unhappy me...Unhappy me: *me miserum...me miserum;* not only not the same word as was translated 'unhappy' at line 633 (and see the note), but it is the same expression that was rendered 'Oh dear me' at 1.508. There, however, the mood was so different that it seems impossible to use the same English expression.

658-9 These are, of course, the standard parental expectations; compare the words of Peneus to his daughter at 1.481-2.

661-2 death...death's: *morte...leti;* see the note on 1.71-3 for a similar situation. See also 4.152-3.

664 starred: *stellatus,* in anticipation of 'starry' *stellantibus* at the end of the story (1.723).

668 Phoronis: i.e. the sister of Phoroneus, Io.

669 bright Pleias: i.e. Maia, daughter of Pleione and mother of Mercury; she is 'bright', *lucida,* because she is a star, *Pleias* being the singular of *Pleiades,* the daughters of Pleione, the well known constellation (Aratus *Phaen.* 254-67).

671-5 The account of Mercury equipping himself for travel comes originally from Hom. *Od.* 5.448 and is picked up by Virgil (*Aen.* 4.239-44). It is typical of Ovid that he should uncercut this famous epic scene by describing how Mercury divests himself of his equipment once he is safely on earth. A different, but equally amusing pastiche on the epic passages occurs at 2.730-36.

673   Jove's son: i.e. Mercury; see the note at 2.697-704.

676   stolen: Mercury was the god of travel and therefore the god both of those who travelled and of those who lived by stealing from travellers. Indeed, the fourth of the *Homeric Hymns* celebrates his thieving tricks at length.

677   a set of pipes: wind instruments achieve different notes either by lengthening and shortening the effective pipe (flutes, trombones, trumpets etc.) or by switching the air to different pipes (organs, mouth organs etc.). This instrument works on the latter principle, being simply a set of pipes of varying length attached side by side and played like a mouth organ. It is known in Greek as the *syrinx* (1.691), and as early as Homer it was associated with shepherds (*Il.* 18.525-6) and in the *Homeric Hymns* (4.511-2) with Hermes. Theocritus (1.1-6) associates it with Pan to whom Virgil (*Ecl.* 2.32-3) attributes its invention (compare Lucretius 4.586-9), hence the English term for it 'Pan pipes'. Marvel (*The Garden* 29-32) is obviously thinking of Ovid:

> *Apollo hunted Daphne so*
> *Only that she might laurel grow.*
> *And Pan did after Syrinx speed,*
> *Not as a nymph, but for a reed.*

682   Atlas' grandson: i.e. Mercury; see the note on 2.697-704.

685-6   sleep...sleep: *somnos...sopor;* see the note on 1.71-3 for a similar situation and compare 1.714-6 for the same situation intertwined with another similar one.

689-712   The story within a story was very much a part of the Hellenistic tradition, and is a device much used in the *Metamorphoses*. This particular story is very pastoral in style; comparison with Theocritus and with Virgil's *Eclogues* is irresistible. The setting in Arcadia is, of course, the obvious clue but a careful reading of *Eclogue* 2, for instance, will reveal much more of interest.

690   Hamadryads: wood nymphs, see Virgil *Ecl.* 10.62.

694-7   Ortygian goddess...Diana's...Latonia...Diana's: three different ways to refer to the same goddess in four lines. Ortygia is an alternative name for Delos where Diana was born to Latona. See also 3.156.

696   she could be thought to be Latonia: an echo, surely, of Nausicaa who also resembled Artemis (Hom. *Od.* 6.102-9, 149-52) as did Dido (Virg. *Aen.* 1.498-502) and, perhaps more surprisingly, Venus (*Aen.* 1.314-29). This resemblance had become an epic commonplace.

700   A typical Ovidian twist that enables him to finish the story swiftly and in a different manner; it also serves to remind the reader that Io's story is still incomplete.

713   Cyllenius': i.e. Mercury's; he was born on Mount Cyllene. See *Homeric Hymns* 4.304; Virgil *Aen.* 4.252.

714-6   eyes...eyes...sleep...sleep...eyes: *oculos...lumina somno...soporem... lumina*; see the note at 1.685-6.

717   curved sword: see the note on 4.666.

720   light...your eyes: *lumina lumen*; the ordinary Latin word for 'light', *lumen* (plural *lumina*), can also be used to mean 'eye'. There is no way to reproduce the pun satisfactorily in English.

721   a single night: *nox una*; Ovid has taken *nox una*, a euphemism for 'death' most famous from Catullus 5.6 (but see also Hor. *Od.* 1.28.15) and set it up in an absurd contrast with Argus' one hundred eyes.

723   her bird: the peacock was sacred to Juno; it appears with Hera on the coins of Samos, Cos and Halicarnassus. Further details can be found in D'Arcy Thompson 164-7.
　　　　starry: *stellantibus*; see note at 1.664.

726   hidden goads: *stimulos...caecos*; in the *Prometheus Vinctus* (597), Io was pursued by goads, but the full phrase is borrowed from Lucretius 3.874.

731   This pathetic image is reminiscent of Virgil's picture of Cassandra (*Aen.* 2.405-6) where Austin's notes are most instructive. Is this raising of the head also a foreshadowing of Io's return to human shape? See 1.86 and the note on 1.84.

732   grief-sounding moo: *luctisono mugitu*; the normal hexameter ending of a dactyl followed by a spondee, 'munching a turnip', is deliberately changed to two spondees, 'munching turnips', and this clearly enhances the onomatopoeic effect of the long vowels of *mugitu. luctisonus* is not found elsewhere and may be an Ovidian coinage.

736   she: *haec*; but *haec* could also be taken with *causa*, 'this sort of case will never etc.' On that hypothesis, as Lee observes:

> *Jove intends Juno to take the*
> *promise in the [second] sense;*
> *he swears to it only in the*
> *[first].*

Bömer, however, reminds us that the gods look indulgently on a lover who breaks his oath, which, according to Apollodorus 2.1.3, was an opinion referred to by Hesiod in connexion with the Io story. It certainly became a commonplace (see Propertius 2.16.47-8 etc.) and, furthermore, we know that Jupiter has already lied to Juno at 1.615.

741   the gape of her mouth: *rictus*, very much an animal word in the *Metamorphoses*; compare 2.481; 3.74, 674; 4.97 etc.

743   Compare 1.612.

747-2.400   Phaethon

The sources for this memorable episode, the longest of the whole *Metamorphoses*, are discussed at length by Otis (1966) 360-6; (1970) 389-95. His essential thesis is that Ovid relied partly on Euripides' *Phaethon*, of which only fragments remain, and partly on a Hellenistic source now lost, but essentially the source of Lucian's *Dialogi Deorum* 25 and of Nonnus' *Dion.* 38.105-434. Phaethon's scepticism about his parentage came from Euripides, his extreme youth from the Hellenistic source. It was Ovid, however, who delayed the Sun's disastrous promise from a solemn undertaking years before to Clymene to a spontaneous gesture to his son and the immediate cause of the disaster.

Earlier in his book (91-2), Otis drew attention to *Fast.* 4.793-4 where Ovid had already linked Deucalion's flood with Phaethon's conflagration, as had Plato (*Tim.* 22b) and Lucretius (5.380-415) before him. For a somewhat different analysis of the history of the myth, see Diggle 4-32. Diggle also discusses in detail the Phaethon story as a favourite motif of Roman plastic art, especially sarcophagi (205-20). In the second volume of Frazer's Loeb edition of Apollodorus there is a fascinating appendix on parallels to this myth in Amerindian folk-lore (388-94).

The word *phaethon* itself first occurs as a Homeric epithet of the Sun (*Il.* 11.735 etc.), later it becomes the name of his son; the word entered English, shorn of its second aspirate, from French as the name of a particular kind of horse-drawn carriage. Sixty years ago, it was widely used in North America as the name for a type of open, touring motor car.

747   The association of Io with Isis is certainly ancient; see Herod. 2.41 (de Selincourt's translation):

> *The statues of Isis show a female*
> *figure with cow's horns, like the*
> *Greek representation of Io.*

the linen-wearing throng: i.e. Egyptian priests; Herodotus 2.37 (de Selincourt's translation):

> *The priests shave their bodies*
> *all over every other day to guard*

> *against the presence of lice, or anything*
> *else unpleasant, while they are about*
> *their religious duties; the priests, too,*
> *wear linen only...*

748   Epaphus: 'Bulls are considered the property of the god Epaphus, or Apis...' Herod. 2.40.

756   Clymene: Phaethon's mother in all extant versions of the myth.

763   Merops, king of Ethiopia and Clymene's second husband, seems to have been a Euripidean invention not taken up by Lucian or Nonnus.

769   which sees and hears us: a commonplace as early as Homer *Il*.3.277 and very often repeated. For the details see Bömer.

775   your spirit moves you: *fert animus,* the very same expression occurs in the first line of the *Metamorphoses.*

778   his Ethiopians: see 2.235-6.

NOTES: BOOK II

1-18   An elaborate ekphrasis; see the note on 1.168 and critique in Wilkinson (156ff.).

2   pyrope that mimics flames: *flammasque imitante pyrope*; in English the word is used only of gems, such as the garnet; in Greek and Latin it seems also to have been used for certain alloys, though which sense is intended here is uncertain. The basic meaning of the word, 'fiery-looking', is paraphrased in the accompanying phrase; see the notes on 3.206-33 and 358.

5-18   When Aeneas visited Cumae, he encountered, according to Virgil, a temple on the doors of which Daedalus had portrayed his own sad history (*Aen.* 6.14-41). Virgil's description of those doors forms part of an ekphrasis; there can be no doubt that our passage is modelled on that one, though, as Austin points out in his note on *Aen.* 6.14-41, an ekphrasis that includes a description of a work of art is by no means uncommon.

5   Mulciber: the 'Softener', one of the titles of Vulcan, the gods' blacksmith and craftsman. He is familiar as Hephaestus from the *Iliad* and celebrated for the shield he made for Achilles (*Il.* 18.478-608). See also 2.106.

7   disk...disk: *orbem...orbi*; see the notes on 1.31 and 33.

8   aquamarine gods: see the note on 1.275.

9   unstable: Golding's solution for *ambiguum*; Proteus, the Old Man of the Sea, was capable of transforming himself into a terrifying variety of forms but could be overcome by a determined attacker who would not let go; Homer gives a most memorable account of him (*Od.* 4.394-461). Philip Howard, writing on the word 'fudge' (*The Times* [of London] 4 April 1985), offers this:

> It is one of those Protean words of English
> slang that have as many meanings as the
> Old Man of the Sea had shapes...only recently
> has it metamorphosed into its new meaning...

Mutability is, in fact, a common attribute of the gods of sea and river; compare for example, Soph. *Trach.* 10 and the commentators.

18   The twelve signs of the zodiac. These are very appropriate for the palace of the Sun since the zodiac is the path through the heavens that the sun seems to traverse in its annual course. See 2.70-5 and 80-3 and the notes there.

34   a child no parent could disown: Phaethon's question is answered before he can even ask it.

36-40   father...father: *pater...genitor;* see the note on 1.71-3.

40-1   In one of Homer's most touching scenes (*Il.* 6.466-73), Hector removes his helmet because its nodding plume is frightening his baby son, Astyanax, whom he was never to see again.

44   ask any favour: at 3.288ff., Jupiter and Semele have an almost identical conversation leading to a very similar catastrophe.

46   the swamp that gods must swear by: the Styx, see the note on 1.189. Ovid cannot resist the humorous observation that the Sun is swearing by an underworld river he can never have seen.

47-8   The contrast between the brevity allotted to the request and the length allowed for the analysis of the reaction to the request is most effective.

48   wing-footed: compare Euripides *Electra* 466.

49   three times or four: *terque quaterque,* an echo of Virgil *Aen.* 1.94, itself taken from Homer *Od.* 5.306. The phrase imparts an epic solemnity to the passage and reminds the reader of Aeneas and Odysseus who used the phrase when they feared they were about to drown. At 1.179, Ovid used the expression in connexion with Jupiter's nod and at *Amores* 3.1.22 of personified Tragedy.

68   Tethys, the wife of Ocean (Hes. *Theog.* 337), is used here to mean 'the sea'. Compare Amphitrite at 1.13 and the note there for another example of what is a not uncommon form of metonymy in Classical poetry. See also the notes on 3.437; 4.258. At 2.156 Tethys appears in her own right.

70-5   As the earth revolves daily on its own axis, the fixed stars, together with the sun, appear to revolve around it. However, the earth's annual revolution around the sun makes it appear that the sun is travelling very slowly through the fixed stars along a path called the zodiac (roughly 'little zoo'), see Aratus *Phaen.* 542-68. The direction of the sun's apparent annual course through the zodiac is opposite to the direction of the apparent daily journey of the fixed stars around the earth.

These instructions, therefore, are both pedantic and perverse, since the distance the Sun would need to travel backwards through the stars on a single day would be negligible. But perhaps the exaggeration of the difficulties is a further element in the Sun's desperate attempt to dissuade the naive Phaethon. For a convenient and attractive book which explores the mythology of the zodiac in greater detail than can be attempted here, see H. Lloyd-Jones and M. Quinton, *Myths of the Zodiac*, London, 1978.

80-3   As should be apparent from the note on 2.70-5, this threat is nonsensical. In any single day, the sun remains almost motionless on the spinning zodiac and therefore would not pass through several signs. At most, it would pass from the very edge of one sign into its neighbour, but there are only twelve days in the whole year when even this can happen.

80   Taurus: the Bull, the second sign of the zodiac, usually identified as the bull responsible for bringing Europa from Sidon (see 2.847ff.); note that the Sun naturally chooses the more terrifying signs.

81   the Haemonian bows: Chiron, one of the Centaurs, was celebrated as Achilles' tutor (Hom. *Il.* 11.831-2); he dwelt in Thessaly (known also as Haemonia, see 1.568) and was taken into heaven as Sagittarius, the ninth sign of the zodiac; see also Lucan 6.393-4.
    savage Leo: the Nemean lion which was eventually killed by Heracles, as the first of his famous Labours, before appearing in heaven as the fifth sign of the zodiac.

82   Scorpio: the eighth sign of the zodiac. Aratus *Phaen.* 636-46 tells the story of how this monster was used by Artemis to kill Orion after which both it and he were taken into heaven, but in such a way that the Scorpio chases Orion for ever.

83   Cancer: the Crab, the fourth sign of the zodiac. He had helped the Hydra, the subject of Hercules' second Labour. See Apollodorus 2.5.2 and the authorities cited by Frazer.

103   Phaethon: *ille*, see the note on 1.58.

106   The Sun's chariot is an ancient concept. (*Hom. Hymn* 4.68-9) and became a commonplace of art and literature, ancient and modern e.g. Milton *Comus* 95-7:

> And the gilded car of day,
> His glowing axle doth allay
> In the steep Atlantic stream.

107   golden...golden...golden: from the *Homeric Hymns* (31.15) to Milton (see the note on 2.106) the Sun's chariot was golden. As for the repetition, it is a device so ubiquitous in all kinds of high literature that examples would be superfluous.

109   chrysolites: *chrysolithi*, a Greek word meaning, literally, 'golden stones' and probably referring to the topaz.

114   Lucifer: i.e. 'Light-bringing', the Morning Star, beautifully described by Homer (*Od.* 13.93-4). It is, in fact, the planet Venus which is visible in the Northern hemisphere either just before the dawn or at dusk when it is known as *Vesper*, the Evening Star. Its lowness in the sky made it seem to be a fallen angel to the Jews (*Isaiah* 14.12) from where it became a term for Satan in Christian poetry e.g. Marlowe *Faustus* 303-5:

> *Unhappy spirits that fell with Lucifer,*
> *Conspired against our God with Lucifer,*
> *And are for ever damned with Lucifer.*

Much more recently, the primary meaning reasserted itself as in the popular song from the First World War which includes the line: 'if you've a Lucifer to light your fag'.

119-20   fire-spewing: *ignemque uomentes*; compare 'flame-producing', *flammiferis*, at 2.155.

120   ambrosia juice: just as nectar was the gods' drink (see the note on 1.111), so ambrosia was their food (Hom. *Il.* 5.369, *Od.* 9.359). See also 4.215.

124   Latinus is similarly decorated with rays upon his head (Virgil *Aen.* 12.161-4) as a symbol of the fact that he is Sun's grandson.

129-33   The five zones are described at 1.45-51. This is an account of the ecliptic, the path of the zodiac (see the note on line 18) which runs across the equator and over the three middle zones. Here again, however, there would be no need for Phaethon to do more than cling to one point if he is to drive the chariot for only a single day (see the note on 2.70-5).

132   North: *Arcton*, literally 'Bear' (see the notes on 2.172; 4.625), but here the metonymy seems too dead to translate literally or to keep as 'Arctos'. Contrast 3.45 and 595.

139-40   Very similar advice is given to Icarus at 8.203-8.

138-9   the coiled Snake...the Altar down below: a traditional star map, such as the one reproduced at the end of the Loeb edition of Callimachus'

Hymns, Lycophron and Aratus, is helpful here. The Snake is clearly Draco, which is coiled around the Bears and is thus one of the extreme Northerly constellations (see also the notes on 2.173 and 3.45); the Altar is one of the most Southerly visible from the Northern hemisphere, hence 'down below'.

146   take my advice and not my chariot: *consiliis non curribus utere nostris*; the similarity of the contrasted words in Latin (*consiliis, curribus*) produces an inimitable effect; but the zeugma is effective in either language, see the note on 2.312-3.

153-4   There seems to have been no set list of names for the Sun's horses; the evidence is discussed by Bömer. The names here are all Greek: Pyrois means 'fiery', Eous 'of the Dawn', Aethon 'blazing' (it is also the name of one of Hector's horses according to Homer *Il.* 8.185), Phlegon 'burning'.

156   Tethys: mother of Clymene (Hes. *Theog.* 351) and (see the note at 2.68) a goddess of the sea. It is natural enough that the sea should be thought of as releasing the sun at dawn. The image is, however, apparently unknown to us before Ovid although Statius imitates it at *Theb.* 3.34-5.

162   heaviness of the yoke: Olympian gods were heavier than men, let alone boys; see Homer *Il.* 5.837-9. See also 4.449-50.

169   Their driver: *ipse*, literally 'he himself', often presents problems to the translator. It can mean 'master', as in Scots dialect, 'it's himself', and has something of that notion here.

170   the horses: *illis*; see the note on 1.58.

171   the cold Oxen: see the note on 1.64.

172   the forbidden sea: as the earth makes its annual journey around the sun, the inhabitants of the Northern hemisphere are able to see a gradually altering array of stars at night as some get lower and lower in the sky until they sink beneath the horizon while others rise from the opposite side. The stars at the very top, however, most notably the constellations known as the Wain or the Seven Oxen (*Septentriones*) or the Greater and Lesser Bear (for that story see 2.514-30 and the note on 2.176-7), are always visible and never 'sink beneath the sea' as we learn from Homer *Il.* 18.487-9.

173   Serpent: *Serpens*, referred to as Snake (*Anguis*) at 2.138-9 where see the note.

176-7   Boŏtes...wagon: see Aratus *Phaen.* 91-3 (Mair's translation):
> *Behind Helice, like to one that*
> *drives, is borne along Arctophylax*
> *[Bear guard] whom men also call*
> *Boŏtes [Ox-driver], since he seems*
> *to lay hand on the wain-like Bear.*

184   boat: *pinus*; see the note on 1.94.

195-6   There is a place...: *est locus...*; another ekphrasis, though a brief one, see the note on 1.168.

195   Scorpio bows out his Claws: according to Aratus (*Phaen.* 546), the two signs of the zodiac immediately following the Maiden are the Claws and Scorpio himself. Virgil (*Georg.* 1.33) fantasises that Scorpio will retract his Claws to make way for a new constellation devoted to Augustus. The sign was also known as the Balance (*Libra*) from the time of Hipparchus, the greatest astronomer of the second century B.C. Indeed, Virgil himself so alludes to it without further comment at *Georg.* 1.208. The name probably alludes to the fact that, in antiquity, the autumnal equinox took place while the sun was in this sign.

202   left the course: *exspatiantur*; see the note on 1.279-85.

208   brother's: see the notes on 1.10 and 2.454.

217-26   The Catalogue of Mountains. Such lists were an integral feature of high poetry from the time of Homer. This particular list is reminiscent of Clytemnestra's famous account of the succession of signal pyres blazing from mountain tops to announce the end of the Trojan War (Aeschylus *Agamemnon* 281-311). Several of the peaks of that list also appear here. Detailed discussion of each mountain can be found in Bŏmer; here, only the more elementary points will be discussed.

218   Ida...abounding in springs: see Homer *Il.* 12.19-22 where no fewer than eight rivers are said to rise on the slopes of Ida.

219   the Virgins: i.e. the Muses who dwelt on mount Helicon in Boeotia, Hesiod's home; hence the elaborate invocation to the Heliconian Muses at the opening of his *Theogony*.
    Haemus (not yet Oeagrian): at 10.77, Orpheus, son of Oeagrus, retreated to mount Haemus in Thrace where, eventually (11.1-53), he was to be torn to shreds; see also Virgil *Georg.* 4.520-7.

222   Rhodope: see Theocritus 7.76-7 for the snows of Rhodope.

224   **Scythia:** its cold was notorious, compare 1.64.

226   **beclouded:** *nubifer,* apparently another Ovidian coinage.

235   **Ethiopians' peoples:** that Africans are black because of their greater exposure to the sun was a commonplace (Herod. 2.22, Lucr. 6.1106-9 etc.), but to attribute it to Phaethon's ride seems to have been an Ovidian invention. For a full discussion of every aspect of race in antiquity, see F.M. Snowden, *Blacks in Antiquity* (Cambridge, Mass., 1970).

241-59   A catalogue of rivers to compare with the mountain catalogue of 2.217-26.

243   **old man Peneus:** see the note on 1.580.

245   **Xanthus that was to burn again:** a reference to the battle between Achilles and the river when Hera enlisted the help of Hephaestus to set fire to it (Hom. *Il.* 21.328-82).

246   **Meander:** *Meandrus,* a Phrygian river with a notoriously winding course that gave its name, even in antiquity, as a word for wandering. 'Here's a maze trod, indeed, Through forth-rights and meanders.' Shakespeare, *Tempest* 3.3.2-3.

251   **Tagus:** a Portuguese river noted for its gold; see Catullus 29.19. In the words of Wyatt, *Of his Returne from Spaine:*
> *Tagus farewel that westward with thy stremes*
> *Turnes up the graines of gold already tried...*

252-3   Even as early as Homer Il. 2.461-3, swans floated and sang on the Cayster. The picture became a commonplace; see also *Met.* 5.386.

253   **Maeonian:** i.e. Lydian. See the note on 3.583.

254-5   A novel explanation for the great mystery of the Nile's source; the question was explored by Herodotus (2.28) and appears constantly in the poets, e.g. Hor. *Od.* 4.14.45-6.

256   **seven riverless valleys:** see the note on 1.422.

258-9   **the Po and the Tiber:** the list of rivers, like the list of mountains (2.226) ends in Italy, and with a patriotic Virgilian flourish.

262-73   **sea...it...water's...waters...sea...ocean:**   *mare...pontus...aequor... aequora...ponto...pelagi;* see the notes on 1.291-2, 330-1; I have tried different solutions here.

263-8   depths...depths...deep: *altum...ima...profundo;*   an   even   more difficult case than the one discussed at 1.71-3.

268   Nereus: one of the marine deities; he was the father of the Nereids, of course (for the list see Hom. *Il.* 18.38-49), who included Thetis, the mother of Achilles. At 1.187, Nereus is used to mean 'sea', compare the use of Amphitrite at 1.13 and of Tethys at 2.68 together with the notes there. Doris was the Nereids' mother.

270-1   Three times...three times: a very Homeric moment, see *Iliad* 5.436-7; 16.702-3.

274   bowels: *uiscera;* see the note on 1.138.

284   all this ash...all this ash: *tantum, tantum...fauillae;* in the Latin, only *tantum,* 'all this' and not *fauillae,* 'ash' is repeated.

286   wounds: see the note on 1.102.

291   your brother: i.e. Neptune, see the note on 1.275. According to Homer, the brothers Zeus (Jupiter), Poseidon (Neptune) and Hades (Dis) drew lots for their respective domains (*Il.* 15.187-93.)

296   Atlas: according to Homer (*Od.* 1.52-4), Atlas held up the great columns of earth and heaven; there is a similar image at Virgil *Aen.* 4.246-7, though there Atlas is already the mountain he is to become at *Met.* 4.657.

299   primaeval Chaos: see the note on 1.5.

312-3   from life and from his wheels: this sort of zeugma (or 'syllepsis' as the pedants prefer) is discussed by Fränkel (197). Compare 1.525-6; 2.146, 462, 505-6, 555-6, 601; 3.7-8, 46-7, 99-100; 4.141-2, 175.

324   Eridanus: normally the Greek for the Po (Latin *Padus* as at 2.258), a point made by Pliny (*N.H.* 37.2.31) in a discussion of this very myth; see also 2.370-1. Pliny also suggests that in Aeschylus' play on the theme (now almost wholly lost) the denouement was set beside a Spanish Eridanus. Be that as it may, it seems clear that an Eridanus was the scene for Phaethon's end from the earliest times (see Euripides *Hipp.* 737-41, Apollonius Rhodius 4.597-600, Aratus *Phaen.* 360 and, for a full discussion, Diggle 27-32. An Italian setting for the end of the Phaethon story would, of course, suit Ovid's tastes (see 2.366 and the notes on 1.171-5 and 2.258-9). Herodotus (3.115) knew that the Eridanus was a source for amber but he disclaims any precise knowledge of its whereabouts.

331-2 A typically absurd consolation.

340 Heliades: literally 'daughters of the Sun'; they are a traditional feature of the myth. Virgil (*Ecl.* 6.62-3) oddly calls them *Phaethontides* which ought to mean 'daughters of Phaethon' but clearly does not. See Diggle 8.

346-8 Phaethusa...Lampetie: one the feminine form of Phaethon, and both names of the Sun's daughters even according to Homer (*Od.* 12.132).

366 Latin brides: see the note on 2.324.

367 Sthenelus' offspring, Cycnus: the father is otherwise unknown; the story of the son, whose name is the Greek for 'swan', is also alluded to by Virgil (*Aen.* 10.189-94). Ovid tells elsewhere (7.371-2 and 12.64-145) of two other men of this name who were transformed into swans.

375 linkage: *iunctura*, a word not otherwise used for 'webbing' any more than 'linkage' is in English.

377-8 to the sky or to Jove: *caeloque Iouique*; a play on words since *Iuppiter*, especially in the phrase *sub Ioue*, can be used to mean 'sky'; see 4.260, 13.707 and the note on 3.363.

380 rivers, the very opposite of flames: *contraria flumina flammis*; no attempt has been made to reproduce the striking word-play of the Latin.

401-530 *Callisto*
As Otis points out (93), the Phaethon story is surrounded by two stories of Jupiter's loves (Io and Callisto) themselves surrounded by two of Apollo's (Daphne and Coronis). In a detailed account of Ovid's sources for these two stories, Otis (1966) 350-66; (1970) 378-9 suggests that some details have been moved from one story to another and that others have been invented by Ovid. The general outlines of the plot, together with a number of variations, are rehearsed by Apollodorus (3.8.2) while Virgil assumes a knowledge of the myth (*Georg.* 1.138). Ovid himself told the story far more briefly at *Fasti* 2.153-92.

405 Arcadia: according to some (e.g. Callimachus *Hymn* 1. 1-7) the birthplace of Zeus and so his special concern. The normal view, as reported by Ovid himself (*Fasti* 1.470), was that the place took its name from Callisto's son, Arcas, so that Arcadia here is something of an anachronism, but no more so than 'Arcadian king' for Lycaon at 1.218-9.

409-10 **Nonacrian:** of Nonacris, an Arcadian mountain and town, see Herod. 6.74, though here the word is used simply as a synonym for 'Arcadian'.

411 **to soften wool by drawing it out:** *lanam mollire trahendo*; for these technical terms for the production of luxurious and sensuous clothing, editors compare *Fasti* 2.742; 3.817-8; 4.773-4; *Her.* 370; *Met.* 6.20-1; 13.511; 14.264-5. As *Matthew* 11.8 reminds us: 'They that wear soft clothing (*mollibus* in the Vulgate) are in kings' houses.'

415 **Phoebe's:** i.e. Diana's, see the note on 1.11.
  soldier: the commonplace that the lover is engaged in a sort of warfare (see *Am.* 1.9.1 for a striking example) is here applied to a devotee of Diana, Venus' rival.
  Maenalos: another Arcadian mountain.

416 **Trivia:** i.e. Diana, compare Catullus 34.15, Virg. *Aen.* 6.13. Diana was identified with Luna (the Moon) and Hecate, and Hecate with the places where three roads meet (*triuia*), hence the title. Compare Virg. *Aen.* 4.609 and Pease's exhaustive note. 'Triviality' is the sort of gossip that can be heard at a *triuium*.

418 That devotees of Artemis (Diana) frequent a virginal, uncut countryside is a notion at least as old as Euripides *Hipp.* 73ff.

423-4 For a picture of the relationship between Jupiter and his wife, see 1.605ff. and the note on 1.606.

425 **Diana's face:** Otis's remarks (117-8) are worth quoting:
  The fact that Jupiter changes his shape
  in order to win the girl suggests, of
  course, his much more radical and
  comical transformation in the Europa
  episode. The introduction of the false
  Diana points ahead to the later appear-
  ance of the true one.
  and her dress: *cultumque*, a word that embraces both clothing and equipment so that the Latin does not have quite the harsh zeugma that the translation would suggest.

428-30 For the humour, compare 2.704-5 and the note there.

435 For a discussion of such apostrophes, see Fränkel 214 n.35. Compare also 3.131-4. and 432-6 and the note there.

438 **guilt:** see the note on 1.600.

441   **Dictynna:** originally a Cretan goddess, later, as here, identified with Diana. See Callimachus *Hymn* 3.189-200 and the note on 1.11.

443-6   **her...she...her...she...her...she...her...she...herself:** i.e. Callisto...Diana...Callisto...Callisto...Diana...Callisto...Diana...Callisto...Callisto; see the note on 1.58.

452   **They say the nymphs did sense it:** a typical Ovidian jest which deliberately and wholly undermines any solemnity the passage might seem to have been endowed with. And yet it is also true, in the words of Otis (118) that:

> Ovid's sly reference to Diana's virginal
> naivete...does not really lessen our sympathy
> with the poor girl.

453   **ninth:** human pregnancies last ten lunar months as Ovid points out with some humour at *Fasti* 2.175-6 in his other account of Callisto's story. This moment occurs, then, during the later stages of the pregnancy when even Diana would not be deceived once the girl had disrobed.

454   **brother's:** insofar as Diana is the moon (see 1.11 and the note there) her brother may be said to be the sun (compare 2.208). Much later, of course, this helped an identification of Apollo with the sun. See J.E. Fontenrose, 'Apollo and the Sun-god in Ovid', *AJPh* 61 (1940) 429-44.

458-65   The bathing scene. Ovid, it seems, first introduced this motif into the Callisto story; it is normally associated with Actaeon (see 3.131-252) and Tiresias. Ovid's source was, no doubt, Callimachus *Hymn* 5 where both of these versions are told.

460   **Parrhasis:** i.e. the Arcadian one, Callisto. The ultimate source for Parrhasia as an Arcadian region is Homer *Il.* 2.608; the immediate source for this term as a synonym for 'Arcadian' is Virgil *Aen.* 8.344 etc.

462   **exposed not just her naked body but her guilt:** for the zeugma, see the note on 2.312-3.

464   **Cynthia:** i.e. Diana from mount Cynthus on Delos noted as the birth place of Apollo and Artemis (*Hom. Hymn.* 3.14-8); see also Hor. *Od.* 3.28.12 and Virg. *Aen.* 1.498. John Gay, in his *Trivia* 3.4 (see the note on 2.416), gives us: 'Now Cynthia nam'd, fair regent of the Night'.

464-5   **Do not pollute my sacred streams:** as Fränkel (211 n.22) points out, this prohibition foreshadows Jupiter's words at 2.530.

466   **The great Thunderer's matron:** i.e. Juno.

481   **gaping wide:** *lato...rictu;* see the note on 1.741.

485   **her original mind remained:** see the note on 1.234.

487   **and she raised whatever sort of hand she had to heaven:** stretching the hand upwards was a standard gesture of supplication; see, for instance, Callimachus *Hymn* 4.107-8. Virgil, in his moving description of the destruction of Troy, relates how Cassandra, unable to raise her hands to supplicate was forced to look up only with pleading eyes (*Aen.* 2.405-6 where Austin's note is, as usual, instructive). Ovid picks up the idea of would-be suppliants unable to raise their arms in several humorous or grotesque contexts. Here, the inability arises only from the transformation of hands to paws; at 1.635-6, Io has temporarily forgotten that a cow's front legs cannot be raised up high, while at 3.723-4, Pentheus' problem is that his arms have been torn away. See also 2.580; 3.241; 4.516. There is a variation on the theme at 4.683-4.

495   **her father:** i.e. Lycaon, see 1.211-39.

504   **would-inducing:** *uulnifico,* a rare word presumably borrowed from Virgil *Aen.* 8.446.

505-6   **suspended both them and the sinful act:** for the zeugma, see the note on 2.312-3.

514-5   **If I'm not lying...you will see:** *mentior...nisi...uideritis;* literally, 'I am lying...unless...you will see'.

524   **Phoronis:** i.e. Io, see the note on 1.668.

527   **foster-child:** compare Homer *Il.* 14.301-3 (Lattimore's translation) where Hera (Juno) says:
> *I am going to the ends of the generous earth, on a visit*
> *to Okeanos, whence the gods have risen, and Tethys our mother,*
> *who brought me up kindly in their own house, and cared for me.*

527-30   See the notes on 1.64, 2.172 and 464-5.

531-632   A complex set of interlocking stories whose central theme is well summarized by Otis (120):
> *a motif very dear to Ovid (it is specifically repeated*
> *in the later Leucothoe and Ascalaphus stories),*
> *the futility of tattling, especially in amatory*
> *matters. The busybodies work nothing but havoc*

> *and themselves suffer for their officiousness.*
> *The anguish they provoke is much worse than*
> *any amount of deception and ignorance.*

It surely cannot be coincidental that the story of the Raven *(Coruus)* telling Apollo of Coronis' infidelity and the story of the Crow *(Cornix)* telling Athene (Minerva) of the wickedness of Herse and Aglauros and then predicting that the Raven will be punished for his tale-bearing by being changed from white to black all appear in fragment 260 of Callimachus' now largely lost *Hecale*. For the details, see Trypanis' Loeb edition pp. 178 and 194-7 and the note on 2.543. Other possible sources for these stories will be discussed as they unfold.

532-3 See the note on 1.723.

537 For the whiteness of doves, see, for instance, Catullus 29.8.

538-9 the geese that were to save the Capitol with their watchful voice: once again, Ovid characteristically introduces a Roman element into this Greek context. The story of the Gauls frustrated in their attempt to storm the Capitol only by the timely cackling of the Sacred Geese is most familiar from Livy 5.47; it is possible, however, that Ovid's word for the original colour of the Raven, *argentea* (i.e. 'silver') at 2.536 is taken from Virgil's use of the word for the colour of the Sacred Geese *(Aen.* 8.655).

539 the river loving swan: see the note on 2.252-3; see also Callimachus *Hecale* fr. 260.56 quoted in the note on 2.543.

543 Larissaean: i.e. Thessalian, from the Thessalian town, Larissa, compare Catullus 64.36, Virg. *Aen.* 2.197. For a detailed account of Coronis' Thessalian origins and other aspects of her story, see Frazer's notes in his Loeb edition of Apollodorus vol. 2, pp.13-16.

Coronis: her story first appears in Pindar *(Pyth.* 3.5-46) but the connexion with the raven was established in Callimachus' *Hecale* fr. 260.55-61 (Trypanis's translation):

> *But it shall be evening or night, or noon, or*
> *dawn, when the raven, which now might vie*
> *in colour even with swans, or with milk, or*
> *with the finest cream of the wave, shall put*
> *on a sad plumage, black as pitch, the reward*
> *that Phoebus will one day give him for his*
> *message, when he learns terrible tidings of*
> *Coronis, daughter of Phlegyas, that she has*
> *gone with Ischys, the driver of horses.*

Coronis is mentioned by no extant Latin poet except Ovid.

544   or unwatched: *uel inobseruata;* note the wry humour; *inobseruata* seems to be another Ovidian coinage.

544-5   Phoebus' bird: i.e. the raven; the identification is attributed to Hesiod by the ancient scholiast to Pindar *Pyth.* 3.28(48) in connexion with this very story. The passage appears as fragment 89 of the *Catalogues of Women and Eoiae* in Evelyn-White's Loeb edition of Hesiod. See also Callimachus *Hymn* 2.65-8.

545   adultery: it is characteristic of Ovid not to restrict this word to infidelity by parties to legal marriage. Compare 4.236.

553   Erichthonius: Apollodorus 3.14.6 (Frazer's translation; his notes also repay study):

> Athena came to Hephaestus, desirous of fashioning arms. But he, being forsaken by Aphrodite, fell in love with Athena, and began to pursue her; but she fled. When he got near her with much ado (for he was lame), he attempted to embrace her; but she, being a chaste virgin, would not submit to him, and he dropped his seed on the leg of the goddess. In disgust, she wiped off the seed with wool and threw it on the ground; and as she fled and the seed fell on the ground, Erichthonius was produced. Him Athena brought up unknown to the other gods, wishing to make him immortal; and having put him in a chest, she committed it to Pandrosus, daughter of Cecrops, forbidding her to open the chest. But the sisters of Pandrosus opened it out of curiosity, and beheld a serpent coiled about the babe.

The story is alluded to in Callimachus' *Hecale* (fr. 260.28-9, Trypanis's translation): 'Meanwhile, the maidens that watched the chest planned to do an evil deed.' See also Euripides *Ion*. Ovid returns to Pandrosus, Herse and Aglauros at 2.708-832.

554   Actaean: i.e. Attic or even Athenian. The adjective occurs in Callimachus (fr. 230) and was taken into Latin apparently by Virgil (*Ecl.* 2.24). Acte was an old name for Attica (Apollodorus 3.14.1).

555   two-formed: Cecrops was half snake and half man, see Apollodorus 3.14.1 with Frazer's notes.

555-6   had given him...together with a rule: for the zeugma, see the note on 2.312-3.

563   expelled from the protection of Minerva: see the note on 2.588.

564   the bird of night: the owl, the bird of Athene (Minerva), depicted on Athenian coins. Her story is told in greater detail at 2.592-5.

569-88   The girl's ravishing by Neptune and subsequent metamorphosis into a crow seems not to be recorded elsewhere. It has, however, many parallels with the story of Daphne (1.452-567).

569   Coroneus: not otherwise known, but the name was presumably chosen to encourage the reader to supply for the name of the crow herself the Greek word for that bird, 'Corone'. Her name is certainly not 'Coronis', as in the plot summaries of some mediaeval manuscripts and renaissance editions, for that would produce intolerable confusion. However, the stories of Coronis, Corone, the Owl and Athene were certainly connected long before Ovid; for the details of a very complex situation, see Frazer's edition of Pausanias, vol. 3, pp. 72-3.

571   Compare 1.478 of Daphne. As Moore-Blunt points out, the rich suitor 'is a stock figure of amatory elegy'; see also F.O. Copley, *Exclusus Amator*, (Madison, Wisconsin, 1956) 104.

572   My beauty hurt me: compare, of Daphne, 1.488-9 and her own words at 1.546.

574-88   Here, the narrative is far more like that of Jupiter and Io (1.597-600) in its speed, though in its outcome, and in the girl's successful petition to a god to save her, it retains its similarity to the Daphne episode.

579   by a maiden: i.e. by Minerva.

580   See the note on 2.487.

588   and given to Minerva: that the owl was the bird of Athene (Minerva) is, of course, a commonplace. The crow's claim is supported by a statue of Athene holding a crow described by Pausanias (4.34.6).

589   Nyctimene: literally 'Night one', i.e. the owl. This is the first extant account of this aetiological tale to explain the shyness of the owl. It is a brief foretaste of the theme of incest to which Ovid returns more fully with the stories of Byblis (9.447-665) and Myrrha (10.298-502). It is worth noting that all three ladies were treated together by Ovid in his *Ibis* (359-62).

592   father's: according to Hyginus (204) and Servius on Verg. *Georg.*

1.403, his name was Epopeus, but according to the scholiast on Statius *Theb.* 3.507, he was called Nycteus, a view possibly arising from the name Nyctimene here.

599   a young Haemonian: Ischys, according to Pindar *Pyth.* 3.31; see also Callimachus quoted in the note on 2.543.

601   For the zeugma, see the note on 2.312-3.

604   ineludible: *indeuitato,* a word found only here.

604-5   A line almost entirely filled with swift dactyls ('munching a') followed by one composed almost entirely of slow spondees ('deep dark).

618   Once again, Apollo's skills are useless to himself; compare 1.491 and the note there.

621-2   for it is not permitted...with tears: editors trace this sentiment back to Euripides *Hipp.* 1396 though it is also contradicted by Ovid himself; see, for example, 1.583-4; 4.426.

623-5   just as when...resounding blow: this memorable simile owes something to the famous description in Lucretius (2.352-66) of the heifer looking in vain for her sacrificed calf, a passage imitated far more closely by Ovid at *Fasti* 4.459-82.

627   the rites that were not right: an attempt at the pun in *iniustaque iusta: iusta,* 'rights', 'deserts', was also used as a term for what is owed to the dead, 'funeral rites'; *iniusta* is simply the opposite adjective, 'undeserved'.

629   snatched his son from the flames: Aesculapius is saved by Apollo just as Dionysius was to be by Jupiter (3.310-5).

630   two-formed Chiron: as early as Homer *Il.* 4.219 we learn that Asclepios (Aesculapius) had learnt medicine from Chiron. See also Pindar *Pyth.* 3.40-6. Chiron was one of the Centaurs, creatures with the body of a horse and the head and shoulders of a man.

632-75   Ocyroe.
This is our first extant account of the metamorphosis of Chiron's daughter into a mare, though it is clearly an ancient tale and was the subject of Euripides' play, *Melanippe Sapiens,* of which only fragments survive. Ovid may have been alone in linking Ocyroe with Aesculapius who is to return as the major figure of book 15.

634   **so onerous an honour:** *oneri...honore;* another example of Ovidian word-play.

636   **Chariclo:** see Pindar *Pyth.* 4.103.

637   **swift river:** Ocyroe is the Greek for 'swiftly flowing'.

639   **she used to sing the secrets of the Fates:** the editors quote Euripides fr. 482 which says much the same about her.

641   **the god:** i.e. Apollo, of course.

645-6   For a full account of Aesculapius' raising of Hippolytus from the dead, see 15.531-46. The earliest known reference to the incident is from the same Pindaric ode that tells the tale of Coronis (*Pyth.* 3.56-8). For Virgil's version, see *Aen.* 7.761-77 with Fordyce's notes.

646   **grandfather's:** i.e. Jupiter's, since he was Apollo's father.

649-54   For an account of Chiron's death, see Sophocles *Trach.* 1095ff.

651-2   **the dreadful snake's blood:** the reference is to the Lernaean hydra with whose blood Hercules' arrows were smeared. See the note on 4.501.

654   **the three-fold goddesses:** the Greek Moirae (Hesiod *Theog.* 903-6), Clotho, Lachesis and Atropos, who gave each mortal his fate at birth, were identified with the Roman Parcae; see, for instance, Catullus 64.306.

655   **Something of his fate was left:** i.e. she had not finished her prophecy. If she had, she would have included his elevation to the stars.

659-60   These complaints are reminiscent of those voiced by Cassandra in Aeschylus' *Agamemnon* (1194-1213). She too was favoured by Apollo and suffered because she displeased him.

675   **a name:** Hippe, which means 'mare' or, in some versions, Melanippe, 'black mare'.

676-707   Battus.
The earliest extant version of this story is to be found at *Homeric Hymn* 4.87-92, 186-212. In that version, an unnamed old man noticed the new born Hermes (Mercury) stealing the cattle of the gods. Hermes promised him a good crop of grapes if he would say nothing of what he had seen. In the event, however, he told Apollo who was pursuing Hermes; nothing is said about either reward or punishment.

According to Antoninus Liberalis, the story was also told by Hesiod in the *Great Eoiae* (most conveniently available in the Loeb Hesiod, 262-7). In that version, the cattle are Apollo's who is in Thessaly, near to the home of Admetus, because he is in love with Hymenaeus, the son of Magnes. Hermes decided to steal the cattle and then drove them far away, eventually passing Battus who demanded and was promised an unspecified reward for his silence. Hermes, however, returned in disguise to test him by offering him a robe if he would tell of any stolen cattle he had seen. Battus took the robe and told what he had seen and was punished by being turned into a rock. It is immediately obvious that Ovid is much closer to the Hesiodic account. Detailed points will be made as they arise.

676   The Philyrean hero: i.e. Chiron whose mother was Philyra; see Hesiod *Theog.* 1001-2.

677   oh Delphic one: Apollo, of course. For the device of addressing a character, a device called apostrophe, see Fränkel 214.

680-1   Perhaps a reference to Apollo's servitude to Admetus (see Apollodorus 1.9.15); more probably, however, Ovid is following the version attributed to Hesiod; see the note on 2.683.

682   an unequal set of pipes with seven reeds: it is, of course, the reeds that are unequal, but this sort of transferred epithet is very common. The instrument, known as the syrinx, is discussed in the note on 1.677.

683   concerned with love: presumably a discreet reference to Apollo's passion for Hymenaeus as recorded in the Hesiodic version.

689   Neleus: the father of Nestor who succeeded him as king of Pylos and was the oldest and wisest of the Greek kings who went with Agamemnon to conquer Troy. Pylos was famous for its horses and cattle. See Homer *Il.* 11.669-83.

691   was afraid of him: *timuit*; i.e. was afraid that he might report the theft; however, the alternative reading, *tenuit* 'stopped him', is tempting.

697-704   Jove's son...Atlas' grandson: i.e. Mercury. Atlas and Pleione were the parents of the Pleiades (see the note on 1.669), one of whom, Maia, became by Zeus the mother of Hermes (Mercury), see *Homeric Hymn* 4.1., Virg. *Aen.* 4.258.

704-5   Fränkel (215-6) discusses such passages well, though I am not persuaded by him that the question marks must necessarily be changed to exclamation marks. See also 2.428-9.

706   touch-stone: *index*, ordinarily 'informer', 'tell-tale' (as at 2.546), is here uniquely applied to a stone. The pun cannot be reproduced in English; translators have traditionally assumed that the stone intended is the touch-stone, a dark coloured stone that can be used to unmask base metals masquerading as gold.

708-832   *Herse and Aglauros*
This is the earliest extant account of this part of the story; for further details, see Apollodorus 3.14.2 and Frazer's notes; see also the note on 2.553.

708   Staffbearer: *Caducifer*, i.e. Mercury, another Ovidian coinage.

709   Munychian: Ovid introduced this adjective into Latin; only Statius (*Theb.* 12.616) followed him. Munychia was a part of the Piraeus, the port of Athens, but the adjective was used by Callimachus (*Hymn* 3.259) of Artemis, because she had a temple in the Piraeus. Here, in a typical 'part for whole' construction, Ovid uses it to mean 'Athenian'.

710   the cultured Lyceum: this was the garden just outside Athens where Aristotle was to set up his school. The introduction of this gross anachronism is, of course, deliberate fun.

711-3   This ceremony, which took place in the Parthenon, Athene's great temple in Athens and was depicted on the temple frieze, was called the Panathenaia. Its origins are clearly extremely old since a primitive Trojan version is described by Homer (*Il.* 6.86-91).

716   kite: D'Arcy Thompson (68) offers a number of references to show that this bird was traditionally regarded as a thief. See also Moore-Blunt:

> The carrying off of sacrificial meats by
> kites was so common a practice, that Aristotle
> (de Miralibus 123), Pausanias (5.14.1) and Aelian
> (N.A. 2.47) all mention it as a remarkable fact
> that it was never known to happen at the altar
> of Zeus in Olympia.

726   Jove's son: i.e. Mercury, see the note on 2.697-704.

727-8   a Balearic sling: the inhabitants of the Balearic Islands were noted for their skill with the sling; see Livy 38.29.6. The sling appears at 4.455-6 in a somewhat different simile.

730-6   A similarly amusing version of the traditional account of Mercury's equipment for travel occurs at 1.671-5 and is discussed in the note there.

749   The story was recounted at 2.552-61.

752   the warrior-goddess: *dea bellica*, i.e. Minerva. Ovid is the first to use this epithet of Minerva but the idea is as old as Homer who puts into the mouth of Zeus these words addressed to his daughter Aphrodite (*Il.* 5.428-30, Lattimore's translation):

> *No, my child, not for you are the works of warfare. Rather*
> *concern yourself only with the lovely secrets of marriage,*
> *while all this shall be left to Athene and sudden Ares.*

754   aegis: Homer *Il.* 5.733-42 (Lattimore's translation):

> *Now in turn Athene, daughter of Zeus of the aegis,*
> *beside the threshold of her father slipped off her elaborate*
> *dress which she herself had wrought with her hands' patience,*
> *and now assuming the war tunic of Zeus who gathers*
> *the clouds, she armed in her gear for the dismal fighting.*
> *And across her shoulders she threw the betasselled, terrible*
> *aegis, all about which Terror hangs like a garland,*
> *and Hatred is there, and Battle Strength, and heart-freezing*
> > *Onslaught*
> *and thereon is set the head of the grim gigantic Gorgon,*
> *a thing of fear and horror, portent of Zeus of the aegis.*

See also 4.799-803. The word has entered English shorn of its mythological associations and meaning merely 'protection', 'defence'.

757   the Lemnos-dweller's: *Lemnicolae* (another Ovidian coinage), i.e. Vulcan's; the association of Hephaestus (Vulcan) with the island of Lemnos can be traced back to Homer *Il.* 1.590-4. See also the note on 2.553.

760-82   An ekphrasis on personified Envy. Ekphrasis was discussed in the note on 1.168. Personification also goes back to Homer. See, for instance, *Il.* 4.439-43 (Lattimore's translation):

> *Ares drove these on, and the Achaians grey-eyed Athene,*
> *and Terror drove them, and Fear, and Hate whose wrath is relentless,*
> *she the sister and companion of murderous Ares,*
> *she who is only a little thing at the first, but thereafter*
> *grows until she strides on the earth with her head striking heaven.*

Even more striking, but too long to quote, is Phoenix' description of Prayer (*Il.* 9.502-12). Latin readers will especially recall Virgil's personification of Rumour at *Aen.* 4.173-97 which itself inspired many imitations; the notes of Pease and Austin give a detailed account of these. Critics have, on the whole, not been kind to Ovid's Envy. Otis's comments (120) may be regarded as not untypical:

> *but the grisly invocation of Envy by Minerva*
> *and Envy's horrible infection of Aglauros...*
> *are meant to excite a kind of melodramatic*

> frisson *in the reader. Ovid was here indebted to Virgilian figures like Fama and, especially, Allecto, but he greatly accentuated the visual and plastic detail...the result is hardly convincing save as a piece of ingenious make-believe.*

765   manly-maid: *uirago*, a striking word based on *uir*, 'man', but indelibly associated with *uirgo*, 'virgin'. Virgil used the word of Juturna (*Aen.* 12.468). 'Manly-maid' is an attempt to capture the two elements that together give the word its peculiar flavour but it is far too clumsy and contrived to do justice to *uirago*. In English, 'virago' has preserved the terrifying connotations of its Latin origin but has lost the sense of an awful purity.

770   Envy: the delay of the word is effective but natural in Latin; it is a little more strained in English.

774   screwed up...sigh: text, and therefore translation, is quite uncertain here, but the general sense is plain.

783   Tritonia: i.e. Minerva; the explanation of this title is disputed but it originates in Homer (*Il.* 4.515) and is not uncommon in Latin poetry; see, for example, Catullus 64.395, Lucr. 6.750, Virg. *Aen.* 2.171.

784-5   Infect...the one: the terseness of this command presumably reflects Minerva's distaste for Envy.

787   She: *illa*, i.e. Envy; see the note on 1.58.

790   thorny: *spinea*, another Ovidian coinage.

794   Tritonis': another form of Tritonia; it is, indeed, the form used by Catullus and Lucretius in the passages referred to in the note on 2.783.

799   bosom: *praecordia*; Golding's 'Lungs and Lights and all' is a more literal rendering, but no longer possible in English.

805   Cecropis: i.e. Cecrops' daughter.

820-4   Fränkel (209):
> *Inuidia had been described before (760ff.) as cold, pallid, sluggish, stiff and hardly able to rise; with almost the same words, Aglauros in the moment of petrification is pictured as cold, pallid, sluggish, stiff and unable to rise (820ff.); the punishment fits the crime.*

831 **sat there, a bloodless statue:** an attempt at Ovid's alliterative *signumque exsangue sedebat.*

833-75 *Europa*
With this story, Ovid begins his great section on the Theban legend that continues till 4.602. Otis (1966) 366-7; (1970) 395-6 assumes that Ovid's version is based on Moschus' *Europa* (which is most conveniently available in the Loeb *Greek Bucolic Poets*); his discussion brings out the differences as well as the similarities, stressing particularly the humour of Ovid and his concentration on the inherent incongruities of the situation. See also the note on 1.568-746.

833 **Atlas' grandson:** i.e. Mercury, see the note on 2.697-704.

834-5 **the lands called after Pallas:** i.e. Athens, called after Pallas Athene.

836 **His father:** i.e. Jupiter.

837 This grand epic line is, of course, deliberately incongruous.

839 **your mother:** i.e. Maia, one of the Pleiades; see the note on 1.669.

843 Note the speed of the narrative.

844 **the great king's daughter:** i.e. Europa, daughter of Agenor, though Moschus and Bacchylides follow Homer (*Il.* 14.321-2) in calling her the daughter of Phoenix. For the details, see Apollodorus 3.1.1 and Frazer's copious notes.

845 **Tyrian:** Tyre and Sidon, the two great cities of the Phoenicians, are often used interchangeably, compare 2.840.

846-7 For a good discussion of this famous contrast between majesty and love, see Otis 122-4.

849 For Jupiter's nod, see the note on 1.179-80.

854 According to Virgil (*Georg.* 3.53) a dewlap was a good sign.

870 **false:** because he was not really a bull.

NOTES: BOOK III

1-137   Cadmus

Cadmus, Thebes and the foundation of the worship of Bacchus (Cadmus' grandson) provide an overall framework for the section from the beginning of Book 3 to 4.603. Otis (128-59) discusses the whole passage and its construction in some detail and a number of his points will be raised in the course of the notes, though no attempt has been made to present his thesis in full. Suffice it to say that he sees this section as the opening panel of a great division of the *Metamorphoses*, a division ending at 6.400 and devoted to 'The Avenging Gods' in contrast to 'The Divine Comedy', the subject of the first two books.

The most familiar source for the legends of Cadmus and his family is Euripides (*Phoenissae* 638-75 and *Bacchae*). Indeed, a full appreciation of the next two books is not really possible without some familiarity with Euripides' last play, *The Bacchae*. However, as will become clear, Ovid is also indebted to many other sources, some of them now lost.

2   Dictaean: i.e. Cretan from mount Dicte, a famous mountain at the Eastern end of the island.

5   dutiful and wicked: *pius et sceleratus*, the oxymoron is, of course, characteristic of Ovid. For *pius*, see the note on 1.149.

7-8   avoided both his native land and his father's anger: *patriamque iramque parentis uitat*; for the zeugma, see the note on 2.312-3. In spite of the word's special and inappropriate associations, it might seem attractive here to use the literal 'fatherland' for *patriam*; on the other hand, *parentis* is, literally, 'parent's' so that Ovid has avoided the obvious jingle that 'fatherland' and 'father's' would suggest.

10-11   lonely: *solis*; 'lonely' is the obvious meaning for *solis* in the immediate context; however, the 'virginal' suggestions implicit in the description of the cow in the next line may well lead to second thoughts. In any case, this virginal cow clearly suggests a contrast with the story of Europa and the bull.

13   Boeotian: the story of the cow is clearly an aetiological legend to explain the name of Boeotia which the ancients derived from the Greek *bous*, 'cow'.

14   Castalian cave: see the note on 1.369 for the spring which gave its name to the cave in which it rises.

15   untended: an inadequate word for Ovid's striking coinage, *incustoditam*, a word whose five long syllables give a slow ponderous beginning to the line highly suggestive of a cow's gait.

19   Panope: this small town is mentioned in Homer's catalogue of ships (in the form *Panopeus*) in connexion with Cephisos (*Il.* 2.520-2). A traveller from Delphi to Thebes might pass Panope and he might even cross the Cephisos if he were planning to pass to the North of Lake Copais. He would, however, be only at the beginning of his journey; Ovid's geography is often imprecise; see the note on 1.369.

28-34   Another ekphrasis; see the note on 1.168.

28   defiled by no axe: in a country with a limited rainfall, trees are comparatively rare and ecologically important. It is not surprising, therefore, that groves of trees were normally protected by religious sanctions.

32   the snake of Mars: according to Euripides (*Phoenissae* 657) the snake was a son of Mars.

33-80   Editors rightly compare this section with Virgil's description of the snakes destroying Laocoon and his sons (*Aen.* 2.199-227).

45   the one that separates the twin Bears: see Aratus *Phaen.* 45-8 (Mair's translation):

> *Between them, as it were, the branch of*
> *a   river,   circles   in   wondrous   ways   the*
> *Dragon, winding infinite around and about;*
> *on either side of his coil are borne along*
> *the Bears, that shun evermore the blue sea.*

See also the note at 2.138-9.

46-7   preparing arms or flight: for the zeugma, see the note on 2.312-3.

60   great...great: *magnum magno*; see the note on 1.33.

95   victor...vanquished: *uictor...uicti*; see the note on 1.33.

98   you too will be a serpent to be looked at: for the fulfilment of this prophecy, see 4.563-608.

99   his colour together with his presence of mind: for the zeugma, see the note on 2.312-3.

101-2   patroness...Pallas: according to Euripides (*Phoen.* 670), it was indeed Pallas (i.e. Athene/Minerva) who advised Cadmus.

101-14   This passage should be compared and contrasted with the description by Apollonius Rhodius (3.1278-1407) of Jason's sowing of another batch of these very teeth. According to Apollonius (3.1183-4), Athene (Minerva) had divided the teeth between Cadmus and Aeëtes (Jason's foe at Colchis) at the time that Cadmus had killed the dragon. For Ovid's account of the story of Aeëtes and Jason, see 7.1-158.

111-4   Roman stage curtains were lowered to reveal the stage and raised to conceal it. Virgil uses the same image at *Georg.* 3.24-5. For the use of Roman imagery here, see the note on 1.171-5. Henderson's comment is very instructive:

> *Ovid has chosen an anachronistic comparison, a favourite trick of his, and one of the ways in which he prevents the reader from practising for long that willing suspension of disbelief which most epic poets are careful to foster; cf. his likening of Apollo (1.533ff.) to a greyhound,* canis Gallicus, *which (as the epithet betrays is out of place in mythological Greece, or of Pyramus' gory suicide (4.121ff.) to the bursting of a lead water-main, an extraordinarily un- (even anti-) epic picture. The simile at the corresponding point in Apollonius' narrative (3.1359-62) is by contrast perfectly conventional and proper--- stars appearing in the sky after a snowstorm.*

123   **in their own war:** *suo Marte;* another metonymy (compare the note on 3.437) but perhaps more dead than the others; hence the decision not to render, 'in their own Mars'. Mars was, of course, the god of war. See also the note on 3.540.

125   **mother:** the earth, compare 1.393. Note the grotesque point that her breast is 'warm' from the fresh blood.

126   **Echion:** picked out because he was to be important as the father of Pentheus by Cadmus' daughter, Agaue. See 3.514, Eur. *Bacche* 507 etc.

129   **The Sidonian exile:** i.e. Cadmus, see 2.840 and the note on 2.845.

131-4   For the apostrophe, see the note on 3.432-6.

132   **Mars and Venus:** see Hesiod *Theog.* 935-7 (Evelyn-White's translation):
> *Also Cytherea [i.e. Aphrodite/Venus] bore*
> *to Ares [Mars]...Harmonia whom high spirited*
> *Cadmus made his wife.*

135-7 One of the great ancient commonplaces; according to Herodotus (1.32), Solon told Croesus (de Selincourt's translation):

> ...*until he is dead, keep the word 'happy' in*
> *reserve. Till then, he is not happy, but only*
> *iucky.*

Compare also Aeschylus *Ag.* 928-9 and Sophocles *O.T.* which not only illustrates this piece of wisdom most poignantly but ends with a most memorable statement of it.

138-252   *Actaeon*

Ovid's treatment of the Actaeon story is discussed at length by Otis (1966) 367-71; (1970) 396-400. He refers in particular to Callimachus (*Hymn* 5.107-18) and Apollodorus (3.4.4). In Callimachus' version, the story is dealt with very briefly and only as a contrast to the much more lenient punishment, blindness, inflicted by Athene (Minerva) on Tiresias when he saw her at her bath. Callimachus makes a point of Actaeon's innocence by stating that he had seen the goddess unwillingly and this is the chief Callimachean element in Ovid's version. Apollodorus cites Actaeon's supposed wooing of Semele as the ultimate reason for his punishment, but this and other improper feeling attributed to him by later authors are not to be found in Ovid; instead, he took from his non-Callimachean sources his picture of a very vengeful goddess.

The story has not infrequently been the subject of plastic art. For two ancient examples, see plates 69c and 86b in Robertson's *A History of Greek Art* (Cambridge, 1975).

Wilkinson (420) discusses the possibility that the Actaeon episode influenced parts of Shakespeare's *Midsummer Night's Dream*; that Shakespeare knew the story is apparent from *Titus Andronicus* 2.3.60-5:

> *Saucy controller of our private steps!*
> *Had I the power that some say Dian had,*
> *Thy temples should be planted presently*
> *With horns, as was Actaeon's; and the hounds*
> *Should drive upon thy new-transformed limbs,*
> *Unmannerly intruder as thou are!*

139 **grandson:** Cadmus' daughter, Autonoe, was, by Aristaeus, the mother of Actaeon.

142 **a mistake:** *error;* in the *Tristia* (2.207), Ovid claims that his banishment from Rome was the result of two things, a poem (*carmen*) and a mistake (*error*). Earlier in the same poem (103-6), he had referred to Actaeon in these terms (Wilkinson's translation):

> *Why did I see it, implicate my eyes?*
> *Why did this guilty secret me surprise?*
> *Actaeon saw Diana's nakedness*
> *By chance: his hounds devoured him none the less.*

This has led some commentators to assume that this line in the *Metamorphoses* also contains a personal reference. Chronological considerations alone make this unlikely, but it is surely safe to infer from all of this something of Ovid's attitude to Actaeon's misfortunes and something of the way he uses the word *error*. For a much fuller discussion and references to other points of view, see Wilkinson 238-9, Otis 145 and the Introduction.

146   the Hyantian young man: i.e. Actaeon; Hyantian is a synonym here for Boeotian; Hyas was the founder of the Hyantes, a Boeotian tribe. The adjective also appears at Apollonius Rhodius 3.1242.

148   The nets and swords: Romans hunted by setting up nets in a forest, driving animals into them and then spearing them to death. There is a good description in Pliny (*Epp.* 1.6). This, then, is another example of Roman practice imposed on an alien context; see the note on 1.171-5.

150   This line is a close imitation of Virgil *Aen.* 12.77.

152   This line picks up the imagery of 3.145.

153   knotted lines: *nodosa...lina*, i.e. the hunting nets.

155-62   Another ekphrasis; see the note on 1.168.

156   Gargaphie: Pausanias (9.2.3) describes the spring where Diana was bathing but he calls it only the bed of Actaeon; later (9.4.3), he discusses Gargaphie but does not connect it with this story.
    girt-up: *succinctae*; Diana was traditionally represented with enough of her tunic tucked in at the waist to leave her lower legs bare. This was the standard way to wear the tunic for those who were involved in strenuous activity such as ploughing or, as in the case of Diana, hunting.

158-9   European taste has long vacillated between a preference for nature obviously dominated and regulated by man's art and what is known as the romantic preference for a more natural and untamed effect. The Roman preference, like that of the seventeenth and eighteenth centuries, was always for obvious human domination of nature.

168   Ismenian: i.e. Boeotian; the Ismenus is a river of Boeotia.

168-72   Crocale...Nephele...Hyale...Rhanis...Psecas...Phiale: all these exotic Greek names have to do with water meaning, respectively, 'seashore', 'cloud', 'crystal', 'drop', 'raindrop' and 'saucer'.

171-3   Water...water: *laticem...lympha*; no attempt has been made to represent Ovid's choice of two rather exotic words for 'water'.

173 Titania: i.e. Diana, grand-daughter, through her mother, Leto, of the Titan, Coeus. Shakespeare borrowed the name from here for his Queen of the Fairies in *A Midsummer-Night's Dream*.

175 wandered: *errans*, which clearly picks up the *error* (mistake) of 3.142; the translation necessarily obscures the reference since there is no satisfactory English word to cover both meanings of the Latin root.

181-2 but the goddess was taller than them: that Diana (Artemis) was taller than her handmaidens is a commonplace, best remembered, perhaps, from Hom. *Od.* 6.105-8 (Lattimore's translation):

> and along with her the nymphs, daughters of Zeus of the aegis,
> range in the wilds and play, and the heart of Leto is gladdened,
> for the head and the brows of Artemis are above all the others,
> and she is easily marked among them, though all are lovely.

It is typically Ovidian to use this famous scene as the basis for his humorour explanation of why the nymphs could not preserve Diana's modesty by surrounding her.

184 facing: *aduersi*; presumably 'facing the dawn', i.e. 'setting'.

194 the horns of a long-lived stag: *uiuacis cornua cerui*, a direct quotation from Virgil *Ecl.* 7.30.

198 Autonoe's hero: i.e. Actaeon, see the note on 3.139.

203 only his mind remained in its original state: compare 2.485 and the note on 1.234.

205 Fear...shame: *pudor...timor*; see the note on 1.618-9.

206-33 Wilkinson (235):

> Ovid indeed has not the face to recite the names
> of all Actaeon's hounds (Hyginus knew eighty-five),
> but he does go so far as thirty-three...before
> relenting with a quosque referre mora est ['and
> others it would take too long to tell']...

The names are all Greek; they are translated in the notes from which it will be possible to see that in many cases clever effects are intended including, particularly, offering a paraphrase for the name in the accompanying adjectives. See the note on 2.2.

206 Melampus: Black-foot.

207   **Ichnobates:** Tracker.

210   **Pamphagos:** Omnivore; **Dorceus:** Gazelle; **Oribasus:** Mountaineer.

211   **Nebrophonos:** Faun-slayer; **Laelaps:** Hurricane; **Theron:** Hunter.

212   **Pterelas:** Winged; **Agre:** Hunting.

213   **Hylaeus:** Forest-one.

214   **Nape:** Glen; **Poemenis:** Shepherd.

215   **Harpyia:** Snatcher.

216   **Ladon:** the name of a river, compare 1.702.

217   **Dromas:** Runner; **Canache:** Clang; **Sticte:** Spotted; **Tigris:** Tiger;
Alce: Strength.

218   **Leucon:** White; **Asbolos:** Soot.

219   **Lacon:** Spartan; **Aello:** Storm-swift.

220   **Thoos:** Quick; **Lycisce:** Wolf-like; **Cyprius:** Cyprian.

221   **Harpalos:** Grasper.

222   **Melaneus:** Black; **Lachne:** Fur.

223   **Labros:** Furious; **Agriodus:** White-tooth; **Dictaean:** see the note on
3.2.

224   **Laconian:** Spartan; **Hylactor:** Barker.

229   **his servants:** *famulos,* a standard word for household slaves, here used
to refer to his dogs.

232   **Melanchetes:** Black-haired.

233   **Therodamas:** Beast-subduer; **Oresitrophos:** Mountain-bred.

241   **as if it were his arms:** see the note on 2.487.

253-315   Semele
That Semele, another of the daughters of Cadmus and Harmonia (see
the note on 2.139), bore Bacchus to Zeus was known to Homer (*Il.* 14.323-5)

and Hesiod (*Theog.* 940-2). That Hera (Juno) caused Semele's death by lightning stroke was known to Euripides (*Bacchae* 1.10). See also Apollodorus 3.4.3.

253-5 This ingenious link passage is in some ways reminiscent of the one at 1.568-87 linking the stories of Daphne and Io. Otis (137) makes much of the moral implications of this dispute and Juno's contemptuous attitude to it.

258 **Agenor:** see the note on 2.844.

258-9 **the Tyrian wench:** *Tyria...paelice*, i.e. Europa; for *paelex*, 'wench' see the note on 1.622.

263-5 **if...if...if:** see the note on 1.377-8.

266 **well sister certainly:** see the note on 1.620.

269-70 **something which has scarcely happened to me:** Hera bore Ares (Hom. *Il.* 5.892-6), the Ilithyiae (*Il.* 11.271) and Hebe (*Od.* 11.604). See also Hes. *Theog.* 921-2. Her bitterness arises primarily from the much greater fecundity of her husband with other goddesses and women; Homer's list of some of his conquests and children (*Il.* 14.317-27) would certainly, in normal circumstances, provoke extreme resentment.

270-1 **trusts...is disappointed:** *fiducia...fallat*; the contrast between the two words, one suggesting 'trust' the other 'betrayal', is greater in the Latin and further accentuated by the alliteration. The translation, however, does attempt to preserve the ambiguity in the Latin as to whether she is to be let down by Jupiter or by her own beauty.

272 **Stygian waters:** at first glance, no more than a clever circumlocution for 'death'; note, however, that the Styx does play a part in Semele's downfall (3.290).

275-8 **she had made herself like an old woman...just like Beroë:** in the *Metamorphoses*, a favourite device of gods and goddesses who wish to approach young women for any purpose; see 4.219; 6.26; 11.310; 14.656. The device is not, however, original to Ovid. Virgil (*Aen.* 5.605-20) sends Iris to give false advice to the Trojan woman and she too adopts the guise of an old woman, Beroë by name; she was clearly Ovid's inspiration for this passage.

278 **Epidaurian:** such mundane details do, in W.S. Gilbert's immortal words, 'add verisimilitude to an otherwise bald and unconvincing tale.' The beginning of Sinon's lying speech (Virgil *Aen.* 2.77-82) is similarly laced with inconsequential details.

288-90   Essentially the same situation as that of Phaethon and the Sun at 2.44-6; in both cases the god swears by the Styx; see the notes on 1.188-9, 2.46 and 3.277.

301   bolt: *fulmen,* usually rendered 'thunderbolt', but that would be very awkward in a line that included 'thundering' and would suggest a repetition not in Ovid.

304   Typhoeus: see the notes on 1.151-62 and 183.

305   For the Cyclopes as thunderbolt makers see the note on 1.259.

313-4   Ino...the Nysaean nymphs: see Hom. *Il.* 6.132-3; they were employed by Jupiter to bring up the infant Bacchus on mount Nysa; for the details see Apollodorus 3.4.3 and Frazer's extensive note; also Fordyce on Catullus 64.252. The punishment suffered by Ino for her involvement is described at 4.421ff.

316-38   Tiresias
The long-lived blind seer most familiar to us from the Theban plays of Sophocles, but important as early as Homer's *Odyssey* (11.90-151). According to Callimachus (see the note on 3.138-252), Tiresias was blinded by Athene (Minerva) because he had seen her naked. Apollodorus (3.6.7) tells the same story and attributes it to Pherecydes, but he also recounts the version told by Ovid and attributes that to Hesiod, an attribution supported by the Scholiast on Hom. *Od.* 10.494 (see the Loeb Hesiod 168). Frazer's notes on the Apollodorus passage are very extensive and include a full discussion on the widespread superstition that it is most unlucky to see snakes copulating.

318   nectar: see the note on 1.111.

323   both Venuses: i.e. ·sexual pleasure both as a man and as a woman.

333   the words of Jove: i.e. that it is women who receive more sexual pleasure.

336-7   for there is not...action of a god: the same sentiment is to be found at 14.784-5 and an analogous one at 2.677.

339-510   Narcissus and Echo
We know little of the antecedent history of these myths and many scholars believe that Ovid was the first to combine them. For a good discussion, see Fränkel (82-5). Wilkinson (434-7) has an account of the way Milton

used Ovid's Narcissus as a model for his Eve (*Paradise Lost* 4.457-69). See also Louise Vinge, *The Narcissus Theme in Western European Literature up to the Early 19th Century* (Lund, 1967); this is a work which ranges far more widely than its title would suggest over the whole subject of the way Ovid in general, and his *Metamorphoses* in particular, were treated and viewed by the European tradition from the Middle Ages to modern times.

342   aquamarine Liriope: *caerula Liriope;* for the epithet see the note on 1.275. Liriope ('lily-like') is probably an Ovidian invention chosen partly for the aptness of her name (the lily belongs to a botanical family related to that of the narcissus) and partly for the beautiful sound it makes with *caerula*.
　　Cephisos: see the note on 3.19; the river confirms the Boeotian background to this tale.

344   he took her violently: see the note on 1.600.

345   loved: i.e. sexually loved, as the context makes plain; the Latin is as non-specific as the English.

348   If he does not get to know himself: 'Know thyself' was inscribed in Apollo's temple at Delphi and was one of the most famous injunctions of Olympian religion. This whole story is, at one level, a humorous commentary upon that piece of advice.

353   As the commentators point out, this line and line 355 are imitations of Catullus 62.42 and 44.

356   nets: see the note on 3.148.

358   sound-repeating: *resonabilis,* another Ovidian coinage to 'explain' the Greek *Echo;* see the note on 2.2.

363   under her Jupiter: *sub Ioue...suo;* the expression *sub Ioue* can regularly mean 'under the sky', 'in the open' (as at 4.260), but the slightly delayed *suo* ('her') makes it plain that here it has a far more literal meaning. The comic effect has not been realized in the translation; there is a similar situation at 2.377-8 discussed in the note. In this passage, some editors read *cum Ioue,* 'with Jupiter', but that destroys the effect.

368   the nymph: *haec;* see the note on 1.58.

371   she saw him and caught fire: *uidit et incaluit,* repeated from 2.574.

382   called...caller: *uocat...uocantem;* see the note on 1.33.

384   do you flee from me? *me fugis?*   Compare Dido's almost identical *mene fugis?* (Virg. *Aen.* 4.314).

386   let us come together: *coeamus*; the Latin word has powerful but not inescapable sexual connotations; he means it one way, she takes it the other way. See also the note on 4.377.

390   fled...fled: *fugit fugiensque*; see the note on 1.33.

391   I would die: *emoriar*; either a subjunctive to give 'I would die' or 'Let me die' (Henderson is wrong to think that the wish would require *utinam*, see 2.818) or a future, as in Golding: 'I first will die ere thou shall take of me thy pleasure', preferred, perhaps rightly, by Henderson.
        I would offer myself to you: *sit tibi copia nostri*, a phrase with the same ambiguity as *coeamus* had at line 386. According to Fränkel 214-5, the use of *copia* in a sexual context is original to Ovid.

401   only: English idiom sometimes requires that an important detail be made explicit, though it can be left implicit in Latin. This is especially true of this sort of 'only', a point more fully discussed by Mayer on Lucan 8.51-2. See also 4.115.

404   one of those he had disdained: the Latin makes it plain that this speaker is male, a point discussed by Fränkel (213 n.32).

406   Rhamnusia: i.e. Nemesis, the Greek goddess of vengeance, who had a temple at Rhamnus in Attica. Compare Callimachus *Hymn* 3.232, Catullus 68.77.

407   There was...: another brief ekphrasis, see the note on 1.168. The passage is discussed by Fränkel 213 n.34 who compares Soph. *O.C.* 676, 683.
        slimeless: *inlimis*, another Ovidian coinage.

412   that let: *passura*; the future participle here suggests habit and custom, 'that would let'; unfortunately, 'a wood that would let' gives a quite inappropriately jarring effect.
        overheat: *tepescere*; the English language developed in a climate that knows little of excessive heat; accordingly, its weather words for warmth tend to have favourable connotations, and those for cold unfavourable ones. Though *tepescere* is far from being an extreme word for heat, it is clear from the context that here it is referring to an unwelcome degree of warmth. Conversely, while *gelidus* can indicate an unwelcome degree of chill (as at 2.171), it can also indicate a pleasant release from heat (as at 1.689 or 4.90).

412-36   Wilkinson (434-7) points out the striking similarities between this passage and Milton's description of Eve in *P.L.* 4.457-69.

419   Parian: the beauty and whiteness of Parian marble were proverbial. For the whole image, compare 4.675.

421   See the note on 4.13.

424-6   admired...was himself admired...praised...was the praised one...he sought...he was being sought...both burning and igniting: *miratur...mirabilis ...probat...probatur...petit petitur...accendit et ardet;* see the note on 1.33.

432-6   The apostrophe elicits a particularly memorable comment from Fränkel (83):

> then he breaks the progress of his narrative with a
> direct address. The poet, like an excited child in
> the theater who tries to help the hero on the stage
> and calls out loud to him to warn him of a trap into
> which he is about to fall, forgets his supposed
> aloofness and talks to his character in order to
> extricate him from his error.

See also 2.435, 3.131-4 and Wilkinson 212.

436   depart...depart: *discedet...discedere,* see the note on 1.33.

437   Ceres: i.e. food; Ceres (Demeter) was the goddess of corn and this is a common and natural metonymy similar to those discussed in the note on 2.68. This particular usage was well established (see Lucr. 2.655 and Bailey's note, Virg. *Aen.* 1.177 and Austin's note) and survives in the English 'cereal'.

442   alas: *io;* see the note on 3.728.

443   many lovers: *multis,* literally just 'many', but English requires the noun more than Latin does. An analogous situation is discussed in the note on 3.401.

446   delighted...see...see...delights: *placet...uideo...uideoque placetque,* a particularly striking example of the device described in the note on 1.33 combined with chiasmus, another trick much favoured by Ovid, where a pair of words is repeated in reverse order, thus suggesting the shape of the Greek letter chi (X). It is, of course, an extremely common effect in all classes of literature; for an example I take, essentially at random, Shakespeare *Sonnet* 129:

> *The expense of spirit in a waste of shame*
> *Is lust in action; and till action, lust*
> *Is perjured...*

447   confusion: *error*, picked up from 3.431.

466   plenty...poor: *inopem...copia*; in a passage especially rich in rhetorical cleverness, this oxymoron is especially memorable.

468   a strange wish in a lover: a phrase that encourages another burst of rhetorical pyrotechnics.

481-2   beat...breast...breast...blows: *percussit pectora...pectora...percussa*: the choice of 'beat' and 'blows' conceals the fact that Ovid is using two parts of the same verb. For the general effect and the chiasmus, see the note on 3.446. For Ovid's striking alliteration of 'p' in these two lines the translation has substituted 'b'.

503-5   A striking example of a victim who learns nothing; the note on 1.234 alludes to other less striking examples.

506   To cut a lock of hair and offer it to a dead loved one was a common practice in antiquity. See, for instance, Propertius 1.17.21. In Aeschylus' *Choephori* and the *Electra* plays of Sophocles and Euripides, much is made of the lock of hair offered to his father's grave by Orestes.

509   but the body was not to be found: like Echo (3.396-9), he was left without a body; see the note on 3.493-501.

511-733   *Pentheus*
The most memorable account of Pentheus is to be found in Euripides' *Bacchae*, his last and, in the eyes of many, his best play. However, Euripides seems not to have been Ovid's principal source. The story of the Tyrrhenian sailors, for instance, is not in Euripides but comes from *Homeric Hymn* 7, while the name Acoetes (3.582 etc.) comes from a lost play on this theme by Pacuvius, the great Latin tragedian of the second century B.C. For the evidence and further details see Otis (1966) 371-2; (1970) 400-1.

514   Pentheus: the most famous of those who rejected Bacchus; Ovid pursues the theme with the daughters of Minyas (4.1-431 and see the note on 4.22) and Acrisius (3.559 and 4.607-14).
    contemptuous of the gods: *contemptor superum*, an echo of Virgil's phrase for Mezentius, *contemptor diuum* (*Aen.* 7.648).

515-6   loss of sight: see 3.333-8.

520 Liber: the word means 'Free' and was the name of an early Italian god of vegetation later identified with Bacchus who was also known in Greek as *Lyaeus* 'Loosener'. See the note on 4.11 and Fordyce on Catullus 64.390.

525 blindness: *tenebris*, literally 'shadows', 'darkness', but this is a common extension; here it echoes 3.515. The contrast between Tiresias' blindness and his visionary powers is a fruitful source of rhetorical jibes much exploited by Sophocles in the *Oedipus Tyrannus*.

531 snake-descended ones: *anguigenae*, another Ovidian coinage. It refers, of course, to the origin of the Thebans as described at 3.95-130.
   offspring of Mars: see 3.32 and the note. The Romans prided themselves on their descent from Mars through Romulus, his son and would, no doubt, see an echo of their own mythology in this line. See, for instance, Livy *Praef.* 7, Virg. *Aen.* 1.276. See also the note on 1.171-5.

537 the lascivious hordes: critics of Bacchic religion consistently accused it of encouraging sexual licence. Euripides' *Bacchae* explores in some depth the psychological problems of Pentheus, a typical holder of such views. There surely was, however, some fire beneath the smoke. See also the note on 4.2.

539 penates: see the note on 1.173-5.

540 without a fight: *sine Marte*, literally 'without Mars'; see the note on 3.123, though the metonymy here is less dead than it is there since this Mars clearly picks up and contrasts with the Mars of 3.531.

542 thyrsi...leaves: the thyrsus was a staff bound in ivy leaves and shaken by Bacchic revellers who also garlanded their heads with ivy; see 3.555, 4.6-8.

555 hair drenched in oil of myrrh: similar language is used of Aeneas in Virgil's *Aeneid* by Iarbas (4.215-7) and by Turnus (12.99-100) to suggest effeminacy.

557 straightway: an archaism to translate the slightly archaic *actutum*; Kenney (120) believes that it may be an echo of Pacuvius; see the note on 3.511-733.

559 Acrisius: this story, which appears in a little more detail at 4.607-14, is known to us only from Ovid. Like all other opponents of Bacchus, Acrisius was to suffer a premature death; it is ironic, therefore, that Pentheus should cite him as an example to follow. It is clear, however, that Pentheus' death preceded Acrisius'.

564   Athamas: the harrowing tale of Ino, another of Cadmus' daughters, and of her husband Athamas is told at 4.416-560.

568 The intrusion of the first person narrator °is very rare in epic but common in elegy. Once again, Ovid undercuts the seriousness of his work; some would argue, correctly, that the *Metamorphoses* is not an epic poem, but the simile here is extremely epic in tone so that the first person is jarringly incongruous with that tone.

576   Tyrrhenian: i.e. Etruscan or, here, Lydian; there is a persistent tradition dating at least from Herodotus (1.94) that the Etruscans were descended from Lydian exiles. See also the note on 3.583.

582   Acoetes: both in Euripides' *Bacchae* and in Pacuvius' play, a Bacchic worshipper is brought before Pentheus for questioning. In the Euripidean version, the prisoner is, at first, anonymous but is eventually revealed as Bacchus himself; in Pacuvius' version, however, he bears the name Acoetes and is presumably not Bacchus in disguise.

583   Maeonia: a part of Lydia; according to Euripides (*Bacchae* 464), Dionysus told Pentheus that he came from Lydia.
        plebs: see the notes on 1.171-5 and 173-5.

594-5   the rainy star of the Olenian she-goat: Aratus *Phaen.* 157-64 (Mair's translation):

> *and if the fame has come to thee of the Goat*
> *herself and the Kids, who often on the darkening*
> *deep have seen men storm-tossed, thou wilt find*
> *him in all his might, leaning forward at the left*
> *hand of the Twins. Over against him wheels the*
> *top of Helice's head, but on his left shoulder*
> *is set the holy Goat, that, as legend tells, gave*
> *the breast to Zeus. Her the interpreters of Zeus*
> *call the Olenian Goat.*

595   Taygete: one of· the Pleiades; see the note on 1.669 and Aratus *Phaen.* 263.
        the Hyades: i.e. the 'Rainy' ones (all the stars in this passage are associated with rain); they are a small group of stars that form part of the Bull; see Aratus *Phaen.* 167-78.

605-91   The Etruscan sailors
The earliest extant source for this story within a story is *Homeric Hymn 7.* There, however, the sailors are unnamed, so that it is presumed that Ovid, like Hyginus later, worked from a Hellenistic source now lost. The story describes a situation pointedly similar to that of its narrator, but Pentheus learns nothing from it.

611-2   See the note on 1.325-6.

613   **Whoever you are:** *quisquis es,* a standard formula in prayers; compare Aesch. *Ag.* 160-2, Cat. 34.21-2 (and Fordyce's note), Virg. *Aen.* 4.576.

617   **fair-haired Melanthus:** the Greek name means 'Black-flower' so that this is presumably a humorous variation on the practice described in the note on 3.206-33.

621   **boat:** *pinum;* see the note on 1.94.

621-2   **defiled by a holy cargo:** the superstitions of sailors are as old as they are inexplicable; except, of course, that it is natural for those engaged in hazardous enterprises to try to formalize their fears.

642   The text in this area is corrupt and a satisfactory solution has not yet been suggested; the general sense is, however, clear enough.

658-665   See the note on 4.394-8.

658   **the god himself...god:** *ipsum...deus;* the first 'god' in the translation is supplied to ease the sense, but it does produce a repetition not in the original.

664-5   Ivy was particularly associated with Bacchus; compare the note on 3.542.

668   **empty images:** *simulacraque inania;* Lucretius (4.994-5) uses the same phrase for dreams; here too they refer to something which is certainly not real.

668-9   **tigers...lynxes...panthers:** all these animals are traditionally associated with Bacchus; see Virg. *Ecl.* 5.29-30, *Georg.* 3.264. In the *Homeric Hymn,* Bacchus is not surrounded by these visions but is himself transformed into a lion.

674   **gaped wide:** *lati rictus;* see the note on 1.741.

675   **scales:** as Henderson points out, dolphins are not fish and have no scales.

690   **Dia:** according to Callimachus (fr. 601), an alternative name for Naxos.

699-700   A similar miraculous release from Pentheus' prison is described in much more detail by Euripides (*Bacchae* 585-659). For two similar outcomes when men are imprisoned for their faith see *Acts* 12.1-11 and 16.19-40.

of their own accord...of their own accord: *sponte sua...sponte sua;* the repetition catches the repeated words of those recounting the tale.

708-10   Another ekphrasis, characteristically at a moment of high drama. See the note on 1.168.

710   sacrilegious: *profanis,* a word which is especially used of the uniniti-ated who should be excluded from a holy ceremony. See 4.390, Hor. *Od.* 3.1.1 and Austin's note on Virg. *Aen.* 6.258.

713   his mother: *mater;* a single word before punctuation at the beginning of a line, known as enjambment, is the most striking position possible in Latin hexameter poetry. It is used with great effect here.

716   noisily: *fremituque;* I have included Tarrant's brilliant emendation for the impossible *trepidumque* of the manuscripts.

720-2   Autonoë...Ino: just for a moment we look back to the story of Autonoë's son, Actaeon (3.138-252) and forward to that of Ino (4.416-562).
    Indeed, the tragedies of Cadmus' four daughters, Semele, Autonoë, Agaue and Ino are all linked at this point.

723-4   See the note on 2.487.

728   Io: a ritualistic cry sometimes, as here, associated with Bacchic worship. Generally it takes its particular sense from its context and has been translated accordingly; compare 3.442 'alas' and 4.513 'Tally ho'.

729-30   This absurdly inappropriate simile in the grand epic manner is, perhaps, ultimately derived from Homer *Il.* 6.146-8. It is, however, as Bömer shows, a favourite Ovidian theme.

732   Ismenides: i.e. Thebans; the Ismenus is a river that flows near to Thebes.

NOTES: BOOK IV

1-415   *The Minyeides*

This section interrupts the story of the house of Cadmus to which we shall not return till 4.416. It serves partly as a continuation of the theme of the wrath of Bacchus against those who oppose him and partly as a framework for a series of contrasting and diverting tales. Otis (128ff.) makes the structure plain. Though this is the earliest extant account of the punishment of the family of Minyas for irreverence to Bacchus, it is clear from the later but very different versions found in Plutarch (*Quaest. Gr.* 38), Aelian (*V.H.* 3.42) and Antoninus Liberalis (10) that the story is very ancient and closely connected with the festival known as the Agrionia.

1   Minyas: the eponymous founder of the Minyae, a tribe which originated in Thessaly but later migrated to Boeotia where Ovid finds them.   The Argonauts were said to have descended from them; see 6.720 and Herod. 1.146; 4.145.

2   orgies: *orgia*; although the word 'orgy' is, of course, derived from the Greek *orgia*, a word adopted into Latin by Catullus (64.260) as well as by Virgil (*Georg.* 4.521, *Aen.* 4.302), its normal usage in both classical languages is as a technical term specifically for the rites of Bacchic worship. The modern sense arises directly out of the normal prejudice felt in antiquity against Bacchic rites (see the note on 3.537) and the reader should be warned to regard the word here as primarily a technical term, though there is no need to suppress entirely the sense of disapprobation associated with the modern word.

6-8   See the note on 3.542.

11   Bromius: Ovid is here listing the Greek (and Roman) names by which Bacchus was known. Bromius is not found elsewhere in Ovid but it is not uncommon in Greek. It derives from a Greek word for noise and may arise from the sound of his rites or from his association with thunder and lightning.

12   the fire-born one: *ignigenam*, a word apparently found only in Ovid, though Ausonius wrote a Greek epigram (29.3) to Bacchus in which he coins a Greek equivalent.

   twice-mothered: a translation of an equivalent Greek term; the whole line is, of course, a reference to the story of his birth; see 3.308-15.

13   Nyseus: both in Greek and Latin this title is normally in the form *Nysaeus*; indeed, *Nyseus* seems to occur only here. For the origin of the title see the note on 3.314.

  unbarbered: long, uncut hair is frequently a characteristic of religions which stress absolute devotion to a divinity who promises to imbue his followers with the pure strength of nature. Samson, the Bacchants, the Sikhs and the 'hippies' of the 1960's are, perhaps, the most familiar examples. See 3.421.

  Thyoneus: according to *Homeric Hymn* 1.21, Thyone was an alternative name for Semele, Bacchus' mother. The epithet is also taken to be cognate with the Greek *thuein*, 'to rage'. It is, in any case, one of Bacchus' more common epithets.

14   Lenaeus: Greek for 'of the wine press'; 'a frequent cult-title for Bacchus', in the words of Austin on Virg. *Aen.* 4.207.

15   Nyctelius: Greek for 'of the night'; another common title for Bacchus.

  Eleleus: found only here. It may be derived from the Greek war-cry, *eleleu* or, possibly, from the Greek *elelizein* 'to shake'; Sophocles (*Ant.* 153) calls Bacchus *elelichthon*, 'earth-shaking', presumably a reference to Bacchic dancing.

  Iacchus: probably a personification of a ritual cry; see Herod. 8.65 (de Selincourt's translation):

> they suddenly heard the sound of voices.
> Dicaeus thought he recognized the Iacchus
> song, which is sung at the Dionysiac
> mysteries...

It is a very common epithet, see Fordyce on Catullus 64.251.

  Euhan: another personified Bacchic cry; see Bailey on Lucr. 3.743.

16   the very many names you have besides: Sophocles (*Ant.* 1115) describes Bacchus as 'with many names'; Ovid's readers will be disinclined to contradict him.

  Liber: see the note on 3.520.

17-28   For the hymnic repetition of 'you', see the note on 1.559-60. Here too, however, some cases reflect only the second person verb.

19   without your horns: in primitive representations, Bacchus tended to be horned; compare *Fasti* 3.499-500, Euripides *Bacchae* 920-2 and Propertius 3.17.19-20.

22   Lycurgus: the story of his attack on Bacchic worship is told by Homer (*Il.* 6.130-40).

23   Tyrrhenians: their story was told at 3.572-700.

25   Bacchae: the female followers of Bacchus.

26   the drunken old man: Silenus, the drunken tutor of Bacchus immortalized in Virgil's sixth *Eclogue*.

27   sway-backed: *pando*, an adjective used elsewhere by Ovid of Silenus' ass; *Ars. Am.* 1.543; *Fasti* 1.399; 3.749.

30   long stop: *longo foramine*, literally 'long hole' referring either to the length of the hollow tube that makes the pipe, or to the length (from the mouth?) of the last stop in the flute. Modern translators introduce the word 'shrill' here which is odd since, the longer the pipe, the less shrill its sound.

33   Minerva: the goddess of all skills, including weaving.

43   For a discussion of this 'Arabian Nights' situation and possible antecedents, see Wilkinson 203; see also the note on 4.276-84. All the stories in this section are of Eastern origin.

44   Dercetis: for the full story of this Eastern goddess of sex and of her daughter, Semiramis, see Diod. Sic. 2.4.2-6.

45   of Babylon: but not yet, see the note on 4.57.

47   her daughter: i.e. Semiramis.

49   a Naiad: the story is fully related by Arrian (*Ind.* 31).

55-166   *The first sister's tale: Pyramus and Thisbe.*
This story clearly had an Eastern origin, like so much else in this book, but nothing is known of its history until it emerges here. To English-speaking audiences the story is most familiar from Shakespeare (*MND* 5.1.108-340); there too, the story is recounted only after others have been alluded to and rejected. However, the story was well known in European literature, including Boccaccio and Chaucer, before it was taken up by Shakespeare; for the details see Rand 117 and Wilkinson 394-427. Ovid recounts the story with an amazing combination of lightness, speed and gentle humour; nevertheless, our sympathies remain engaged with the innocent lovers throughout. No wonder Ovid's tale was so widely imitated.

57   the lofty city: Babylon, founded by Semiramis (Diod. Sic. 2.7.2-10.6); she is a figure who is partly mythological (as at 4.44-8) but largely, no doubt, founded on the famous 9th to 8th century Queen Sammu-ramat of Assyria.

64 hidden...hidden: *tegitur, tectus;* see the note on 1.33. The notion of hidden love, using the verb *tegere*, 'to hide', recurs at 4.159 and 192.

68 (what does love not sense?): *(quid non sentit amor?);* there is a very similar parenthesis, *(quis fallere possit amantem?)* '(who could deceive a lover?)' in Virgil's *Aeneid* (4.296), though, as Otis (1970) 336-7 points out, Ovid goes on immediately to address the lovers, just the sort of authorial intervention favoured by Ovid but avoided by Virgil.

88 Ninus' tomb: Semiramis was the widow of King Ninus (Nineveh) and the tomb she built for him was one of the most famous monuments of antiquity (Diod. Sic. 2.7.1).

89 tree...tree: *arboris: arbor;* see the note on 1.33.

90 a cool spring: *gelido...fonti;* see the note on 3.412.

91 they approved this plan: *pacta placent;* the translation offers a faint echo of Ovid's neat alliteration.

107 Pyramus: to achieve the delay and the enjambment (see the note on 3.713), it has been necessary to give the translation a rather strained structure not to be found in Ovid. The delay of the name is, however, a most effective device to underline the fatal delay in his arrival.

115 only: see the note on 3.401.

122 a pipe with faulty lead: for this simile see Henderson's comments quoted in the note on 3.111-4.

126 blood...blood: *caedis...sanguine;* see the note on 1.157-8.

133 tremblingly: *tremebunda;* a rare English word for a rare Latin one. It is also possible that *tremebunda* is to be taken with *membra*, 'she saw a body writhing tremblingly...'

148 ivory: i.e. ivory scabbard. Her speech closely mirrors Pyramus' at 4.108-15.

151-2 For the zeugma see the note on 2.312-3.

152-3 See the note on 1.325-6.
   death...death...death: *letique...morte...morte;* see the notes on 1.73 and 661-2.

159 will cover: *tectura;* see the note on 4.64.

167-270   Second Sister's Tale: The Loves of the Sun.

Leuconoё's tale comes in two parts, the Sun as a witness to the love
of Mars and Venus, and as himself the lover of Leucothoё and victim
of the jealousy felt by Clytie. As Ovid himself makes clear (191-3),
the unifying theme of this section is the disastrous effect of jealousy.

169-70   Sun...Sun: *Solem: Solis;* it is often difficult to reproduce this sort
of juxtaposition properly (see the note on 1.33); here, however, it has
proved impossible even to bring 'Sun' and 'Sun' close together.

171-89   Mars and Venus

This story originates in Demodocus' song to the Phaeacians and Odysseus
(Hom. *Od.* 8.266-366). Ovid had retold the story at length before (*Ars
Am.* 2.561ff.) in a highly discursive manner only loosely based on Homer;
this version is very brief and very different both from the young Ovid's
and from Homer's, though far more faithful to Homer's in its details.

171-2   For the Sun as the tell-tale who told Hephaestus (Vulcan) of
the adultery of his wife, Aphrodite (Venus) with Ares (Mars), see Hom.
Od. 8.271-2.

173-4   the Juno-born husband: i.e. Vulcan; *Iunonigena*, 'Juno-born', does
not occur elsewhere, but the mythology is, of course, Homeric, see *Il.*
1.571-2.

175   For the zeugma see the note on 2.312-3.

178-9   Homer *Od.* 8.279-80 (Lattimore's translation):
while many more [of Hephaestus' chains] were suspended overhead,
from the roof beams,
thin, like spider webs...

185   the Lemnian: i.e. Vulcan; Hom. *Od.* 8.283-4 (Lattimore's translation):
...Lemnos, the strong-founded citadel,
which of all territories on earth, was far dearest to him.

187   one of the unabashed gods: *aliquis de dis non tristibus;* according to
Homer (*Od.* 8.338-42), it was Hermes (Mercury). Contrary to the possible
implication of Otis (155), Ovid used *aliquis* for Mercury at the correspond-
ing point in his earlier version too (*Ars Am.* 2.585).

190-273   The Sun and Leucothoё and Clytie

Leucothoё's story, which is perhaps of Persian origin (see 212 and Wilkinson
203n.), is no longer extant in any source before Ovid. The same is also
true of Clytie's story, although there was a (different?) nymph of that
name known to Hesiod (*Theog.* 352) only as a daughter of Tethys and
Oceanus.

190   Cythereia: i.e. Venus, one of whose sacred islands was Cythera; see Virg. *Aen.* 1.680 and Austin's note; see also Hesiod *Theog.* 196-8 quoted in the note on 4.537-8.

192-208   For this 'unusually elaborate' apostrophe (in the words of Fränkel 214, n.35), see the note on 3.423-6.

192   hidden: *tectos*; see the note on 4.64.
son of Hyperion: i.e. the Sun; see Hes. *Theog.* 371-4.

202-3   Anaxagoras (and not Thales, as was once believed) seems to have been the first to identify the true cause of eclipses.

204   Rhodos: a personification of the island of Rhodes which was (and, in a more modern idiom, still is) a great centre of sun-worship. Pindar (*Ol.* 7.14) calls her, 'bride of the Sun'.

205   According to Homer (*Od.* 10.135-9), Circe lived on the island of Aeaea and was the daughter of Perse and the Sun.

209-12   Eurynome...Orchamus: otherwise unknown, just like their daughter, though the names are not unfamiliar elsewhere. The possibilities are discussed at length by Bömer.

209   perfume-bearing: *odorifer*; presumably to suggest 'Persian'; this is, however, partly an aetiological legend, see 4.253-5.

212   Achaemenian: Achaemenes was the mythical founder of the Persian royal family. See Herod. 1.125; 7.11; Hor. *Od.* 2.12.21.

213   Belus: for this name, which was a Hellenization of the name we meet in the Old Testament as Baal, see Austin on Virg. *Aen.* 1.621. The word meant 'lord' and, as such, was commonly used for Eastern kings.

214   the pastures of the Sun's horses: notorious from Homer *Od.* 12.260ff.

215   ambrosia: see the note on 2.120.

219   having been turned into the likeness of Eurynome, her mother: see the note on 3.275-8.

226-33   For the clinical efficiency of this seduction, or rape (238-9), see the note on 1.600.

234-5   her...her: i.e. Clytie's in both cases. See the note on 1.58.

236   **adultery:** see the note on 2.545.

238   **stretched her hands up to the Sun's light:** the context makes this conventional gesture peculiarly appropriate; see the note on 2.487.

250   **nectar:** see the note on 1.111.

251   **and after many precomplaints:** *multaque praequestus:* another Ovidian coinage; unlike many of his others, this one was never imitated and presumably struck his successors as an unnecessary and unpleasing formation.

256-7   **spite...spite:** *dolorem...dolor;* see the note on 1.33.

258   **Venus:** i.e. sexual love. For this sort of metonymy, see the note on 2.68.

261   **beneath Jove's sky:** *sub Ioue,* literally 'beneath Jove'; for the metonymy, disguised in the translation, see the note on 2.68; for the expression, see the note on 3.363.
      bare...bare: *nuda...nudis;* see the note on 1.33.

269-70   **turned towards her sun:** *uertitur ad Solem,* a Latin translation of the Greek *heliotropion,* 'heliotrope', more familiarly known as the sunflower. This is, then, another aetiological tale.

270   **though transformed, she kept her love:** see the note on 1.234.

271-3   A reminder that this whole section is a description of how the daughters of Minyas passed the time while their neighbours were foolishly wasting time, as they thought, on Bacchic worship. Homer introduced a similar, but much longer interlude (*Od.* 11.333-84) to remind his audience that the wonderful tales of Odysseus' wanderings were from his narrative to the Phaeacians on the isle of Scheria.

274   **Alcithoë:** the last of the sisters to tell a story and also, it seems, the prime instigator of the refusal to worship Bacchus (4.1).

276-84   The first sister, never named, wondered quietly to herself which of several named stories to relate, thus emphasising the breadth of Ovid's repertoire; see the note on 4.43. Here, Alcithoë indulges in *praeteritio,* a rhetorical device in which a speaker mentions something only to assert that he will not deal with it. Once again, the breadth of Ovid's repertoire is drawn forcefully to our attention.

276   **Daphnis:** a mythical Greek shepherd best known from the pastoral poetry of Theocritus (especially *Idyll* 1) and Virgil (especially *Eclogue* 5).

His story is obscure but, essentially, it seems that he was loved by a nymph and punished for his infidelity to her by blindness or petrification. For the details, see Gow on Theocritus *Id.* 1.

280   Sithon: otherwise unknown.

281   Celmis: an obscure name sometimes appearing in the form *Scelmis.* This is its only occurrence in Latin and the Greek references are too slight to be of help.

    adamant: *adamas,* a Greek word used as early as Hesiod (*Theog.* 161) for a very hard, mythical substance; literally, the word means 'that cannot be overcome'. Virgil introduced the idea into Latin, see *Aen.* 6.552 and Austin. The concept is found frequently in English literature from Chaucer on; more recently, however, a metaphorical adjectival sense for the word has developed, 'stubbornly inflexible'.

282   the Curetes: Callimachus (*Hymn* 1.51-3) tells the story of how the Curetes drowned the infant cries of Zeus so that his father, Cronos (Saturn), should not hear him or, as we learn from Lucretius' account (2.633-9), eat him.

    born from a heavy shower: Ovid's source for this notion is unknown.

283   Crocos and Smilax: neither Ovid's source for this story nor its details are known. Crocos, the familiar crocus, may well here be the autumnal version from which saffron is obtained. Smilax is the bindweed.

285-388   Salmacis and Hermaphroditus
This story is introduced as a 'novelty' (*nouitate* 284), a word that can also suggest something strange. Certainly, the antecedents of this story are unknown (Fränkel [183 n.37] even believes that it may be an Ovidian invention), and it certainly is a strange reversal of the male-dominated loves we have seen hitherto. Otis (156-7) develops the point well and illustrates the way that Hermaphroditus' innocence reminds us of Daphne's. For the geographical background, see Strabo 14.2.16.

288-91   a boy born to Mercury and the goddess of Cythera...took his name from them: i.e. a son of Mercury (Hermes) and, see the note on 4.190, Venus (Aphrodite), i.e. Hermaphroditus; see 4.382.

297   Carians: the pool or well, known as Salmacis, was near the temple of Aphrodite in Halicarnassus, one of the principal cities of Caria.

306-9   See the note on 1.325-6.

311   Cytorian comb: probably made from boxwood from the hills behind the port of Cytorus in Paphlagonia. See Catullus 4.11.

320-8 This speech, amazingly outspoken for a woman, is very closely based on Odysseus' speech to Nausicaa (Hom. *Od.* 6.149-60, Lattimore's translation):

> *I am at your knees, O queen. But are you mortal or goddess?*
> *If indeed you are one of the gods who hold wide heaven,*
> *then I must find in you the nearest likeness to Artemis*
> *the daughter of great Zeus, for beauty, figure and stature.*
> *But if you are one among those mortals who live in this country,*
> *three times blessed are your father and the lady your mother,*
> *and three times blessed your brothers too, and I know their spirits*
> *are warmed forever with happiness at the thought of you, seeing*
> *such a slip of beauty taking her place in the chorus of dancers;*
> *but blessed at the heart, even beyond these others, is that one*
> *who, after loading you down with gifts, leads you as his bride*
> *home.*

Yet the Homeric speech is a model of propriety compared to Ovid's pastiche of it. In particular, Odysseus' speech has nothing to correspond to the last few words of Salmacis' speech.

301 grass that was always green: unusual in a Mediterranean climate and possible only beside a reliable source of water.

303 the relieving bronze: there was a belief that the clashing of brazen cymbals would restore an eclipsed moon. For more details, see D.E. Hill, 'The Thessalian Trick', *Rh.Mus.* 116 (1973) 232-6.

342 went here and there and everywhere: *huc it et hinc illuc;* the translation does not quite catch the tripping speed effected by Ovid's string of four monosyllables. The form *it*, 'went', is unusual and, when used, often suggests something special as, for instance, at Catullus 3.11 where it suggests the hop of Lesbia's bird in the underworld.

345 soft: *mollia*, see the note on 2.411.

356-72 Fränkel 216-7 n.49:

> *This is the only passage in Ovid's works, I believe,*
> *which has a touch of sultry sensuality...The reason*
> *is that the water of the Salmacis pond was supposed*
> *to induce that quality, cf. 4.385-6; 15.319.*

362 the king of birds: *regia...ales*, literally 'royal bird'; the eagle, compare Virg. *Aen.* 1.394 and Austin's note.

362-4 entwines...entwines: *implicat...implicat:* the word also occurs in the immediate Virgilian model for this image (*Aen.* 11.751-6), a simile to illustrate violent warfare, itself based on a horrific Homeric portent

(*Il.* 12.201-7). For Ovid's characteristic trick of taking an image familiar from one context and introducing it into a wholly different one, see the note on 1.533.

365   or like ivy: the eagle and snake simile gives way to the far more conventional (almost hackneyed) simile of the ivy wrapped around its tree; see Hor. *Od.* 1.36.20 and the note of Nisbet and Hubbard. In Shakespeare's *M.N.D.*, not long before the Pyramus and Thisbe scene, Titania, another forward lady lover, addresses her beloved so (4.1.44-6):

> the female ivy so
> Enrings the barky fingers of the elm.
> O, how I love thee! how I dote on thee!

366   or like an octopus: with this simile, Ovid reverts to the unconventional. Neither in antiquity, nor in modern times would an octopus be an acceptable image in an erotic context. See, for instance, Hom. *Od.* 5.432-5 (Lattimore's translation) where Odysseus is attempting to cling to the rocks to save himself from the violence of the sea:

> As when an octopus is dragged away from its shelter
> the thickly-clustered pebbles stick in the cups of its tentacles,
> so in contact with the rock the skin from his bold hands
> was torn away.

368   Atlas' great-grandson: i.e. Hermaphroditus, see the note on 2.697-704.

374-5   puts on...puts through: *inducitur...conducat; inserere,* not *conducere,* is the normal word for 'grafting', but Ovid has pressed *conducere* into service presumably· to form a link with *inducitur;* the translation attempts to represent this. For grafting see Virg. *Georg.* 2.32-4.

377   had come together: the literal meaning of *coierunt,* a word which, however, is especially, but not exclusively, associated with sexual union; compare the note on 3.386 where the ambiguity is more obviously exploited.

389-415   *The fate of the Minyeides*
See the note on 4.1-415.

390   profaning: *profanat:* see the note on 3.710 where the cognate adjective has been rendered 'sacrilegious'.

**391-3   **This list of Bacchic instruments and other paraphernalia should be compared with Pentheus' contemptuous words at 3.531-42.

**394-8   **The transformation of the looms into vines is very similar to the fate of the sailors at 3.658-65; furthermore, both are introduced by nearly identical formulae: 'as true as it is beyond belief' (*tam...uera...quam* *ueri maiora fide)* and 'an event beyond belief' (*resque fide maior).*

415 evening: *uespere,* a word that provides the root for *uespertilio,* 'the evening creature', 'the bat'.

416-562 Ino
Here Ovid reverts to the story of the house of Cadmus which he had broken off at the end of book 3. Ino, the last of his daughters, has already been alluded to at 3.313 and again at 3.722 (see the note on 3.720-2). Ino's story was well known and is told, or alluded to, by Homer (*Od.* 5.333-5), Herodotus (7.197), Pindar (*Ol.* 2.30; *Pyth.* 11.2), Euripides (*Med.* 1284ff.) and Callimachus (fr. 91), also by Ovid himself at *Fast.* 6.485-550. Euripides' tragedy, *Ino,* survives only in a few fragments. For a full discussion of Ovid's sources see Otis (1966) 372-4; (1970) 401-3. As Otis points out, this passage includes many Virgilian touches, some of which will be discussed as they arise.
    For Ovid, Juno's anger arises solely from Ino's role as foster mother of Bacchus, see 3.313; 4.421, 524; he is silent on the other cause usually cited for the madness of Ino and Athamas, that is punishment for Ino's atempted sacrifice of Athamas' children, Phrixus and Helle, by his previous wife, Nephele; see Apollodorus 1.9.1-2 and Frazer's notes. Ovid's Ino is a far more sympathetic character than the traditional stepmother figure she is elsewhere.

417 his aunt: i.e. Ino, though the name does not emerge until 4.430.

418 alone of so many sisters: i.e. Autonoe, Semele, Agaue, see 3.719-25.

421 her divine foster-child: Ino had fostered Bacchus after he had been born from Zeus' thigh; see the notes on 3.313-4.

422-7 This part of the speech is modelled on Juno's similar speeches at Virg. *Aen.* 1.39-40; 7.286-322. See also the note on 4.432-80.

422 the wench's son: i.e. Bacchus, Semele's son.

424 give a mother her son's bowels to tear at: Agaue and Pentheus whose story is told at 3.701-31.

428 taught...learn: *docet...doceri;* see the note on 1.33. The point could have been made clearer by rendering *doceri* literally 'be taught' but that gives too awkward an effect. The sentiment, 'it is right to learn from an enemy', appears to have been proverbial, see Aristoph. *Birds* 375.

432-80 Juno's trip to the Underworld
Homer (*Od.* 11) and Virgil (*Aen.* 6) were both responsible for famous

descriptions of visits to the Underworld, Ovid owes much to both. His greatest debt here, however, is to Juno's visit to Allecto (Virg. *Aen.* 7.323ff.). Once again, Ovid has taken a passage of high drama from Virgil and used it in a context of strikingly petty behaviour; see also the notes on 1.163-252, 171-5. The differences between Virgil and Ovid here are brought out very clearly by Brooks Otis, *Virgil, A Study in Civilized Poetry* (Oxford, 1964) 325.

432   There is a downward path....: *est uia decliuis;*   a typical ekphrasis, see the note on 1.168.

funereal yew: *funesta...taxo;* perhaps because it is poisonous (Virg. *Georg.* 2.257), the yew was always associated with death in Latin literature. Matthew Arnold *The New Sirens* 267-70.

> *Strew no more red roses maidens,*
> *Leave the lilies in their dew:*
> *Pluck, pluck cypress, O pale maidens:*
> *Dusk, O dusk the hall with yew.'*

436   The place is drear: *loca senta;* the adjective, *sentus,* is archaic and this striking phrase has been borrowed from Aeneas' moving words to Dido in the Underworld (Virg. *Aen.* 6.462 where Austin's note is instructive).

443   The bloodless shades...without bodies or bones: as Odysseus' mother, Anticleia, explains to him in the Underworld (Hom. *Od.* 11.218-22, Lattimore's translation):

> *but it is only what happens, when they die, to all mortals.*
> *The sinews no longer hold the flesh and the bones together,*
> *and once the spirit has left the white bones, all the rest*
> *of the body is made subject to the fire's strong fury,*
> *but the soul flitters out like a dream and flies away.*

449-50   groaned beneath the weight of her sacred body: see the note on 2.162. See also Virg. *Aen.* 6.412-4 where Charon's boat, used only to ghosts, groaned (*gemuit*, here Ovid uses *ingemuit*) under the weight of the living Aeneas.

450   Cerberus: the three-headed dog of the underworld is familiar from Virg. *Aen.* 6.417-25 where Austin's note is very full. The dog does not appear in Homer's description of the Underworld though it is alluded to, though not by name, at *Il.* 8.368. The earliest extant reference to the name is Hes. *Theog.* 311.

452   the sisters that were born to Night: i.e. the Furies, primitive goddesses of vengeance fully described in Aeschylus' *Eumenides.* There is also a memorable Virgilian description (*Aen.* 12.845-51).

453   adamant: see the note on 4.281.

456   the Accursed Place: *Sedes Scelerata*, a phrase borrowed from Tibullus 1.3.67-8, unless Austin (on Virg. *Aen.* 6.563 where there is a similar expression) is right in thinking that there was a 'traditional phrase' that all three are relying on.

457-63   The punishments of the damned are taken from Hom. *Od.* 11.576-600 and Virg. *Aen.* 6.595-607. For a general discussion of the traditional account and how various poets treated it, see Austin on Virg. *Aen.* 6.601. See also Tib. 1.3.67-80.

457   Tityos: according to Homer (*Od.* 11.576-80) he was punished by being tied down while two vultures pecked eternally at his entrails. A similar account, but without the explanation, appears at Virg. *Aen.* 6.600. The 'nine acres' is a feature of all three accounts as well as Tib. 1.3.75.

458   Tantalus: the origin of the English 'tantalize'. Homer gives the same punishment for him (*Od.* 11.582-92) but makes room for far more elaboration. In other versions (e.g. Pind. *Ol.* 1.55ff.) he was punished by having a stone set over him that constantly threatened to crush him. He does not appear in Virgil though a similar stone does, apparently attributed to others (*Aen.* 6.202-3).

459   the branch: it is a branch of grapes; Tantalus can never either eat or drink.

460   Sisyphus: see Hom. *Od.* 11.593-600, again a far more elaborate account. His punishment, but not his name, appear briefly at Virg. *Aen.* 6.616.

461   Ixion: he does not appear in Homer. His name is given by Virgil (*Aen.* 6.601) and his punishment is vaguely attributed to 'others' (*alii*) fifteen lines later. Previously, however, (*Georg.* 4.484) Virgil had connected the two together as had Tibullus (1.3.73-4). Pindar's account (*Pyth.* 2.21-48) is, perhaps, the fullest. For his offence see the note on 4.465.

462-3   Belides: the fifty daughters of Danaus (the Danaids) were forcibly betrothed to the fifty sons of Aegyptus but avenged themselves by murdering their bridegrooms on their wedding night. For this they were punished by having to fill leaking vessels for ever. Their story is the plot of Aeschylus' *Suppliants.* They appear neither in Homer's Underworld nor Virgil's but they are described by Tibullus (1.3.79-80). See also Hor. *Od.* 3.11.23-32 where they are mentioned together with Ixion and Tityos. Belides, 'daughters of Belus', because Danaus, their father, was (like his twin, Aegyptus) a son of Belus (Apollod. 2.1.4.); for the name, 'Belus', see the note on 4.213; for more of the genealogy, see the note on 4.607.

465 **and, above all, at Ixion:** he was being punished for attempting to seduce or ravish Juno.

466 **of the brothers:** Athamas and Sisyphus were both sons of Aeolus; this point was specifically made as early as Hesiod (*Catalogue of Women and Eoïae* fr. 4 in Evelyn-White's Loeb edition).

480 **Thaumantian Iris:** she was the rainbow (see 1.270-1), the messenger of the gods and daughter of Thaumas (Hes. *Theog.* 780-1; Virg. *Aen.* 9.5); here she is performing a ritual to remove the taint of death, for which see Virg. *Aen.* 6.229 and Austin's note.

481 **Tisiphone:** one of the Furies; the picture owes something to Tibullus (1.3.69-70), something to Virgil (*Aen.* 6.570-2) and something to her sister Allecto as described by Virgil at *Aen.* 7.324ff. where Fordyce's note is particularly full and illuminating.

482-3 **blood...blood:** *sanguine...cruore*; see the note on 1.157-8.

484-5 **Grief...Fear...Fright...Madness:** a similar, but much longer, list of personified evils is to be found in Virgil's house of Dis (*Aen.* 6.274-81) and it too begins with *Luctus*, 'Grief'. This sort of personification is as old as Homer (*Il.* 4.440).

486 **Aeolus' doorposts:** i.e. Athamas' doorposts, see the note on 4.466.

492-5 **snakes...snakes:** *colubrae...angues*; a similar problem to the one discussed at 1.71-3.

501 **Echidna:** a peculiarly unpleasant figure who was the mother of Cerberus, the Lernaean hydra and other monsters (Hes. *Theog.* 304-14); note that all these creatures are literally venomous.

513 **Tally ho:** *io*; see the note on 3.728. There may, however, be a hint of Bacchic frenzy here too; compare 4.523.
   nets: *retia*; see the note on 3.148.

516 **laughing:** *ridentem*; a pathetic allusion to the laugh or smile traditionally associated with the baby's first recognition of his mother and most memorable from the last two lines of Virgil's *Eclogue* 4.
   stretching his little arms out: see the note on 2.487; though here, the gesture may well be no more than the natural reaction of an infant.

523 **Euhoe:** the characteristic cry of the Bacchants.

524 **foster-son:** see the note on 3.313-4.

525-7   A short ekphrasis; see the note on 1.168. Although the translation begins with the characteristic, 'There was a cliff...', it should be noted that this is not, in fact, one of those ekphrases that begins *est...*

531   grand-daughter: i.e. Ino, daughter of Cadmus and his wife, Harmonia, who was the daughter of Mars and Venus; see the note on 3.132.

532   uncle: i.e. Neptune; according to one view of the birth of Venus (Aphrodite), she was the daughter of Jupiter (Zeus) and Dione (Hom. *Il.* 5.348-71) and so niece of Neptune (Poseidon), her father's brother. See 1.275.

533   to whom befell the power: a reference to Hom. *Il.* 15.189-91 (Lattimore's translation): Poseidon is speaking of the allotment of responsibilities given to himself and his brothers, Zeus and Hades:
> All was divided among us three ways, each given his domain.
> I when the lots were shaken drew the grey sea to live in
> forever.

537-8   This is based on the other view of Aphrodite's birth. According to Hesiod (*Theog.* 147-87), Earth instructed her son, Cronos, to cut off the genitals of his father (Uranus); from the blood that dripped from the wound onto the earth were born the Furies, the Giants and the Melian Nymphs. The story continues (*Theog.* 188-98; Evelyn-White's translation):
> And as soon as he had cut off the members with
> flint and cast them from the land into the surging
> sea, they were swept away over the main a long time:
> and a white foam spread around them from the immor-
> tal flesh, and in it there grew a maiden. First she
> drew near holy Cythera, and from there, afterwards,
> she came to sea-girt Cyprus, and came forth a lovely
> goddess, and grass grew up about her beneath her
> shapely feet. Her gods and men call Aphrodite, and
> the foam-born goddess and rich-crowned Cytherea,
> because she grew amid the foam, and Cytherea because
> she reached Cytherea...

Aphrodite is not a name of Greek origin but the Greeks could not resist imposing a Greek etymology upon it; *aphros*, the Greek for 'foam' is, accordingly, pressed into service. The scene described by Hesiod is, of course, the inspiration for Botticelli's famous painting, 'The Birth of Venus'.

542   Palaemon...Leucothoe: for the names see Apollod. 3.4.3; Cic. *de Nat. Deorum* 3.15.39 and Hom. *Od.* 5.333, 'Ino called Leukothea'.

560-1   the one...in...on that: *in illo...in illo;*   no attempt has been made in the translation to represent what is surely a fortuitous (and ugly) repetition in Latin.

561   birds: according to Homer (*Od.* 5.337), Ino came to Odysseus like an *aithuia* ('gannet' or 'gull') and it has been suggested that this lies behind the story of her metamorphosis. See Bömer.

563-603   *The transformation of Cadmus and Harmonia into snakes*
This story is most familiar from Euripides *Bacchae* 1330ff. See also the notes of Dodds. With this story, Ovid brings to an end his account of the house of Cadmus that he had begun at 2.833 with the story of Europa. Note how at 4.571-3 Ovid prepares us for the end of this section by bringing us back almost to the beginning. See also 3.98 and the note.

568   the Illyrian borders: according to Apollonius Rhodius (4.516-7), the tomb of Cadmus and Harmonia was by the Illyrian river. See also Frazer's note on Apollod. 3.5.4.

571   a sacred serpent: see 3.35-94.

573   the viper's teeth: see 3.101-30.

575-6   See the note on 1.325-6.

604-5.249   *Perseus*
The various tales of Perseus will be discussed separately. For an interesting discussion of the whole Perseus section, see Otis (1970) 346-9. He believes that it is 'deliberate bathos, a true parody of epic'.

604-13   Acrisius: already briefly discussed in the note on 3.559. His function here is to be a typically ingenious link, see Otis (1970) 346.

607   sprung from that same stock: see Apollodorus 2.1.4-2.4.2 for those parts of this genealogy that are not already familiar:

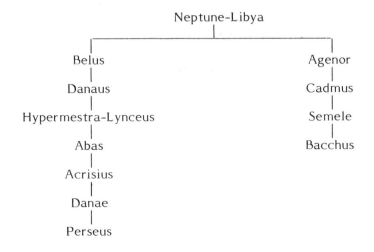

Neptune-Libya

Belus — Agenor

Danaus — Cadmus

Hypermestra-Lynceus — Semele

Abas — Bacchus

Acrisius

Danae

Perseus

610-1   Early references to Danaë, mother of Perseus by Zeus who came to her in a shower of gold, include Pindar *Pyth.* 12.11-18 and Sophocles *Ant.* 944ff.

614-20   *Perseus and Libya*
Apollonius Rhodius 4.1513-7 (Seaton's translation):
> For when over Libya flew godlike Perseus...
> bearing to the king the Gorgon's head newly
> severed, all the drops of dark blood that
> fell to the earth produced a brood of those
> serpents.

615-8   the snaky monster...the Gorgon's head: the reference is, of course, to Medusa; see 4.699, 741-3.

620   For the snakes of Libya, see, for example, Herod. 4.191. Lucan (9.619ff.) not only alludes to the snakes of Libya but refers to the same aetiological legend.

621-62   *Perseus and Atlas*
Many elements in this account are traditional, as will be shown, but this is the first extant account of a confrontation between Perseus and Atlas. Lucan 9.654-5, however, (a passage that follows the one on Perseus and Libya referred to in the last note), picks up the story again.

625   the cold Bears: they are cold because they are the most Northerly ('arctic' derives from *arctos* 'bear'); see the notes on 2.132, 172.
   the Crab's arms: see the note on 2.83.

629-30   For this scene, see 2.111-5 and the notes there.

632   Atlas, son of Iapetus: Hesiod *Theog.* 507-12 (Evelyn-White's translation):
> Now Iapetus took to wife the neat-ankled maid
> Clymene, daughter of Ocean, and went up with
> her into one bed. And she bare him a stout-hearted
> son, Atlas: also she bare very glorious Menoetius
> and clever Prometheus, full of various wiles, and
> scatter-brained Epimetheus who from the first was
> a mischief to men who eat bread.

643   Themis: see the note on 1.321. This particular prediction is otherwise unknown.

647   a huge snake: according to Apollonius Rhodius 4.1396-8, its name was Ladon. For other references and a full discussion, see Bömer.

652   he: i.e. Perseus.

656   Medusa: for her story see 4.771-86.

657-66   This description of Atlas' transformation into a mountain should be compared closely with Virgil's picture (*Aen.* 4.246-51) to which it clearly owes much. Virgil's Atlas is the mountain and not the person, and yet his picture is laced with references to the 'head', 'shoulders', 'chin', 'beard' etc. from which commentators have speculated that Virgil was drawing on an artistic representation of a personified mountain. Pease (on *Aen.* 4.250) is especially helpful here. Virgil continues to confuse mountain with person by referring to Mt Atlas in the next breath (*Aen.* 4.258) as Mercury's grandfather (see the note on 2.697-704). Ovid's metamorphosis, then, has its roots in Virgil and yet, as usual, he stamps his individuality upon his model, making it entirely his own.

660   raised up: *altus*; the Latin word normally means 'high' (or 'deep') but, in origin, it is the perfect participle passive of *alere*, 'to nourish' or 'to raise' (in the U.S. sense), and it is more in that sense that it is used here.

663-803   *Perseus and Andromeda*
The story of Andromeda was the subject of tragedies by both Sophocles and Euripides, though both survive now only in a few fragments. Herodotus too (7.61) has a passing reference to Perseus' marriage to Andromeda, daughter of Cepheus. For a full discussion of Ovid's sources, see Bömer; for a sensitive discussion of Ovid's treatment of the story, see Otis (1970) 346-7. His suggestion earlier in the book (159-60) that Perseus/Andromeda/Cepheus/Phineus (see 5.1ff.) are to be compared with Virgil's Aeneas/Lavinia/Latinus/Turnus seems less convincing.

663   Hippotes' son: *Hippotades*, from *Od.* 10.2 where begins Homer's account of Odysseus' encounter with Aeolus, son of Hippotes, and king of the winds. He also has a memorable place in Virgil's *Aeneid* (1.50-91).
    prison: *carcere*; the same word is used for Aeolus' cave by Virgil (*Aen.* 1.54).

665   he: *ille*; i.e. Perseus, see the note on 1.59.

665-7   Perseus' accoutrements are much the same as those of Hermes (Mercury) as described by Homer (*Od.* 5.44-5) and Virgil (*Aen.* 4.239-46).

666   curved sword: *teloque unco*; presumably the same as the 'curved sword', *falcato ense*, attributed to Mercury at 1.717; indeed, according to Apollodorus (2.4.2), it was Mercury who gave it to Perseus. It was called a *harpe* (see 5.69) in Greek.

669   Cepheus: son of Belus and father of Andromeda; see Herod. 7.61.

670   Ammon: sometimes Hammon, the Jupiter of North Africa; see Fordyce on Catullus 7.5 and, for a savage but brief portrayal, Virg. *Aen.* 4.198ff.

671   a penalty for her mother's tongue: the story is at Apollodorus 2.4.3 (Frazer's translation):

> *For Cassiepea, the wife of Cepheus, vied with the Nereids in beauty and boasted to be better than them all; hence the Nereids were angry, and Poseidon, sharing their wrath, sent a flood and a monster to invade the land. But Ammon having predicted deliverance for the calamity if Cassiepea's daughter Andromeda were exposed as a prey to the monster, Cepheus was compelled by the Ethiopians to do it, and he bound his daughter to a rock.*

Cassiepea is variously Latinized; Ovid's preference is for *Cassiope*.

672   Abas' descendant: *Abantiades*, here, Perseus, though at 4.607 the term referred to Acrisius; see the genealogy in the note on that line.

675   Compare 3.419.

677   Typically, Ovid introduces a humorous touch which makes his attitude to this tale quite plain.

682   a virgin, to address a man: *adpellare uirum uirgo*; the contrast is even more effective in the Latin because of the play on the words *uirum uirgo* which is impossible to represent properly in English.

683-4   See the note on 2.487.

691-4   This picture of the parents clinging to their daughter as the monster approaches is more pathetic than plausible.

697-705   This bargaining by Perseus again lowers the emotional temperature of the scene.

697-8   her whom Jupiter made pregnant with fertile gold: i.e. Danaë, see the note on 4.610-1.

699   the Gorgon with the snaky hair: i.e. Medusa. See 4.615-8, 741-3.

714   the swift bird of Jove: i.e. the eagle, see the note on 1.338.

719   Inachus' descendant: i.e. Perseus; Danaë, Perseus' mother, was the daughter of Acrisius, King of Argos (4.607-11) and Inachus was the great river of Argos; see the note on 1.579-83.

723   noisy...all round: *circumsona*, another Ovidian coinage.

740-52   This seems to be the earliest extant version of this story of the origin of coral; Ovid returns to the theme, though without reference to Perseus or Medusa, at 15.416-7.

741   hard: a good example of what is known as a proleptic (anticipatory) adjective. The sand will not in fact be hard unless it is exposed to the head. In the very next line, 'made...soft', *mollit*, the antonym, again draws attention to the theme which dominates this brief section.

743   Phorcus: the Greek form, *Phorcys*, is also found in Latin. She is referred to by Homer (*Od.* 1.72) and, as the mother of Medusa and others, by Hesiod (*Theog.* 270-6).

754   Mercury: he had given Perseus the 'harpe' (see the note on 4.666).
warrior maiden: *bellica uirgo*; i.e. Minerva; compare 2.752; 5.46; *bellicus* is a favourite Ovidian word not found in Virgil. According to Apollodorus (2.4.2) Athene (Minerva) had helped Perseus to decapitate Medusa. See also the note on 2.754.

755   Jupiter: as Perseus' father, presumably.

755-6   cow...calf...bull: to reflect the sex and status of the three divinities.

756   the wing-footed one: i.e. Mercury; see 1.671 and the note on 1.671-5.

757-64   Typically, Ovid moves very fast from the period before an important event to a detailed description of that event. The *hymenaeus*, 'wedding song', is as early as Homer (*Il.* 18.493) but, for a full discussion, see Fordyce on Catullus 61.

765-71   After Odysseus had been entertained at length by the Phaeacians, he was finally asked, at the end of a banquet, for the story of his voyage (Hom. *Od.* 8.536-86) and the next four books were devoted to his very full reply. In Virgil's *Aeneid* (1.723-56), Dido made a similar request to Aeneas, also at the end of a banquet, and she too received a very full reply encompassing the whole of the next two books. This, then, is an imitation of those famous scenes, but on a very small scale.

765   The gift of high-born Bacchus: i.e. wine.

766   Lynceus' descendant: i.e. Perseus; see the note on 4.607.

767-70   The textual problems here are considerable, and line 768 is universally condemned.

772   Agenor's descendant: i.e. Perseus. Elsewhere, Ovid uses the term only for Cadmus but Agenor, if not a direct ancestor of Perseus, was the brother of his remote ancestor, Belus. See the genealogy in the note on 4.607.

772-89   For this story, see Hesiod *Theog.* 270-83. According to him, there were two sisters, known as the Graiae (though he does not mention the single eye). According to Aeschylus (*P.V.* 792-7), there were three and they shared a single eye and a single tooth. According to Apollodorus (2.4.2), Perseus took both the eye and the tooth from the three Graiae and withheld them until they directed him to the Gorgons. Ovid's version is essentially a perfunctory rehearsal of the traditional story and relies on some degree of previous acquaintance. Note that in all versions the Gorgons, including Medusa, were sisters of the Graiae.

782   The notion that Perseus could protect himself from petrification by looking only at a reflected image of Medusa does appear in Apollodorus, but not in Hesiod.

786   Pegasus and his brother: Hesiod *Theog.* 280-1 (Evelyn-White's translation):

> And when Perseus cut off her [Medusa's] head,
> there sprang forth great Chrysaor and the horse
> Pegasus.

As Hesiod himself implies ('Now Pegasus flew away' [284]), he was a winged horse.

790-803   Hesiod (*Theog.* 278) reports that Poseidon (Neptune) slept with Medusa, and Apollodorus (2.4.3) that there was a belief that Medusa was beheaded because she vied with Athene (Minerva) as a beauty. Ovid (or his source) has neatly combined these stories.

799   aegis: see also the note on 2.754.

BIBLIOGRAPHY

To save space in the notes, authors frequently cited are cited only by name and page number together with date of publication or other suitable indication where more than one work is involved. The references are fully expanded here:

Austin

P. Vergili Maronis Aeneidos Liber Primus with a commentary by R.G. Austin, Oxford, 1971.

P. Vergili Maronis Aeneidos Liber Secundus with a commentary by R.G. Austin, Oxford, 1964.

P. Vergili Maronis Aeneidos Liber Quartus edited with a commentary by R.G. Austin, Oxford, 1955.

P. Vergili Maronis Aeneidos Liber Sextus with a commentary by R.G. Austin, Oxford, 1977.

Bailey

Titi Lucreti Cari de Rerum Natura Libri Sex edited etc. by Cyril Bailey, Oxford, 1947.

Bömer

P. Ovidius Naso Metamorphoses Kommentar von Franz Bömer, Heidelberg, 1969-

de Selincourt

Herodotus the Histories translated and with an introduction by Aubrey de Selincourt, Penguin Books, 1954.

Diggle

Euripides Phaethon edited with Prolegomena by James Diggle, Cambridge, 1970.

Dodds

Euripides Bacchae edited with introduction and commentary by E.R. Dodds, Oxford, 1944 (1st edition), 1960 (2nd edition).

Evelyn-White

Hesiod The Homeric Hymns and Homerica with an English translation by Hugh G. Evelyn-White (Loeb Classical Library), London and Cambridge, Mass., 1914.

Kenney

'The Style of the *Metamorphoses*' by E.J. Kenney in *Ovid edited by J.W. Binns*, London and Boston, 1973.

Kirk and Raven

G.S. Kirk and J.E. Raven, *The Presocratic Philosophers*, Cambridge, 1971.

G.S. Kirk, J.E. Raven and M. Schofield, *The Presocratic Philosophers* (2nd edition), Cambridge, 1983.

Lattimore

The Iliad of Homer Translated with an introduction by Richmond Lattimore, Chicago, 1951.

The Odyssey of Homer Translated with an introduction by Richmond Lattimore, New York, Evanston and London, 1965.

Lee

P. Ouidi Nasonis Metamorphoseon Liber I edited by A.G. Lee, Cambridge, 1953.

Mair

Callimachus with an English Translation by A.W. Mair, Aratus with an English Translation by G.R. Mair (Loeb Classical Library), London and Cambridge, Mass., 1921.

Mayer

Lucan Civil War VIII Edited with a Commentary by R. Mayer, Warminster, 1981.

Moore-Blunt

J.J. Moore-Blunt, *A Commentary on Ovid Metamorphoses II*, Uithoorn, 1977.

Nisbet and Hubbard

R.G.M. Nisbet and Margaret Hubbard, *A Commentary on Horace: Odes Book 1*, Oxford, 1970.

Oldfather

Diodorus of Sicily with an English Translation by C.H. Oldfather (Loeb Classical Library), Cambridge, Mass. and London, 1923.

Otis

Brooks Otis, *Ovid as an Epic Poet*, Cambridge, 1966 (1st edition), 1970 (2nd edition).

Fordyce

Catullus a Commentary by C.J. Fordyce, Oxford, 1961.
P. Vergili Maronis Aeneidos Libri VII-VIII with a commentary by C.J. Fordyce, Oxford, 1977.

Fränkel

Hermann Fränkel, *Ovid, a Poet between two Worlds,* Berkeley and Los Angeles, 1945.

Frazer

Apollodorus The Library with an English Translation by James George Frazer (Loeb Classical Library), London and Cambridge, Mass., 1921.
Pausanias's Description of Greece with a commentary by J.G. Frazer, London, 1913.

Geer

Letters Principal Doctrines and Vatican Sayings Epicurus translated, with an Introduction and Notes, by Russel M. Geer, Indianapolis, 1964.

Golding

The Fyrst Fower Bookes of P. Ouidius Nasos worke, intitled Metamorphoses, translated oute of Latin into Englishe meter by Arthur Golding Gent. A woorke very pleasaunt and delectable, London, 1565. The complete translation followed in 1567. See also *Ovid's Metamorphoses The Arthur Golding Translation 1567 edited, with an introduction and notes, by John Frederick Nims,* New York, 1965.

Gow

Theocritus edited with a Translation and Commentary by A.S.F. Gow, Cambridge, 1950.

Gransden

Virgil Aeneid Book VIII edited by K.W. Gransden, Cambridge, 1976.

Henderson

Ovid Metamorphoses III with Introduction, Notes and Vocabulary by A.A.R. Henderson, Bristol, 1979.

Herescu

Ouidiana Recherches sur Ovide publiees...par N.I. Herescu, Paris, 1958.

Hollis

Ovid Metamorphoses Book VIII edited with an Introduction and Commentary by A.S. Hollis, Oxford, 1970.

Pease

Publi Vergili Maronis Aeneidos Liber Quartus edited by Arthur Stanley Pease, Cambridge, Mass., 1935.

Rand

Edward Kennard Rand, Ovid and his Influence, London, 1925, New York, 1963.

Seaton

Apollonius Rhodius The Argonautica with an English Translation by R.C. Seaton, (Loeb Classical Library), London and New York, 1912.

Smith

Dictionary of Greek and Roman Biography edited by William Smith, London, 1849.
Dictionary of Greek and Roman Geography edited by William Smith, London, 1854.

Thompson

D'Arcy Wentworth Thompson, A Glossary of Greek Birds, Oxford, 1895.

Trypanis

Callimachus Aetia etc. Text, Translation and Notes by C.A. Trypanis, (Loeb Classical Library), Cambridge, Mass. and London, 1958.

Wilkinson

L.P. Wilkinson, Ovid Recalled, Cambridge, 1955.

Williams

P. Vergili Maronis Aeneidos Liber Tertius edited with a commentary by R.D. Williams, Oxford, 1962.

INDEX

This index is based on the translation. The references are normally to explanatory notes. Where there is no such note a brief explanation is offered. The diaeresis mark indicates that the vowel is to be sounded as a separate syllable.